ISRAEL & THE WORLD AFTER 40 YEARS

Also by Aaron S. Klieman

Israel's Global Reach: Arms Sales as Diplomacy
Foundations of British Policy in the Arab World
Soviet Russia and the Middle East
Emergency Politics and the Growth of Crisis Government
Israel-Jordan-Palestine: The Search for a Durable Peace
Statecraft in the Dark: Israel's Practice of Quiet Diplomacy
The Chaim Weizmann Papers (co-editor)
The Rise of Israel: A Documentary History (co-editor)

Also in Hebrew:

Divide or Rule: Great Britain and the 1937 Palestine Partition Plan
Unpeaceful Coexistence: Israel and the Jordanian Option

ISRAEL & THE WORLD AFTER 40 YEARS

Aaron S. Klieman

PERGAMON-BRASSEY'S
International Defense Publishers, Inc.
WASHINGTON • NEW YORK • LONDON • OXFORD • BEIJING
FRANKFURT • SÃO PAULO • SYDNEY • TOKYO • TORONTO

Pergamon-Brassey's books are available at special discounts for bulk purchases for sales promotions, premiums, fund-raising, or educational use through the
Special Sales Director,
Macmillan Publishing Company,
866 Third Avenue, New York, N.Y. 10022.

Pergamon-Brassey's International Defense Publishers, Inc.

Editorial Offices
Pergamon-Brassey's
8000 Westpark Drive, 4th Floor
McLean, VA 22102

Order Department
Macmillan Publishing Co.
Front and Brown Streets
Riverside, NJ 08075

Klieman, Aaron S.
Israel & the world after 40 years / Aaron S. Klieman.
p. cm.
Bibliography: p.
Includes index.
ISBN 0-08-034942-0
1. Israel—Foreign relations—Philosophy. I. Title. II. Title:
Israel and the world after 40 years.
DS119.6.K54 1989
327.5694—dc20 89-34182
CIP

British Library Cataloguing in Publication Data
Klieman, Aaron S.
Israel & the world after 40 years.
1. Israel, Foreign relations, history
I. Title
327.5694

ISBN 0-08-034942-0

10 9 8 7 6 5 4 3 2 1
Printed in the United States of America

to Adrian

על הדבש... ועל העוקץ

both for "the honey and
the sting . . ."

CONTENTS

LIST OF ILLUSTRATIONS

Figures

PREFACE

Altneuland—the old-new land—was the name Dr. Theodor Herzl chose in 1902 for his futuristic novel about a dynamic Jewish state rebuilt on the soil and foundations of biblical Zion. Little could he have known then how singularly appropriate his choice of book title would be for observers of Israeli life and political affairs at present. So much of contemporary Israel retains Herzl's theme of sharp dualism by combining elements of the ancient and the modern. The country is rich in paradox, even contradiction. From its society, culture, and economy to its domestic politics and foreign relations, Israel in its fifth decade of independence provides a fascinating study in contrasts.

Take, for example, the Israeli economy, which is "mixed" or transitional. It still features strong traces of prestate experimentation in socialism (the kibbutzim, the Histadrut labor federation, national health coverage) in the midst of unabashed capitalism, growing class distinctions, and an entrepreneurial free market. On the social scene one cannot help but note the obvious demographic divide between Israeli Arabs and Jews. The Jewish community itself is split in turn along both religious and ethnic lines: pietists and secularists, Ashkenazim and Sephardim. Culturally, too, there is basic ambivalence. Poised between East and West, not quite in the mold of traditionalism but neither wholly modernized, Israel fuses Third World backwardness and inefficiency in some areas with a technological sophistication equal to that of the most advanced European and Asian industrial nations. Qualifying among the oldest world civilizations, Israel is also a charter member of the newly emergent countries to have reached independence after the Second World War.

What better proof though of Israeli dualism than the deep cleavages in its political life? Leftists and rightists . . . hawks and doves . . . Labour against Likud . . . "Peace Now" versus "*Gush Emunim*" (bloc of the faithful). Bipolarization dominates national politics and has been protracted since the 1967 victory by fiercely contested issues:

- the final status of the administered (occupied? conquered? liberated?) West Bank (Judea and Samaria);
- the validity/the wisdom of Jewish settlement there;
- the formula of "territory for peace" and the range of options from annexation to unilateral withdrawal; and
- by no means least, contradictory assessments—ranging from extreme optimism to extreme pessimism—about the prospects for eventually resolving the long-standing historic Arab-Israel conflict.

Nothing so captures this meeting of extremes as the first and second national unity governments (1984–88; 1988–), an uneasy power-sharing framework imposed by a divided electorate on the two traditional party adversaries, Labour and Likud. Signs of tension and contradiction thus abound wherever one looks in Israel.

Why should we expect Israeli foreign policy therefore to be any different? And in fact, Israel's standing in international affairs possesses its own distinctive set of sharp contrasts. From the first moments of independence on 14 May 1948 until the very present the country and its people remain suspended between the two poles of ideal and reality in relating to the rest of the world.

Israel manages somehow to gain reproach for acting beyond its borders far too assertively and at the very same time for acting too timidly. Equally frustrating are outside accusations of Israeli militarism and expansionism aimed at nothing less than regional hegemony that sound incredible next to the individual Israeli's abiding sense of collective national insecurity and his perception of Israel as militarily besieged and diplomatically isolated. It is hard to play both David and Goliath.

Still, one paradox follows another. Physical geography may have placed Israel squarely in the Middle East, but it has yet to become truly *of* the Middle East in other than the military sphere. In a further example of dissonance, national leaders may insist on Israel's capacity for independent choice and complete freedom of action befitting a sovereign state even as Israel grows more reliant on the United States—a benefactor to be sure, and Israel's most trusted friend in the international arena, yet a foreign power all the same. But of Israel's many foreign policy incongruities, probably none is more indicative of the lost Zionist dream of normalcy than the overall international standing of the Jewish commonwealth. Herzl and the founders of modern Israel may have envisioned that at forty the country would be fully integrated within the family of nations; in reality, Israeli representatives still must contend with those opponents who would reduce Israel to the status of outcast—a pariah state threatened with exclusion from the world community and, ultimately, with extinction.

Nor does the dualism, or the irony, end here. One further jarring contrast deserves mention in introducing the subject of Israeli foreign policy. Granted that possibly no other country rivals Israel in crisis, war, and diplomacy over the last forty years. Even so, there is something odd, and to the author personally troubling, about Israel in global affairs. The country "enjoys" a prominence in world politics far exceeding what its small size and limited capabilities warrant. It is also unbelievably, embarrassingly conspicuous in the Western and world media, the center of controversy and an object for close outside scrutiny. Whether this habitual interest and saturation coverage is necessarily good for Israel or not is beside the point. The fact is that this twentieth-century *altneuland* has a remarkable propensity for drawing and exciting wide attention.

How strange and totally inconsistent to discover, therefore, that pitifully few scholarly attempts have been made in all this time to go beyond the Israeli-related crisis of the day or the fleeting sensational newspaper headline to address Israel as an important world actor. Remarkably, nearly twenty years have passed since the previous in-depth study of Israeli foreign policy was published—either in English or Hebrew!—by Professor Michael Brecher. Otherwise, all that the curious or concerned student of world affairs finds are (a) several biographies and memoirs on or by Israeli statesmen and generals, (b) firsthand military accounts of Israel's wars, (c) some excellent scholarly articles tucked away in professional academic journals, and (d) monographs dealing in a limited way with a single specific issue, like Israeli–American relations, Israel and Middle East conflict, Israel's campaign against international terrorism, or its possible nuclear option.

What is missing though is an overview of Israel's defense and foreign affairs, but particularly the latter, that tries to address the apparent anomalies and numerous question marks surrounding Israeli statecraft. A book, in short, that insists upon treating Israel as a normal state actor stripped of superlatives . . . but also of diatribe.

This is, therefore, definitely not a book for beginners. The author seriously doubts whether any reader comes to the subject of Israel and the world in complete innocence, without having opinions already formed, either for or against. Israel does not encourage halftones. Nor is the author himself a beginner, retaining any illusions about emerging unscathed from the hands of critics: both those who atavistically cling to an idealized vision of an Israel that can do no wrong and those who do not count Israelis among their friends.

The wish to fill the twenty-year gap in the scholarly background literature has been the stimulus for undertaking this book. And what an instructive two decades these represent for Israel, its foreign affairs, and its pursuit of those elusive goals: normalcy, peace, security. This more recent period takes us through the full range of individual and national experience from the traumatic days of the 1973 Yom Kippur War to the heady moments of the 1977 peace breakthrough with Egypt.

Such comprehension means that Israeli foreign policy must also be analyzed within a broader and comparative foreign policy framework. Does Israel conform, for example, to the norms, rules, and conventions of international behavior? Are Israeli national interests similar to those of other countries? Or is its conduct perhaps deviant owing, for starters, to its being the only Jewish state and to its having to survive, for added measure, in an external environment of unrelieved hostility? Again, Israel's preoccupation with security: Is that atypical? Or should it be taken as indicative of the kind of political and security dilemmas plaguing small states in a climate of international insecurity?

In essence, what follows is written with four purposes in mind. First, to locate and elucidate the principal sources for Israeli statecraft (i.e., national memory, economic capabilities, political system, and external situation) along with an historical overview of its actual performance. Second, to trace the internal decision-making process by which foreign policy is made and then implemented through various instruments and channels. Third, to review Israel's most important and strategic bilateral relationships before concluding, fourth, by charting a possible future course in foreign affairs for Israel based on its experience and current diplomatic situation.

In conceptual terms, Israel is presented here in several capacities: as a member of the international system, as a decisional body, and as a partner in both warmaking and peacemaking. Accordingly, the book divides into three main parts. A section each is devoted to (a) national interests and attitudes, or how Israel *reacts* to the external setting; (b) internal processes, or how Israel *acts* at home in fashioning specific policy moves; (c) and last, its political relations, or how Israel *interacts* with other international actors.

In following this research design, part one deals with the foundations of Israeli foreign policy. Chapter 1 identifies core foreign policy objectives that define "the national interest" and that are then measured against the resources or "national power" available to Israel for the pursuit and fulfillment of these goals. The different ways Israeli publics and leaders see themselves in terms of the world is the focus of chapter 2. Expectations at the time of statehood in 1948 are contrasted with current attitudes. The disparity between ends and means in the case of Israel, and its influence upon policy makers, is then underscored in chapter 3, which presents a balance sheet of diplomatic success and failure drawn from the historical record since 1948. Chapter 4 continues this survey, using the 1984–88 national unity government to illustrate some important continuities that suggest a distinctive Israeli diplomatic style.

Part two is devoted to the main domestic sources for initiatives by Israel across, and far beyond, its borders. Chapters 5 and 6 approach foreign policy as a function of coalition constraints, the decision-making process itself, and bureaucratic politics waged among competitive government agencies. Chapter 7 takes this policy process one essential step further by considering how internal policy decisions are then executed and put into effect.

Among the preferred implementation strategies, those to be singled out for closer examination include Israeli economic statecraft, foreign military assistance programs, and not least, the brand of quiet, back-channel diplomacy practiced from Jerusalem.

The next section directs attention to Israel's different diplomatic arenas. What becomes clear is the extent to which the Israeli diplomatic map is highly prioritized. To be sure, envoys on behalf of Israel persist in forging the greatest possible number of worldwide links. As a consequence, Israel has registered a degree of success in extending its global reach into just about every political constellation and geographic region; two worthy of mention surely are the United Nations and its affiliated specialized agencies and the network of Diaspora Jewry. All this notwithstanding, the chief focus of interest lies, as it always has, with, first, the central superpower equation and, second, the Arab-Israeli dispute.

Chapter 8 concentrates on the problematic Soviet connection and on Israel's vital relationship with the United States. In the same vein, chapter 9 turns to strategies used by Israel for penetrating the Middle East subsystem and for interacting in its politics and diplomacy. Here our thesis is that for much of Israel's troubled history a quite extraordinary and complex de facto relationship has evolved with its eastern neighbor, the Hashemite Kingdom of Jordan. To the extent this unpublicized, tacit relationship translates into a tangible commitment, and not merely a political preference, it has constituted a serious disincentive against the quest for an alternative Palestinian option.

The book ends with some final observations and tentative conclusions about Israel as a state actor. These insights, plus the larger historical, theoretical, and political perspectives offered in the earlier sections, sufficiently embolden the author to hazard volunteering the outlines for a revised foreign policy agenda designed to see Israel safely and securely through its first half-century. Only then will Israeli foreign policy have achieved its highest assignment and greatest reward: an Israel at peace—at peace with its Arab neighbors, with the world at large, and not least, with its own Jewish heritage.

❑

In a sense this book is over forty years in the making. For all of that time the center of my childhood and adult experience has been occupied by the rebirth of Israel, its evolution, and struggles at home, on the battlefield, and in the global arena. What the reader finds here consequently represents a sustained learning period of reading and observation, listening and arguing, teaching and reflection.

Along the way I have accumulated a heavy debt of gratitude, thanks for which are sincerely, even if inadequately, expressed at long last to the community of scholars whose writings have been assimilated into my own thinking; to a generation and more of Israeli soldier-students; to friends and colleagues at my home institution, Tel Aviv University, and also at Georgetown University who hosted me on two occasions as visiting Israeli professor in the Department of Government. I do wish to single out, however, Avi Ben-Zvi, Gideon Doron, and Joel Migdal because of their good counsel and helpful comments on this particular project; also my research assistant, Amir Horkin, for supplying the finishing touches to the manuscript. A word of acknowledgment as well to Sylvia Weinberg of the Social Sciences Faculty typing service who has word-processed the book so patiently and to

Pamela Yacobi for tackling the selected topic readings; despite the many corrections and revisions they have not yet declared me persona non grata.

The last word of praise is reserved for my wife, who for the last twenty-five years has been at my side. This book is one way of letting her know how much it means always to have found her also on my side.

Aaron Klieman
Ra'anana
2 June 1989—28 *Iyar* 5749
Jerusalem Reunification Day

PART ONE

ISRAEL AS A STATE ACTOR

To the outsider, Israel and the individual Israeli present a strange combination of worldliness with traces of insularity. The two qualities, rather than being irreconcilable, are intimately related. In some ways Israel is an island. Cut off since birth from its immediate Arab precinct, so much of its political behavior—like the thinking of its people—stems from this abiding sense of Middle Eastern rejectionism that is only further compounded by the difficulty Israel has had in explaining itself to the rest of the world. After forty years Israel's place in the world remains unsecured and undefined.

There is thus about Israel a suggestion of somehow being worlds apart: of being out of step and out of touch. Such "distance," which is as much psychic as physical, has only increased the desire to be part of the wider world and to be a party to whatever goes on internationally. Maybe this has to do with the country's Jewish and prophetic roots; perhaps the cause is entirely temporal, owing to a basic dependence on international ties and assistance. Whatever the reason, Israelis are tireless in countering this imposed remoteness. Consider, for instance, the flood of Israeli tourists to Egypt once the barriers came down in 1979 and a land bridge spanned to an Arab neighbor; or the annual summer flow of travelers to Europe and beyond—at times equaling one out of every seven or eight Israelis! Additional indicators are disproportionately high subscription rates to foreign magazines like Time, Newsweek, *and* National Geographic; *strong representation at professional conferences abroad; and protecting El Al, Israel's national airline, as an invaluable link to the world beyond.*

Being an island fortress was unforeseen by Israel's founders, and yet every Israeli government has had to confront this most basic of all realities. Each prime minister has entered and left office with security and peace as the number one unfulfilled issue on the national agenda, to the neglect of other pressing social and economic priorities.

Israel's political elites and diplomatic statesmen are in a still less enviable position, given the heavy responsibility that falls upon them in taking on the outside world. First, they have the weight of Jewish history on their shoulders. History in the case of Israel not only precedes diplomacy but accompanies it constantly. Second, they bear responsibility for the future of the state and, consequently, indirectly for the survival of the Jewish people. This does not leave much margin for error. Third, they have got to define the range of national objectives and then to pursue them with few material assets and even fewer exciting options. Fourth, the nation's leaders operate under the burden of previous decisions, commitments, and procedures inherited from those who came before, further reducing their independence of choice and action.

As if this legacy of confusing traditions, ambitions, and political inhibitions was not enough, two more intrude at present. As Israeli foreign policy moves toward its first half-century, the international climate of world affairs is changing, and not entirely to Israel's advantage. It faces a watchful and increasingly critical, impatient world, tired of the Arab–Israeli conflict and anxious for its resolution. This outside pressure also comes at a time in Israel's own history when the domestic consensus has become frayed. The national resolve confronts a twofold challenge: there is a certain softening—a weariness and loss of direction—on the one hand; and, on the other hand, a certain hardening of Israeli views toward international affairs, toward Arab and Middle Eastern affairs, even toward Jewish affairs.

The following four chapters take a closer look at the transformations currently under way in each of the areas that comprise the general setting for foreign policy and diplomatic relations by Israel as a state actor.

CHAPTER 1

❑

THE NATIONAL INTEREST

Now we believe that in the struggle for time we will win. We believe that time is with us . . . Israel will ultimately emerge triumphant. This may take long and arduous years, but sustained by the unity and faith of world Jewry, with patience, and, above all, with a sense of balance and with the realization that we are in danger, we will come through and move ahead.

–the late Dr. Yaakov Herzog, 1970

Foreign policy debate in Israel is framed by multiple diplomatic traditions. Fundamental attitudes are rooted in Jewish history and extend from one of two extremes, either amity or deep enmity, to a posture of studied detachment. At a deeper level, patterns of Israelite encounters in the ancient Near East with alien cultures (Assyrian, Babylonian, Egyptian) and foreign powers (Greece, Persia, Rome) still retain a surprising hold on thought processes and images in the modern secular Jewish state toward the outside world. But in the immediate sense, what really determines policy choices and specific decisions in Jerusalem is the country's set of multiple and concrete national interests.

FOREIGN POLICY GOALS

Diplomacy is the art of promoting one's national interest through persuasion. However, no state, regardless of how small or underdeveloped, possesses but a single interest. Rather, all states are alike in acting on behalf of complex interests: social and economic as well as political and strategic, domestic but also external. Where states differ is in their mix of objectives and in the priority assigned each of the often conflicting interests. By this standard Israel's definition of its national interest is distinctive on at least two counts.

In the first instance, Israeli foreign relations are dictated by no less than seven vital "issue-areas" or clusters of primary objectives. In existence since 1948, these core diplomatic aims are legitimacy, peace, security, developing commerce, winning foreign endorsement for government policy positions, constructive engagement in international projects, and finally, links with world Jewry. The latter concern is in itself a mark of distinctiveness, calling our attention to the fact that Israel is, and will always remain in the future, the only Jewish state. In the second instance, the order of priority among these seven permanent goals has changed over time, shifting rather dramatically during Israel's first forty years.

More specifically, the following insights are offered into Israel's pursuit of the national interest:

- As a state actor Israel has shown constancy of purpose. It combines a strong commitment to core objectives with flexibility in the choice of means for their realization.
- Achievements in each of the seven issue-areas, nevertheless, have come comparatively early in Israel's diplomatic history, followed by a loss of momentum and even major setbacks.
- Since the first decade, diplomatic victories have been rather few and far between.
- As a consequence, Israeli leaders were forced into readjusting the country's set of priorities. Far greater weight is given to physical and immediate security than to winning endorsement overseas for government policies, for example, or to enjoying popularity in world opinion, or even what seems in moments of despair to be the elusive goal of peace.
- The same downward slope from long-term, abstract goals to concrete, short-term ones applies to a lowering of sights *within* each cluster of goals.
- Instead of insisting upon the full realization of these ends, Israeli diplomacy has moved into a defensive mode. Accordingly, the thrust of Israeli foreign policy has concentrated in recent years primarily on averting further erosion of the country's international position or the loss of whatever precious gains had been achieved earlier in each of the seven diplomatic assignments.

In a word, with time, Israel's foreign policy has become less rather than more ambitious. The impression as well as the reality is of a country badly chastened by experience and appreciative of the obstacles it faces and therefore intent upon holding the line. These generalizations are confirmed by looking briefly at each of the specific policy areas.

Legitimacy

Legal diplomatic recognition nowadays tends to be almost instantaneous, as well as something of a formality. Under existing conditions the procedure is for a people's claim to self-determination to be established conclusively at the moment of its declared independence. This right of statehood is then confirmed by individual foreign governments rushing to extend recognition and through prompt admission into the United Nations. Their struggle for sovereignty and legitimacy thus quickly behind them, the new states, with few exception, become an accepted fact of international life, are integrated into the world community, and can look forward to getting on with other affairs of state heading their particular national agenda.

Israel, unfortunately, happens to be one of the exceptions. For other established countries, their sovereign existence within the international system is a given. Exact boundaries or regime may be disputed, but not the state's very political existence, whereas Israel's most fundamental right of nationhood is still being actively contested.

Present reminders of this controversial and unsettled international status abound even after more than four decades. They come in various forms of physical attack, verbal abuse, and symbolic insult; they also take place at both the national and the individual, personal level. Perhaps because the anti-Israel campaign has been going on for so long, Israelis by now are conditioned to being excluded from Middle Eastern regional groupings and even to being singled out as targets for Arab terrorism. What seems to rankle Israelis most, though, are seemingly minor acts as the Soviet authorities' decision not to fly the Israeli flag, as is customary in European Cup basketball competitions, when the Maccabi Tel Aviv team played in Moscow in January 1988—the first time in twenty-one years! Or, to cite another example, Israelis had a hard time comprehending the scene at the 1988 (Handicapped) Paraolympics in Seoul when Kuwait's gold-winner in one of the competitions refused to shake the outstretched hand of the Israeli who took second place before the eyes of an incredulous stadium and TV audience. Such things still hurt Israelis.

The quest for recognition began auspiciously enough. UN endorsement for Jewish statehood came in 1947. This was followed in fairly rapid succession by American and Soviet recognition in 1948 (in one of the rare instances of cold war superpower concurrence). UN membership was bestowed on Israel in 1949.

The "highest seal" of recognition, Foreign Minister Moshe Sharett called it. Immediately following the historic vote, Sharett addressed the General Assembly. Speaking for the new state and Jews throughout the world, he described Israel's admission into the world body as the fifty-ninth member "the consummation of a people's transition from political anonymity to clear identity, from inferiority to equal status, from mere passive protest to active responsibility, from exclusion to membership in the family of nations." At the time, when representing Israel in the international forum as head of the delegation, Abba Eban felt certain that after admission to the UN, "it was no longer possible for Israel's juridical legitimacy to be denied." How wrong he was.

As of May 1949, some fifty-four countries had already extended recognition to Israel. Israel confidently went on to enjoy several further successes. Most notable: repairing relations with the estranged former Palestine mandate power, Great Britain; exchange of ambassadors with the Federal Republic of Germany in 1965; and a diplomatic offensive toward the new Afro-Asian states in the late fifties and sixties. By 1967 the number of states having formal diplomatic relations with Israel reached an all-time high, ninety-eight countries.

Nevertheless, the professed goal of moving on to full, normal relations with all countries was frustrated. The number of active ties fell to a low of sixty-five after 1973. But then toward the end of 1986, Israel's standing, at least in the formal sense, showed improvement, with the total number of official bilateral ties inching to 79. Notwithstanding these inroads, however, the Israeli diplomatic register and map continued to compare unfavorably with the PLO—its rival claimant for world recognition—which was claiming as of 1989 to have been recognized by at least 92 countries.

Almost from the beginning Israel came up against determined resistance from various quarters and had to learn how to contend, diplomatically and not only militarily, with the very real threat of political rejection. Foremost, Israel faced in 1949 (and, with the single exception of Egypt, still faces) a categorical denial of its legitimacy and existence by the Arab world, supported by a wider circle of Muslim countries. This bloc of states, deeply hostile and unreconciled toward Israel, not only challenges Israel's claim to legitimacy but disputes the Zionist entity's very right to exist (see Map 1). This cardinal fact of Arab rejectionism, as we shall see, has immensely

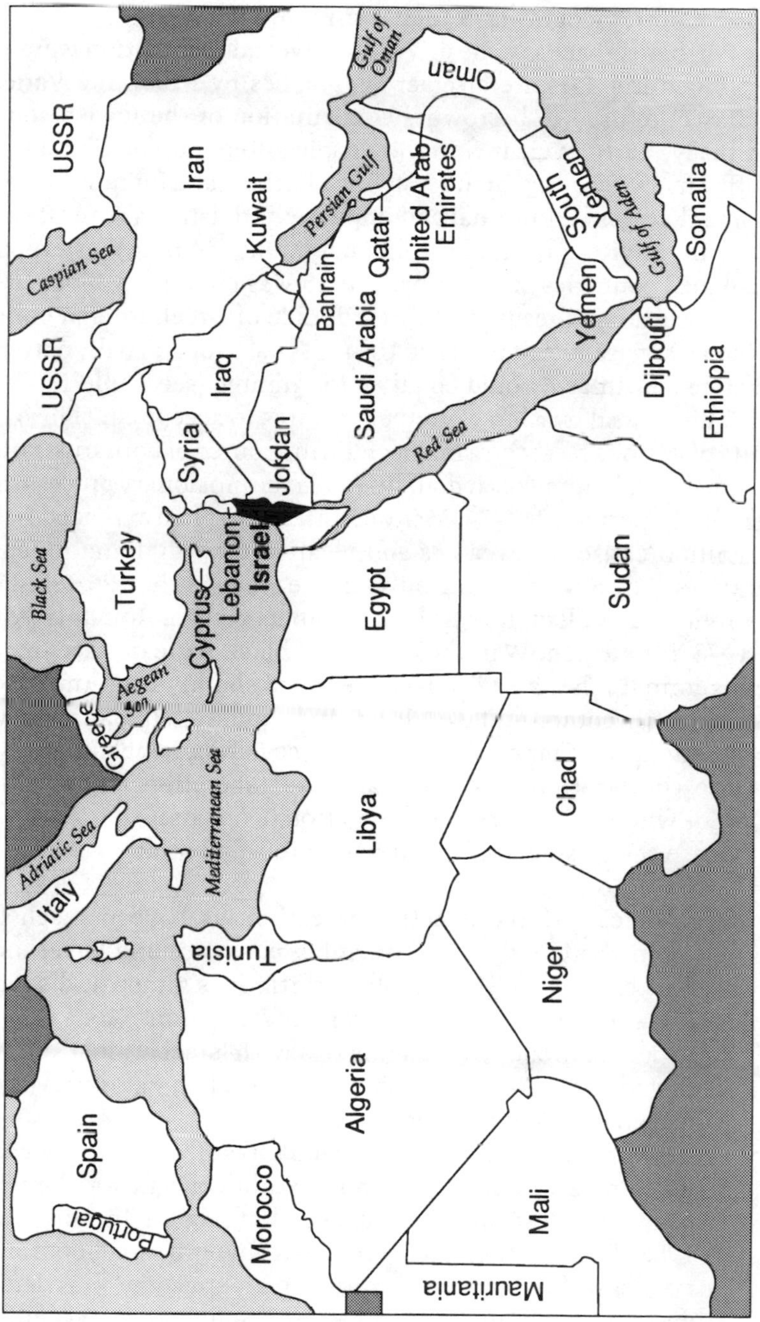

Map 1. Israel and the Middle East

complicated efforts at securing undisputed legitimacy while distorting the hierarchy of other domestic-diplomatic targets.

Further setbacks in the drive for universal recognition were not long in coming. Despite discreet approaches by Israel, the Vatican steadfastly refused to bestow its confirmation of the Jewish state's legitimacy. Early overtures to the People's Republic of China were rebuffed in 1950 and again in 1954. Iran, Turkey, and India studiously insisted that ties be minimal and unpublicized. Israel's request to be among the invitees to the founding conference of non-Western and nonaligned countries at Bandung in 1955 was effectively blocked by Arab opposition. Already in the first decade of Israeli foreign policy, it became apparent that not even the most basic of all goals, national and state legitimacy, could be taken for granted (see Table 1).

This refusal by a large number of states to accept Israel into the family of nations has been a major enduring source of both frustration and concern. What makes it doubly so was the erosionary process that began in the period 1967–74. Many countries that had extended Israel recognition chose to sever ties and recalled their diplomatic representatives. The Soviet Union did so in the wake of the 1967 Six-Day War, followed by all of the East bloc members save for Romania. After the 1973 Yom Kippur War, the number of black African states maintaining formal relations with Israel dropped sharply from thirty to a mere three (Lesotho, Malawi, Swaziland). Indeed, so alarming was this deterioration that by the close of the seventies Israel found itself in close competition with the Palestine Liberation Organization (PLO) for who enjoyed greater international support.

Since then, Israeli policy stresses a fourfold strategy:

a. to defeat efforts at delegitimization, as happens each fall when the UN General Assembly convenes and Israel must beat back Arab-Muslim block initiatives aimed at disqualifying the credentials of the Israeli delegation;
b. to persuade countries having ties with Israel against submitting to either Arab blandishments or Arab threats by revoking recognition and cutting off ties;
c. to check the Palestine Liberation Organization's new political offensive aimed at gaining world consent for the independent Palestinian state declared at Algiers in November 1988. When Turkey, a country with whom Israel does have ties, saw fit to extend recognition, Jerusalem was left to express its "disappointment, regret, and dissatisfaction." Israeli diplomats at every other post abroad were instructed to work at convincing other friendly countries, especially in the

Table 1. Israel's Diplomatic Register

A. UN Member States

	Country	Recognizing Israel	Suspended relations	Denying recognition
1.	Afghanistan			+
2.	Albania	+	+	
3.	Algeria			+
4.	Angola			+
5.	Antigua and Barbuda*	+		
6.	Argentina	+		
7.	Australia	+		
8.	Austria	+		
9.	Bahamas*	+		
10.	Bahrain			+
11.	Bangladesh			+
12.	Barbados*	+		
13.	Belgium	+		
14.	Belize*	+		
15.	Benin	+	+	
16.	Bhutan			+
17.	Bolivia	+		
18.	Botswana	+	+	
19.	Brazil	+		
20.	Brunei Darussalam			+
21.	Bulgaria	+	+	
22.	Burkina Faso	+		
23.	Burma	+		
24.	Burundi	+	+	
25.	Byelorussian Soviet Socialist Republic**			
26.	Cameroon	+		
27.	Canada	+		
28.	Cape Verde			+
29.	Central African Republic	+		
30.	Chad	+	+	
31.	Chile	+		
32.	China			+
33.	Colombia	+		
34.	Comoros			+
35.	Congo	+		
36.	Costa Rica	+		

Table 1. (Continued)

A. UN Member States

Country	Recognizing Israel	Suspended relations	Denying recognition
37. Cuba	+	+	
38. Cyprus	+		
39. Czechoslovakia	+	+	
40. Democratic Kampuchea	+	+	
41. Democratic Yemen (South)			+
42. Denmark	+		
43. Djibouti			+
44. Dominica*	+		
45. Dominican Republic	+		
46. Ecuador	+		
47. Egypt	+		
48. El Salvador	+		
49. Equatorial Guinea	+	+	
50. Ethiopia	+	+	
51. Fiji	+		
52. Finland	+		
53. France	+		
54. Gabon	+	+	
55. Gambia			+
56. Germany, Democratic Republic (East)			+
57. Germany, Federal Republic (West)	+		
58. Ghana	+	+	
59. Greece	+		
60. Grenada*	+		
61. Guatemala	+		
62. Guinea	+	+	
63. Guinea Bissau			+
64. Guyana			+
65. Haiti	+		
66. Honduras	+		
67. Hungary	+	+	
68. Iceland*	+		
69. India	+		
70. Indonesia			+

Table 1. (Continued)

A. UN Member States

	Country	Recognizing Israel	Suspended relations	Denying recognition
71.	Iran	+	+	
72.	Iraq			+
73.	Ireland	+		
74.	Italy	+		
75.	Ivory Coast	+		
76.	Jamaica	+		
77.	Japan	+		
78.	Jordan			+
79.	Kenya	+		
80.	Kuwait			+
81.	Lao People's Democratic Republic (Laos)	+	+	
82.	Lebanon			+
83.	Lesotho	+		
84.	Liberia	+		
85.	Libyan Arab Jamahiriya			+
86.	Luxembourg*	+		
87.	Madagascar	+	+	
88.	Malawi	+		
89.	Malaysia			+
90.	Maldives			+
91.	Mali	+	+	
92.	Malta*	+		
93.	Mauritania	+		
94.	Mauritius	+	+	
95.	Mexico	+		
96.	Mongolia			+
97.	Morocco			+
98.	Mozambique			+
99.	Nepal	+		
100.	Netherlands	+		
101.	New Zealand	+		
102.	Nicaragua	+	+	
103.	Niger	+	+	
104.	Nigeria	+	+	
105.	Norway	+		
106.	Oman			+

Table 1. (Continued)

A. UN Member States

Country	Recognizing Israel	Suspended relations	Denying Recognition
107. Pakistan			+
108. Panama	+		
109. Papua New Guinea*	+		
110. Paraguay	+		
111. Peru	+		
112. Philippines	+		
113. Poland	+	+	
114. Portugal	+		
115. Qatar			+
116. Romania	+		
117. Rwanda	+	+	
118. Saint Kitts and Nevis*	+		
119. Saint Lucia*	+		
120. Saint Vincent and the Grenadines*	+		
121. Samoa*	+		
122. São Tomé and Principe			+
123. Saudi Arabia			+
124. Senegal	+	+	
125. Seychelles			+
126. Sierra Leone	+	+	
127. Singapore	+		
128. Solomon Islands	+		
129. Somalia			+
130. South Africa	+		
131. Spain	+		
132. Sri Lanka	+	+	
133. Sudan			+
134. Suriname*	+		
135. Swaziland	+		
136. Sweden	+		
137. Syrian Arab Republic			+
138. Thailand	+		
139. Togo	+		
140. Trinidad and Tobago*	+		
141. Tunisia			+
142. Turkey	+		

Table 1. (Continued)

A. UN Member States

Country	Recognizing Israel	Suspended relations	Denying recognition
143. Uganda	+	+	
144. Ukrainian Soviet Socialist Republic**			
145. Union of Soviet Socialist Republics	+		
146. United Arab Emirates			+
147. United Kingdom of Great Britain and Northern Ireland	+		
148. United Republic of Tanzania	+	+	
149. United States of America	+		
150. Uruguay	+		
151. Vanuatu			+
152. Venezuela	+		
153. Viet Nam	+	+	
154. Yugoslavia	+	+	
155. Yemen (North)			+
156. Zaire	+		
157. Zambia	+	+	
158. Zimbabwe			+
TOTAL:	115	33	41

B. Representation Elsewhere (Including Nonmembers of UN)

Country	Recognizing Israel	Suspended relations	Refraining from recognition
1. Andorra			+
2. Curaçao*	+		
3. Gibraltar*	+		
4. Hong Kong	+		
5. Kiribati	+		
6. Korea, Democratic People's Republic (North)			+

Representation Elsewhere (continued)

Country	Recognizing Israel	Suspended relations	Refraining from recognition
7. Lichtenstein*	+		
8. Marshall Islands*	+		
9. Monaco*	+		
10. Nauru			+
11. Republic of (South) Korea*	+		
12. San Marino*	+		
13. Switzerland	+		
14. Taiwan			+
15. Tonga*	+		
16. Tuvalu	+		
17. Vatican			+
18. West Samoa	+		
TOTAL:	13	0	5

* Nonresident ambassador or representative
** Represented by the USSR

Source: (1) *Yearbook of the United Nations*, 1984, vol. 38.
(2) *United Nations Chronicle*, June 1988, vol. 25, no. 2.
(3) Israel's Ministry for Foreign Affairs.

West, not to recognize the would-be West Bank entity nor to raise their level of contacts with the PLO. But already that December the UN General Assembly voted 104–2 (Israel and United States), with thirty-six abstentions, to change the designation of the PLO Mission to that of "Palestine";

d. in what has become a slow and arduous uphill struggle, to encourage once friendly states in Eastern Europe and Africa to renew direct contacts, countries cool to Israel (such as India) to upgrade their representation, and still recalcitrant states (as Spain) to establish relations for the first time.

The main thrust, however, remains essentially defensive (see Table 2).

Policy objectives concentrate on arresting any erosionary trend and on firming up existing ties while probing for fresh openings. "A significant victory," pronounced Israel's UN representative at the outcome of a General Assembly vote in October 1988 defeating an

Table 2. Recent Diplomatic Inroads

Relations Established
Spain (1986)
Solomon Islands (1989)
Relations Renewed
Zaire (1982)
Liberia (1983)
Ivory Coast (1986)
Cameroon (1986)
Togo (1987)
Central African Republic (1988)
Kenya (1988)
Relations Upgraded
Poland (1986)
Hungary (1987)

Arab resolution to disqualify the Israeli delegation's credentials. The "great step forward," as he put it, was that the number of countries voting for the resolution had increased only by two (forty-one instead of thirty-nine in 1987), while those standing alongside Israel and the principle of universality in opposing the anti-Israel measure grew from eighty the year before to ninety-five. Of such are Israeli diplomatic "victories" made. The UN, Sharett's "highest seal," in more recent years has tended to make Israel's delegitimization one of its principal enterprises. Even after four decades the legality of the Jewish state is still subject to question by important segments of the international community.

Peace

Since Israel does not enjoy full international recognition, it cannot succeed in the second core function ordinarily assigned to diplomacy and foreign policy: peace. Achieving a full state of peace with the neighboring Arab countries, too, eludes Israeli statecraft. Born three short years after the European Holocaust, no nation could have yearned for peace and tranquility more than Israel. Yet in forty years Israel has never known a single day of true peace.

As a result, early definitions of the peace goal have had to be scaled down appreciably. Again the pattern is one of limited success early on, followed by disappointment, stalemate, and policy reverses.

Negotiations conducted on the island of Rhodes under UN auspices at the end of the War for Independence resulted in a series of armistice agreements reached separately by Israel with Egypt, Lebanon, Jordan, and Syria in that order, between February and July 1949. Members of the Israeli delegation saw no need at the time to press urgently for an immediate peace. Viewing peacemaking as a logical progression, they felt confident that peace was imminent since reason left the Arabs no alternative but to accept the reality of Israel's existence and to sue for peace without Israel having to rush things or to make painful territorial concessions. This confidence proved short lived, however, as Arab leaders in the years after 1949 refused to reconcile themselves to Israel's existence, rendering Arab-Israeli conciliation impossible.

Ironically, therefore, the armistice regime that after all had been meant to provide a brief stepping-stone in the logical progression toward a comprehensive, contractual peace endures today as the main legal instrument governing Arab-Israeli relations. Egypt is the only Arab country to have exchanged the armistice accords for a peace treaty. And this took thirty years to achieve. Moreover, in our longer perspective the Sadat initiative looks more like a momentary peak of renewed optimism toward peace prospects in 1977–79 than any final peace breakthrough. In the decade that followed, many Israelis who had supported a positive response by Israel at the time came to express deep reservations as to the treaty's true political value. In their view, instead of being an inspiration, the "cold peace" was a disappointment in light of the tangible assets given up in the Sinai and in comparison with the informal, nonbinding, yet functional working relationship with Jordan.

With the loss of a real peace momentum, the emphasis in recent years has shifted back to holding the line. The principal objective of this preventive posture has been to ensure against a breakdown of the Israel-Egypt peace regime or, at a minimum, Cairo's return to the Arab rejectionist fold.

Insecure and unrecognized borders are a constant reminder to Israelis of diplomacy's failure to achieve lasting peace. Israelis still basically live within provisional partition lines drawn in 1948 under the force of arms rather than by negotiation (see Map 2).

This unnatural and unsettled state of affairs is best seen in the status of Jerusalem. For nineteen years, from 1948 to 1967, it was a divided city arbitrarily separated by jagged coils of barbed wire and isolated enclaves. It was a tense no-man's land, and the Arab Legion sandbagged positions atop the Old City walls. This intolerable situ-

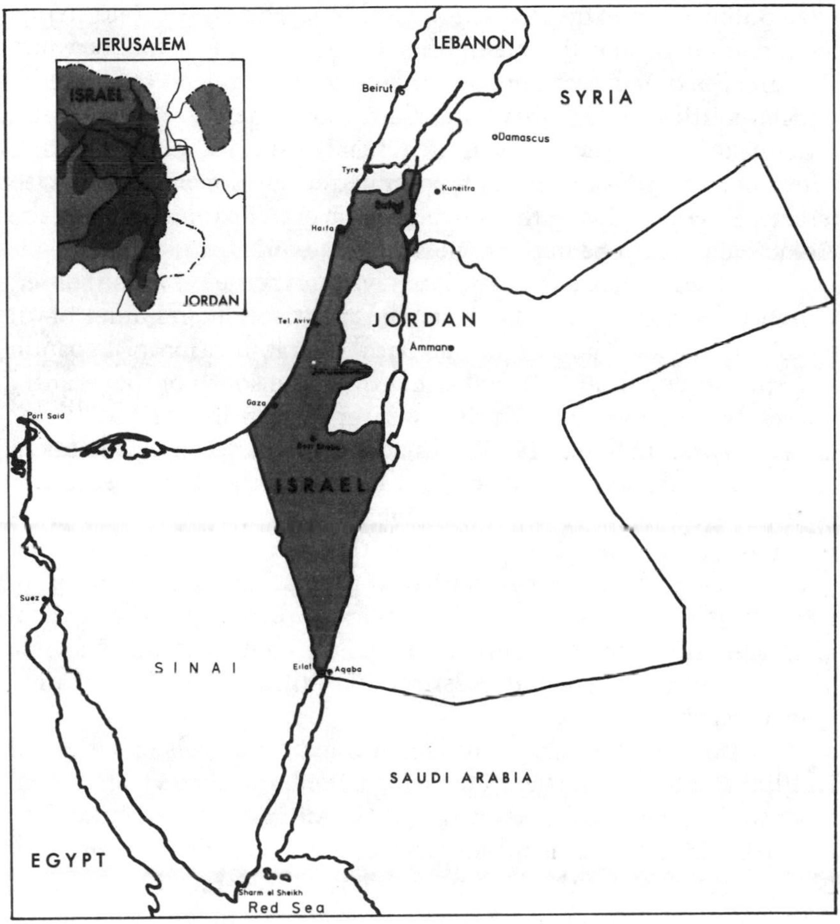

Map 2. 1949 Armistice Lines

ation ended with reunification of the city under Israeli rule in the 1967 fighting. Even so, international acceptance of Jerusalem as the capital of Israel has not been forthcoming, and most foreign governments still insist on keeping their diplomatic missions in Tel Aviv.

In effect, the provisional and improvised 1949 armistice lines remain to the present along Jordan, Syria, and Lebanon. The eastern frontier question, far from being resolved, is a divisive issue at home, with public opinion divided as to whether (a) the pre-1967 armistice demarcation, or so-called green line, (b) the Jordan River, or possibly (c) a modified, redrawn border somewhere in between ought to be Israel's political and security border. Similarly, the frontier with Syria remains to be negotiated, given the refusal of successive regimes and rulers in Damascus to entertain possible recognition and peace with Israel. As a consequence, the concentration of troops and armor on the Golan Heights is one of the highest in the world.

Also problematic since the late seventies is the Lebanese border, which in previous years had been the most stable and quiet of all Israel's frontiers. The internal political destabilization of Lebanon and the buildup of PLO armed strength in the south of the country bordering on Israel led to military intervention by the IDF (Israel Defense Force) in March 1978 and again in June 1982 in the mistaken belief that Lebanon's politics could be restructured and peace imposed. A draft treaty between the governments of Israel and Lebanon was actually negotiated in May 1983 with American assistance. In the end, however, the agreement failed to gain Lebanese ratification in the face of Syrian opposition. Thus, instead of symbolizing the goal of good-neighborliness, southern Lebanon continues to present a security threat for Israel, necessitating a military rather than a political response.

In sum, on the peace front Israeli maximum goals of definitive conflict resolution and genuine peace have long since yielded to an essentially narrower concentration on conflict management and on war avoidance through military deterrence. In realistic terms, for Israel as much as for the Arab participants, the name of the game is stability; stability as opposed to peace and comity in the fullest sense. The difference between peacekeeping (assuming one exists to be kept!) and peacemaking, of course, is profound.

The actual record on Arab-Israeli peacemaking indicates that in the post-1948, post-1956, post-1967, and post-1973 periods one diplomatic offensive after another began auspiciously enough only soon to bog down in the lower reaches of what is known in Middle East parlance as "no war, no peace." This grey area has drained international goodwill and exhausted mediatory efforts on behalf of limited or marginal gains: from cease-fire, truce, and armistice through separation of forces, demilitarization, and interim agreements to, perhaps at best, grudging pledges of nonbelligerency. Fighting over each little concession and abiding by the rules of the game, Israel has been willing—or forced—to settle for less.

The 1979 precedent of peace with Egypt for a while rekindled earlier Israeli hopes for a prompt settlement, for "peace now." When this most promising of all previous Middle East initiatives fizzled out too, it brought the peace debate within Israel full circle. At the close of the eighties national expectations and the foreign policy agenda had returned to the gradualist approach associated with the cheerless era of the fifties and sixties. One heard more about slow processes (of functional frameworks on the Israeli-Jordanian model, of small confidence- and security-building measures, of long-term reconciliation between Israelis and Palestinians), and of a ripening process than of either bold gestures or dramatic breakthroughs to peace.

Security

Frustrated in peacemaking and confronted from the outset by an unanticipated, constant Arab militarization, Israel's entire definition of security has had to be revised. New states usually begin by addressing national security in absolute terms but then learn to live with the global reality of insecurity. While this "security dilemma" is therefore familiar, it is considerably more acute in Israel's case. Instead of being able to concentrate exclusively on promoting the country's prosperity, Israeli governments have had a hard time just defending the lives and property of its inhabitants.

During David Ben-Gurion's premiership in the 1950s, the outlines of a political-military doctrine emerged in response to the Arab threat. This policy continued to express the desire for peace while also stressing that if the Arabs insisted on "no peace" then Israel had the right to demand, at a minimum, "no war."

The government of Israel would not tolerate acts of violence against its territory or citizens launched from across the permeable armistice lines. In defending the country, Israeli leaders cited Article 51 of the UN Charter assuring the right of individual self-defense. This position has had at least three major foreign policy consequences. First, in the last forty years, Israel has managed its security affairs from a perceived sense of vulnerability (see Map 3). Its insecurity is heightened militarily by (a) long, exposed frontiers and (b) Arab numerical superiority, strategic depth, material resources, and outside sources of arms (see Table 3). This insecurity is further height-

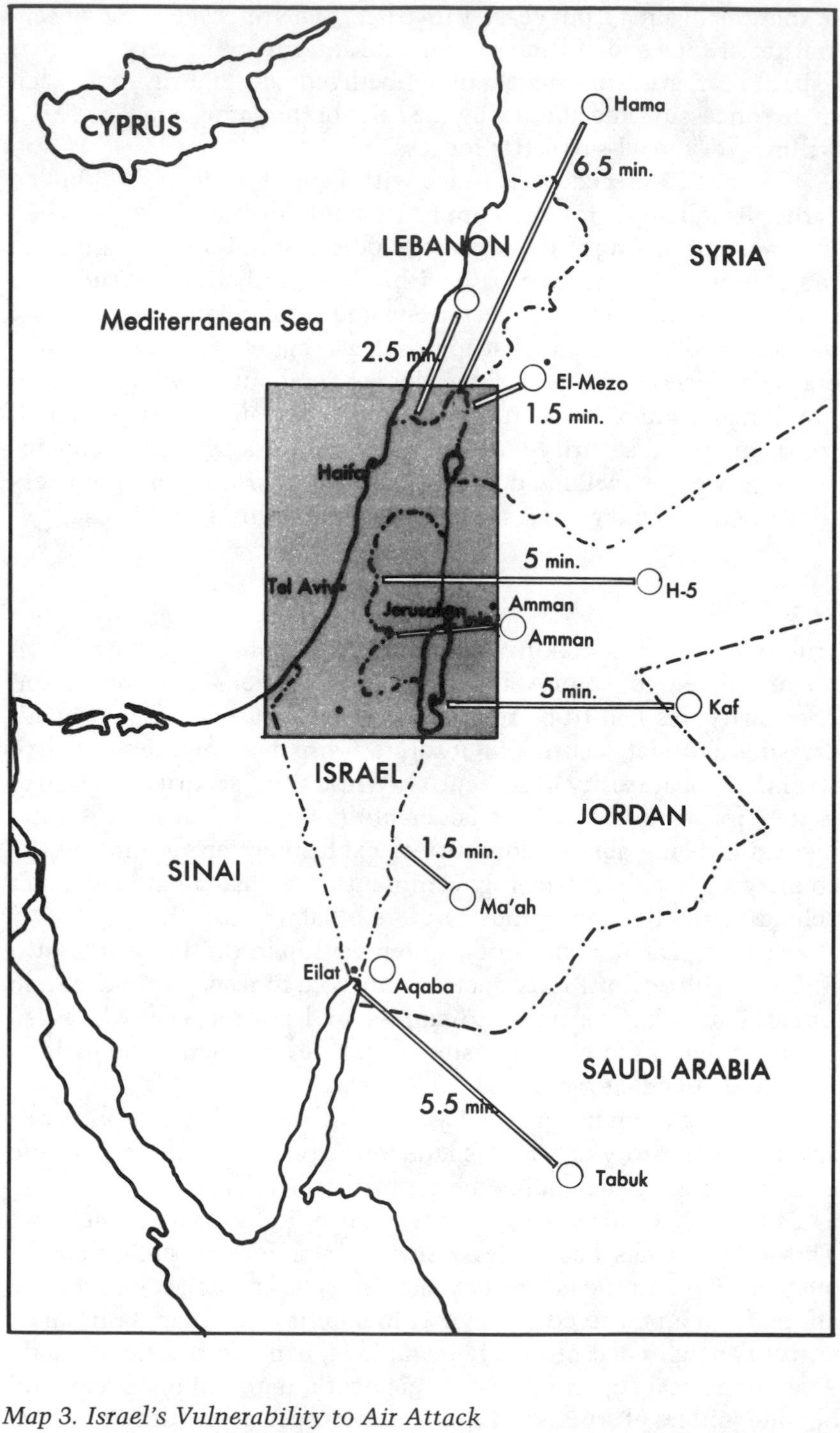

Map 3. Israel's Vulnerability to Air Attack

Table 3. Israel and the Arab States—A Comparison of Defense Expenditure and Military Manpower (1984–87)

Country	Defense Expenditure: $ Million 1984	$ Million 1986	$ Million 1987	$ Per Capita 1984	$ Per Capita 1986	$ Per Capita 1987	% of Government Spending 1984	% of Government Spending 1986	% of Government Spending 1987	% of GDP/GNP 1984	% of GDP/GNP 1986	Numbers in Armed Forces (000) 1984	Numbers in Armed Forces (000) 1986	Numbers in Armed Forces (000) 1987	Est. Reservists (000) 1987	Para-military (000) 1987
Algeria	929	1,161	1,198	43	51	51	4.4	5.2	5.4	1.8	1.7	130.0	169.0	169.0	150.0	30.0
Bahrain	346	135	143	1,295	468	481	24.1	9.2	9.6	6.9	3.4	2.8	2.8	2.8	—	2.2
Djibòuti	27	30	34	68	74	83	22.4	n.k.	n.k.	n.k.	n.k.	2.7	4.5	4.2	—	1.2
Egypt	3,786	5,215	4,572	80	105	89	16.3	18.3	15.8	8.2	8.3	2.7	4.5	4.2	—	1.2
Iran	20,582	5,904	8,956	469	124	179	45.3	11.9	15.8	12.3	30.4	550.0	704.5	654.5	350.0	45.0
Iraq	13,835	11,583	13,996	929	752	880	n.k.	n.k.	n.k.	51.2	31.7	642.5	845.0	1,000.0	170.0	5.0
Israel	5,798	5,559	5,136	1,380	1,263	1,154	39.1	24.8	20.8	22.4	18.9	141.0	149.0	141.0	504.0	4.5
Jordan	533	714	745	209	262	270	26.6	30.2	24.9	13.7	15.5	76.3	70.2	80.3	35.0	6.5
Kuwait	1,655	1,381	1,400	2,527	1,995	1,950	12.5	9.1	11.6	7.6	8.1	12.5	12.0	15.0	—	—
Lebanon	312	n.k.	n.k.	115	n.k.	n.k.	18.6	n.k.	n.k.	n.k.	n.k.	20.3	15.3	n.k.	—	8.0
Libya	n.k.	1,409	1,386	n.k.	371	365	n.k.	14.4	13.9	n.k.	6.8	73.0	71.5	76.5	40.0	2.5
Mauritania	n.k.	n.k.	n.k.	23	n.k.	n.k.	3.5	n.k.	n.k.	9.8	n.k.	8.0	8.4	14.8	—	6.4
Morocco	476	751	860	20	33	37	9.5	13.5	13.4	4.0	5.1	144.0	170.0	203.5	—	35.0
Oman	1,960	1,731	1,508	2,362	1,919	1,596	38.5	35.6	36.0	21.3	28.4	21.5	21.5	21.5	1.0	5.0
Qatar	166	n.k.	n.k.	615	n.k.	n.k.	5.0	n.k.	n.k.	2.5	n.k.	6.0	6.0	7.0	—	—
Saudi Arabia	22,674	17,306	16,235	3,637	2,599	2,360	37.5	46.9	35.8	21.5	22.4	51.5	67.5	73.5	—	8.5
Somalia	104	83	n.k.	23	18	n.k.	33.4	51.8	n.k.	n.k.	11.0	62.5	42.7	65.0	—	29.5
Sudan	269	376	391	12	16	17	13.1	17.0	16.2	3.5	n.k.	58.0	56.8	58.5	—	3.0
Syria	3,210	3,623	3,949	309	322	351	30.5	32.4	37.2	16.7	14.5	367.5	392.8	407.5	272.5	34.8
Tunisia	437	521	524	62	71	74	13.9	17.3	15.6	5.4	5.9	30.0	37.0	42.1	—	9.0
UAE	1,867	1,880	1,580	1,436	1,446	1,215	43.8	49.2	64.4	6.7	8.8	43.0	43.0	43.0	—	—
North Yemen	598	503	530	80	65	66	39.1	37.4	39.9	16.6	12.5	36.6	36.6	36.8	40.0	25.0
South Yemen	194	n.k.	n.k.	88	n.k.	n.k.	20.9	n.k.	n.k.	17.7	n.k.	27.5	27.5	27.5	45.0	45.0

Source: IISS. *The Military Balance, 1988–1989* (London: The International Institute for Strategic Studies, 1988), p. 255.

n.k. = not known

ened politically because Israel is one of the few countries unaffiliated formally with any bilateral, regional, or international military alliance system.

Second, while the national security doctrine stresses defense, in certain key respects it is also offensive in nature. If attacked, Israel pushes the battlefield back onto enemy ground. In the past it has pursued a firm policy of reprisal and retaliation. Preemption has also been a favored strategic option best demonstrated by the Six-Day War in June 1967. In much the same way leaders have acted aggressively, ignoring international legal conventions, in their counterterrorism campaign, for example, or in the air strike against the Iraqi nuclear reactor in 1981. Such controversial force demonstrations inevitably create a political storm, thereby further complicating the task of Israeli diplomats.

A third consequence of the self-defense posture is the militarization of foreign policy. Early on Israel's military establishment laid claim to national security as its exclusive preserve, supported by prevailing and incontestable military facts on the ground. Preoccupation with security—the image of an Arab noose always poised around Israel's collective neck—has translated into a high state of military alert, resource mobilization, budget allocation, and indigenous defense industries.

Foreign policy considerations take a back seat to military options as a result of this larger, overriding security preoccupation. Judging from past performance, Israeli pragmatic, down-to-earth decision makers are more inclined to downplay arguments based on diplomatic niceties, legal nuances, or reliance on others in favor of direct, unilateral action. Particularly in stressful situations, diplomacy is dismissed as inappropriate, time consuming, and possibly even detrimental and counterproductive. In the 1976 Entebbe plane-hijacking crisis, the Israeli government preferred risking a dangerous air rescue operation to negotiating with Arab terrorists. Again, in the case of the 1981 Iraqi reactor strike, Israel opted to take out the nuclear facility alone rather than wait for international pressure to mount against Baghdad.

Also reflecting this pattern of diplomacy's subordination, the Ministry for Foreign Affairs traditionally has played a secondary role in policy making to its bureaucratic counterpart, the Ministry of Defense, as shall be discussed in part 2. Perhaps the Soviet Union's Georgi Arbatov had this in mind in June 1988 when he noted wryly how once it was fashionable in Europe to say the Jews made excellent diplomatic envoys and terrible fighters, whereas today they are known for being superb soldiers but poor diplomats.

Arguably, Israeli statecraft's greatest contribution in the field of security is its strategic relationship with the United States. Yet, such are Israel's insecurities that this, too, has come to be viewed as a source of uncertainty. First, because the relationship also implies excessive dependence on Washington. Second, because it lacks iron-clad safeguards should Israel's security be compromised and the country's existence become threatened by a massive attack from the Arabs and not the Soviets.

The security interest, in short, conforms to a regressive pattern. Like peace and legitimacy, it still eludes Israel. The effect is seen in national security definitions that focus almost exclusively on the physical dimension—on military strength and deterrent capability. The staying power of this force approach to complex military-political problems appears to have survived even the 1982–84 armed invasion of Lebanon and subsequent disillusionment. More than a year into the Palestinian uprising in the administered territories that began in December 1987 (the *intifada*), the government almost exclusively emphasized military and police efforts.

The average Israeli will nod in agreement that the best guarantee of security is normalized interstate relations, only to add ruefully that given declared Arab intentions he or she no longer looks with confidence to the UN Security Council or any other international actor. Israelis in the past preferred the more visceral, the more emphatic response, choosing to arm themselves and to go it alone. Such a narrow concept of the "security dilemma" clearly does not often leave much room, or esteem in Israeli eyes, for the diplomatic art.

Commerce

Foreign trade is at least one area where Israelis could see and appreciate diplomacy's contribution to the national interest of economic strength and development. This economic dimension of foreign policy, after all, is vitally important for Israel.

Being deficient in nearly every category of raw materials, the country has always been dependent upon imports. In recent years, as an industrializing country with a small home market, Israel's economic planners have adopted an aggressive export-oriented strategy and argue the need for overseas outlets if Israel is to pursue continued industrial growth. Also, from both an ideological and symbolical standpoint, flourishing international trade relations partially allay Israeli insecurities. These relations suggest the country really does have a global contribution to make after all, such as in offering a paradigm for Third World modernization, and confirm its active participation in international affairs as a desirable trading partner.

Nevertheless, from the beginning Israel encountered various barriers to free trade, informal as well as formal. Middle East antagonism denied Israel access to its logical and natural trading partners, the geographically proximate Arab countries. This blow to economic prospects has been considerably damaging because Arab ostracism of Israel goes much further than simply refusing to deal directly with the Zionist entity. Following 1948 an entire economic boycott apparatus was set up under the Arab League, its expressed purpose being to dissuade other countries from dealing with the Zionist state and, if necessary, to impose sanctions against those governments and corporations either selling to or purchasing from Israel. This blacklist even extended to foreign flag vessels destined for Israeli ports.

As part of this "war by other means" against Israel, Egypt took the lead in barring the Suez Canal to Israeli goods and merchant shipping. It did so in direct defiance of a UN Security Council resolution in September 1951 calling upon Egypt to end its violation of the 1888 Constantinople Convention pledging freedom of navigation through this international waterway to all states. As justification for this discriminatory action, the Egyptian government insisted that as an artificial, unlawful entity Israel could not be entitled to the rights and privileges accorded legitimate states by the convention. When the resolution remained inoperative, it served as a lesson in Israel's international education. The United Nations would never again be looked to as Israel's savior or guarantor of security.

During the late sixties and seventies, economic warfare against Israel expanded. Arab oil wealth enabled countries like Saudi Arabia and Libya to dangle offers of monetary aid to Afro–Asian countries like Uganda in exchange for their willingness to terminate commercial and diplomatic agreements with Israel.

Objections by Israel to such flagrant discriminatory measures largely fell on deaf ears. Not eliciting an international response in defense of free trade, and aside from U.S. congressional legislation opposing cooperation by American firms with Arab League strictures, Israel for the most part has had to gear itself to countering the Arab boycott unilaterally. The economic-diplomatic strategy long in effect in Jerusalem offers a riposte built around a range of tactics that includes (a) taking pains to retain traditional trading partners by suggesting economics be divorced from politics so that differences in the latter not be allowed to interfere with bilateral commercial cooperation, (b) diversifying sources of supply and export, and (c) struggling to enter new regional markets such as the Far East and to establish new trade relationships.

The strategy can claim not a few economic payoffs. Israel's exports, for instance have increased from $300 million in 1950 to just over $1 billion in 1968 and $8.2 billion in 1987. Such achievements are impressive considering the barriers and problems Israel faces—which is exactly the point, for the major thrust of its economic statecraft still lies with containment. The decline in foreign economic investment in the last decade has not been reversed. A good percentage of overseas trade has had to be transacted in secret, as was the case with China in the late 1980s, and through the use of third parties in order to circumvent Arab boycott-monitoring organizations. In 1988 the tourist sector, one of Israel's largest, suddenly found itself in a grave crisis after a serious drop in foreign tourism, reduced El Al flight bookings, and canceled hotel reservations prompted by the surge of unrest and violence on the West Bank (the *intifada*). This meant the government had to redirect its efforts. Once again, the direction was toward holding the line: from expanding hotel and other facilities to handle earlier projected tourist inflows to damage control and fighting to save the entire tourist trade.

On the economic front we can conclude, therefore, that the most basic aims—unrestricted access and free competition—are considered more as future targets for Israeli foreign policy than fulfilled goals. Many countries remain reluctant to buy Israeli products or to sell their products in Israel for fear of irritating the Arab and Muslim nations. The same must be said for the fifth goal of Israeli diplomacy which is to persuade foreign governments to support Israeli positions or actions. Once again, there is far more room for concern than for satisfaction among Foreign Ministry officials.

Foreign Endorsement

Simply put, Israel has had an increasingly hard time mounting an effective propaganda or information (*hasbara*) campaign in support of state policies. The record, although mixed and uneven, shows the early period to have been better than the more recent one.

Consistent with the optimism in 1948, the original premise was that Israel could expect to receive a fair hearing from the world community. Hence the initial positive attitude toward the United Nations as an impartial forum for presenting Israel's viewpoint on national, regional, and global issues and its case concerning aspects of the Arab-Israeli dispute. If anything, one might say that international opinion in the early years showed a bias in favor of Israel: sympathizing on the one hand with the historical circumstances attending its birth and, on the other, making allowance for its inexperience as well as special security plight. Thus, while by no means problem free, the first years found the infant state enjoying both a positive image and a sympathetic audience. The prevailing perception placed Israel in the role of underdog, popularized in the image of a diminutive yet courageous David pitted against the Arabs' Goliath.

Since then, of course, the roles have been reversed. The change took place gradually, beginning toward the close of the first decade. As signposts for this erosion in world support, we recall the following:

1949—Arab propagandists embarked on a programmatic campaign to discredit Israel in every way possible, which later widened to include Muslim and Third World critics.

1956—Collaboration with Britain and France against Egypt, regardless of its logic or compelling necessity at the level of the local Arab-Israeli conflict, further played into Arab hands by linking Israel in the eyes and mind of outside spectators with Western imperialism.

1967—A convincing victory in the June war ended the image of Israeli military inferiority, substituting for it the impression of preponderant strength.

After 1967 Israel's portrayal by the world media shifted to that of an occupying power bent on possessing Arab lands and denying Palestinian rights. Israeli representatives failed completely in pressing home the historic claim to a Jewish presence across the old, pre-1967 "green line." Historic roots, religious attachment, and future economic potential were all understated in stressing the primacy of the security factor. In public relations terms, where impressions and stereotypes count for everything, it was as simple as this: David had become Goliath.

The image problem only became worse in the next two decades, to such an extent that not even so positive and constructive an accomplishment as Israel's 1979 treaty of peace negotiated with Egypt had the power to arrest the decline in Israeli prestige, let alone to reverse it. Two particularly calamitous *hasbara* events best record this downward slope:

1975—Endorsement by seventy-two UN members (thirty-five against, with thirty-two abstentions) of a General Assembly resolution designating Zionism to be a form of racism and of racial discrimination; and

1982—International criticism heaped on Israel for its armed incursion into Lebanon, capped by photographs of the

> shelling of residential Beirut and indirect responsibility for the slaughter of Palestinian civilians in the refugee camps of Sabra and Shatilla by Christian militia.

Nor were the intervening six years exactly free of contention.

The IDF's temporary seizure of southern Lebanon as far as the Litani River (March–June 1978) did not help promote Israeli public relations. Destruction of the Iraqi nuclear reactor in June 1981 likewise could not be expected to sit well with champions of international law and organization who always have had difficulty subscribing to Israeli definitions of legitimate self-defense. In the same mold, application of Israeli law to the Golan Heights in December 1981, in effect unilaterally annexing them to Israel, reverberated badly. Then again, Israel's perceived obduracy on peace-related questions, or its policy of authorizing new West Bank settlements as well as "thickening" existing ones, represent merely two of the numerous other ongoing and contentious issues that could be counted on to fill the interludes between one dramatic episode and another, both before and after the Lebanon war.

Just when it seemed as though the international climate might be improving, Israel unexpectedly found itself once more in the public eye—and not in a complimentary sense. Tough measures used in putting down Palestinian disturbances (the *intifada* uprising) on the West Bank and in the Gaza Strip in the months after December 1987 brought renewed censure in the United States, at the UN, and elsewhere that Israeli representatives had considerable difficulty in countering.

Living for so long with criticism can hardly be expected not to leave its traces on policy. Israelis have conditioned themselves against such combined verbal and media attacks through a combination of public impatience with the world and studied indifference. David Ben-Gurion, when asked to comment on one-sided condemnations of Israel by the UN ("oom" in Hebrew abbreviation), replied derisively: "Oom-shmoom." Israel's first premier on another occasion postulated: "Never mind what the Gentile world thinks or says—all that really matters is what the Jews do!" Translated into contemporary policy terms, this attitude has lowered expectations that other governments will endorse Israeli policies.

Here, holding the line is best reflected in the refusal by successive governments to authorize sufficient funding needed for waging a more effective, more persuasive campaign—one geared to winning friends, to influencing world opinion favorably, and to refurbishing Israel's image abroad. Failure to assign information a higher priority fits the pattern of foreign policy defensiveness. It also constitutes a self-fulfilling prophecy by, in effect, abandoning this sensitive, politically relevant arena of *hasbara* to enemy propagandists. The result could be Israel's loss of the important media or information (image) war.

Constructive Engagement

By this point in the discussion the thrust of the argument should be clear. Israeli foreign relations proceed overall from a constricted rather than expansive, "the sky's the limit" framework, both conceptually and operationally. Nowhere is this broad retreat more apparent than by what has happened to Israel's pledge in 1948–49 to dedicate itself to improving the lot of mankind and to exercising an affirmative influence upon international relations.

So far removed is this objective from recent political reality that it is almost impossible now to recapture for the younger reader what this sixth diplomatic aspiration meant to the founding generation. At Israel's creation, the Jewish state confidently assumed that it would be part of the solution, not the problem.

Reporting to the Knesset on 15 June 1949, Israel's first foreign minister, Moshe Sharett, addressed the historic significance for Jews of the UN admission just awarded Israel: "It brought Israel *back* into the community of nations." It also "conferred upon the Jewish people regathered in their ancient land equal rights with all free nations." To Sharett, it "*closed* the dark chapter of persecution, degradation, and discrimination." By this "*revolutionary* change," a "new and complex *responsibility*" had devolved upon Israel as it confidently entered what he called "the ring of international contest and mutual dependence."

Driven in part by idealism and in part by the anti-Semitic stereotype of the parasitic Jew, Zionist diplomacy's explicit aim was to act as a catalyst for realizing Israel's full integration into the world economy and into the world society. Almost obsessively, Zionist leaders felt an inner need to prove both to themselves and to the rest of the world the potential of the Jewish people. If only provided the opportunity to do so through sovereign statehood, the Jews had a major contribution to offer mankind.

Accordingly, many smaller states see UN membership of intrinsic value, a foremost goal in and of itself, conferring both status and pride. For Israel in its infancy, as Sharett was arguing, admission to the international organization was regarded as merely the start, as but a means to fulfilling the larger end.

In his first address to the General Assembly of the United Nations on 11 May 1949, Sharett made this particular point. In extending a hand of true friendship to all peace-loving nations, Israel, he said, was fully conscious of the fact that poverty and ignorance were hereditary enemies of lasting peace and therefore pledged its cooperation under UN auspices.

> The Government of Israel was determined to do all it could to root out those twin evils, to raise the standard of living of the common man, without distinction of race or creed, to ensure equal rights to all, to safeguard the equality of status of men and women, to raise the dignity of labour, to guarantee freedom of enterprise, individual and collective, without the framework of a progressive State, to ensure full religious freedom and to add its proof that true democracy could be as fully operative for the commonweal in Asia as in any other part of the world.

For this reason more than any other, Israel sought to be heard on a wide range of global and Middle East issues aimed at fostering world progress and international understanding.

Indeed, for a brief time Israel's initial experience in the field of sociocultural and economic cooperation encouraged these lofty pretensions. Its impressive outreach program during the 1950s and 1960s proved quite successful. In those years Israel could be found at the forefront of worldwide efforts at international development. It played an assertive role at multilateral conferences sponsored by the UN Educational, Scientific, and Cultural Organization (UNESCO) and in the framework of activities by other UN specialized agencies. Offers by Israel to share its experience and techniques in specific fields as agriculture and desert reclamation, absorption and education, lowering infant mortality and other health programs, and urban development met with a warm reception in Africa, Asia, and Latin America, and aid from Israel was often sought after.

Again, however, the general pattern of decline affecting foreign relations soon repeated itself by the second decade. Humanitarian, political, functional collaboration could not be kept divorced for long from politics. Consequently, Israeli fortunes shifted much for the worse, and early gains in constructive engagement were dissipated, leading to a narrowing of policy emphasis. So much so that in more recent years Israeli policy makers are accustomed, even if not entirely reconciled, to finding both Israel and Zionism referred to in world forums in largely negative terms. The UN body, in particular, has long since become a place of unremitting hostility.

Were the United Nations to be believed, Israel would be confirmed as "not a peace-loving member state." UN documents contain an extensive list of declarations charging Israel with acting contrary to international legal norms and conventions and with continued disregard of UN resolutions. All too frequently Israel finds itself described as a primary threat to world peace and security. By the unwritten rules of politics in the United Nations, for all intents and purposes Israel is barred from serving as a rotating nonpermanent member on the Security Council; no Israeli jurist has ever been appointed to a term as judge on the fifteen-member International Court of Justice. For many people the Middle East conflict, and Israel in particular, is perceived as a menace to international order and stability.

As an indication of this tremendous gap, consider the wording as well as the lopsided margins of three UN resolutions adopted all in one working day, 7 December 1988. The first declared that Israel was not a peace-loving country and called upon all members to sever diplomatic, trade, and cultural ties with the Jewish state. It was approved by a vote of 83 in favor, 21 against, 45 abstaining. The second condemnation reaffirmed that, contrary to the view of Israel, the question of Palestine was the core of the Middle East conflict. It, too, passed: 103–18–30. The third resolution declared Israeli law null and void in its capital, Jerusalem, and was supported by 143 members, with 7 abstentions. Only El Salvador stood by Israel.

International integration, in short, has been part of Israel's monumental ambitions and—so far—unrealistic expectations. True to form, Israel's reaction to such attacks and ostracism has been to withdraw into its own protective shell. Fighting back for the most part has meant replying to criticism by others. It means averting a situation of being relegated to the status of a pariah state. And at times it means boycotting no longer hospitable international bodies. Whatever else, this is a far, far cry from the constructive engagement foreseen in 1948.

Links to World Jewry

It is a final testimony to overall depressed foreign policy goals—the gap between expectation and achievement—that what was once taken to be axiomatic and self-evident, i.e., Israel as the centerpiece of contemporary (post-exile and post-Holocaust) Jewish life, is now open to question . . . and from within the Jewish fold. Goal revision with respect to Israel and the Jewish people traces itself through perhaps three consecutive stages.

The initial Israel-Diaspora relationship postulated several

things. First, that the now sovereign Jewish state, with a defense capability and diplomatic contacts of its own, henceforth would serve as defender of the Jewish people. Israel offered a haven of refuge for the oppressed or imperiled Jew anywhere in the world, the only physical guarantee against a repeat of the Holocaust nightmare. A second premise emphasized that Israel and Zion represented, in addition, a spiritual and cultural center—if not for the entire world then at least for the Jewish world. Third, that ultimately Israel was the only place for Jews to live. In effect, Israel felt justified—nay, duty-bound—in arrogating to itself the fourfold function of acting as guardian, representative, magnet, and homeland. In return, Israel asked fellow Jews in the Diaspora (*gola* or *galut*) for their full identification and support.

In the beginning, this role of primacy and of undisputed Jewish leadership was taken for granted in Israel and by Israelis. The Jewish Agency, headquartered in Jerusalem, acted as coordinator and catalyst for a host of educational, cultural, and humanitarian projects undertaken jointly with Diaspora leaders. More important, each Israeli envoy, apart from his or her regular diplomatic mandate, accepted a special mission to act as an emissary to the indigenous Jewish community. And in this first stage Israeli representatives couched their appeal to Jewry in uncompromising terms of solidarity: political backing in crisis, lending a hand in its epic story of Jewish renaissance, and above all, the ultimate personal commitment of immigration (*aliya*). The country, after all, had been built through *aliya* and "the ingathering of the exiles" (see Table 4).

As a result of this stress on the theme of maximum commitment to the Zionist enterprise, two major waves of immigration took place during the first twenty-five years. Between 1948 and 1951 the Jewish population of Israel doubled in size from the original 650,000. Then 1968 to 1973 became the prime years of immigration from the West.

Table 4. Immigration to Israel by Region of Birth (1919–48)

Region	Numbers	Percentage
Europe	377,487	87.81%
Asia	40,776	9.48%
America and Oceania	7,579	1.77%
Africa	4,033	0.94%
TOTAL	429,875	100.00%

Source: Central Bureau of Statistics, *Israel Statistical Abstract*, no. 39 (1988), p. 161.

These were to be the high-water marks, however (see Table 5). *Aliya* figures peaked and then declined instead of progressively increasing with time.

The seventies marked a second or transitional stage in Israel's special relationship toward world Jewry. During those years the emphasis shifted from sole leadership to a greater sense of copartnership. Close collaboration continued, with Israel serving as a prime sealer, uniting Jews otherwise divided on theological, denominational, political, or cultural lines in a single common cause, that of ensuring the Jewish state's viability. Nevertheless, rumblings could be heard in this dialogue in reaction to the lopsided nature of the relationship, with discreet calls from the Diaspora for a more equal partnership. Specifically, Jewish leaders asked to be consulted on certain issues, especially decisions by Israel that might influence, either directly or indirectly, the delicate standing of Jewish communities abroad. It was also then that the message of *aliya* becomes distinctly muted. Rather than insisting on *aliya*, as Ben-Gurion had done, Israeli representatives showed a willingness to settle for less. Other tangible expressions of solidarity with Israel became substitutes for the personal long-term commitment of individual Jews to settle in Israel: purchase of Israel bonds and similar fund-raising campaigns, private Jewish economic investment, perhaps some pro-Israel political lobbying in home countries, tourist visits to the Holy Land, possibly even a year's study or work program in Israel. The main thing was "to have a foothold in Israel." Almost imperceptibly the foreign policy of Israel toward its only natural ally—the Jewish people—pulled back to more defensible positions.

Yet even these minimalist positions, still resting on Israel's preeminence within this Jewish partnership, have become less tenable over the last decade or so. For one thing, some Jews outside Israel found the image of Israel and the message it sought to spread flat and uninspiring. After forty years Israel-Diaspora relations had come to be

Table 5. Immigration to Israel by Region of Birth (1948–88)

Region	Numbers	Percentage
Europe	832,676	47.12%
Africa	445,849	25.23%
Asia	358,825	20.30%
America and Oceania	129,631	7.33%
TOTAL	1,766,981	100.00%

Source: Central Bureau of Statistics, *Israel Statistical Abstract*, no. 39 (1988), p. 162.

marked by an increased number of fractious issues that, on several notable occasions, even resulted in embarrassing public acrimony. The recent impression is of distinguished world Jewish figures as well as organizations distancing themselves from Israeli policies to an unprecedented degree. Some are troubled by Israeli political trends that surfaced in 1977, highlighted by the Likud party's electoral triumph, which suggest a less liberal, more nationalist mood; others by Israeli government positions toward the territories, settlement policy, and the peace process. Whatever the reason, clearly Jewish leaders abroad refuse to remain silent, to align themselves unquestioningly alongside Israel, or to take their marching orders, so to speak, from Jerusalem.

The specific *aliya* issue is a case in point. In this third stage, the notion of large-scale Jewish immigration to Israel is no longer really contentious (see Table 6).For all of 1988, only 13,464 *olim* (people who immigrate to Israel) settled in Israel—a mere increase of 46 people over the previous year. Instead, it is the Jewish demographic flow in the opposite direction—from Israel (*yerida*) to the *gola* (Diaspora), and to North America in particular, rather than the other way around—that arouses extreme sensitivities on both sides (see Table 7).

Government authorities, for example, differ sharply with Diaspora leaders over Soviet Jewry. Initially, they disagreed as to the best approach for influencing the Kremlin to allow its Jews to go—whether by public protests and mass demonstrations, or as Israel has argued, through quiet overtures. Then, in the mid-1980s the issue became one of whether Soviet émigrés and "prisoners of Zion" should be permitted to resettle anywhere they chose or, as Israel maintained, to be brought first to Israel. From the beginning of the 1970s through

Table 6. Immigrants to Israel by Period of Immigration (1919–88)

Years	Numbers of Immigrants
1919–48 (May)	482,857
1948–51	686,739
1952–60	294,488
1961–64	228,046
1965–71	197,821
1972–79	265,582
1980–84	83,637
1985–86	20,147
1987	12,965
1988	13,464

Source: Central Bureau of Statistics, *Israel Statistical Abstract*, no. 39 (1988), p. 161.

Table 7. Immigration—Emigration Percentages (1968–88)

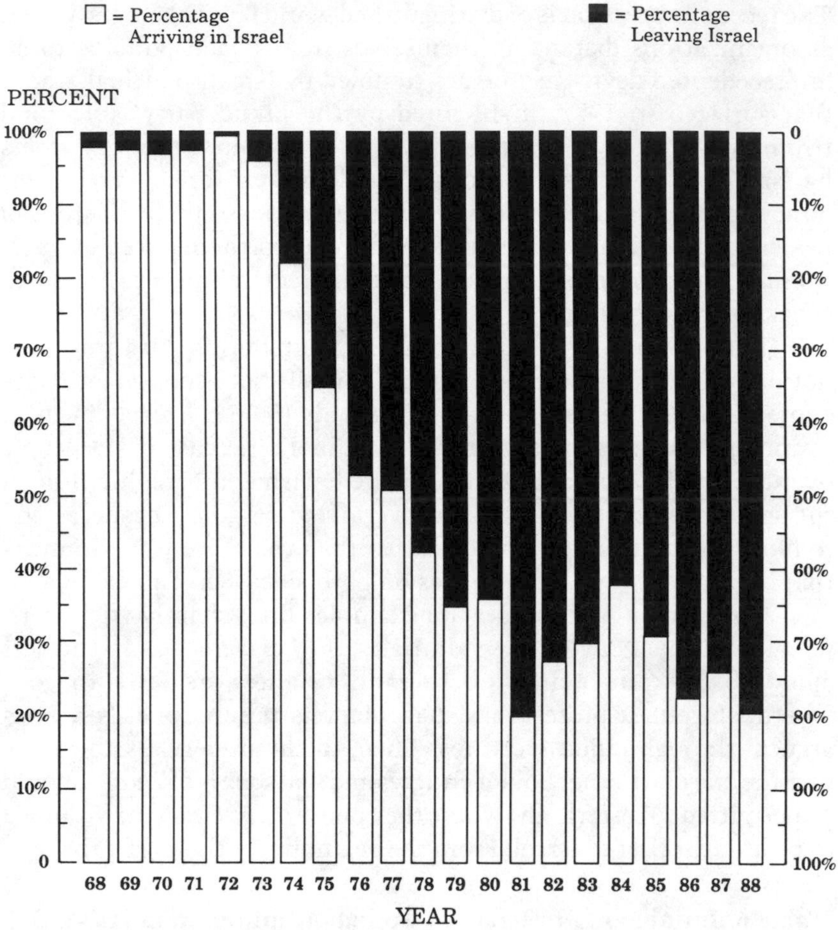

Source: *Maariv*, 20 June 1988.

1988, a total of 270,000 Jews left the Soviet Union, of whom 170,000 (62.9 percent) came to live in Israel. Recent dropout (*neshira*) rates show a major attrition, with Soviet Jewry opting in large numbers for destinations other than Israel (see Table 8). A new low was reached in May 1988 when figures indicated that of the 1,116 Jews leaving the USSR that month a mere 110 (9.5 percent) came to Israel.

More sensitive still, from the standpoint of Zionist ideology, is the fairly new hypothesis advocating that world Jewry maintain two main centers. As articulated by Professor Jacob Neusner and others,

Table 8. Soviet Jewish Immigration (1968–87)

Year	Jews Leaving USSR	Jews Arriving in Israel
1968	231	231
1969	3,033	3,033
1970	999	999
1971	12,897	12,839
1972	31,903	31,652
1973	34,733	33,277
1974	20,767	16,888
1975	13,363	8,435
1976	14,254	7,250
1977	16,833	8,350
1978	28,956	12,090
1979	51,331	17,278
1980	21,648	7,570
1981	9,448	1,762
1982	2,692	731
1983	1,314	861
1984	896	340
1985	1,140	348
1986	904	201
1987	8,060	2,015
Total	275,402	166,150

Source: Moshe Zak, *Israel and the Soviet Union—A Forty Year Dialogue* (Tel Aviv: Sifriat Maariv, 1988) (Hebrew), p. 459.

the argument briefly is that Israel cannot claim to be the sole, or even leading, center of Jewish cultural creativity; nor is it self-evident that the survival of the Jewish people as such would be impossible without the Jewish state. Other liberal countries may serve as an alternative national home, with the United States currently rivaling Israel as a magnet (see Table 9). A final irony is the invitation before and during the 1988 Knesset election campaign from certain Israeli political representatives to the Diaspora to see itself as an overseas Jewish constituency with a right to participate in determining Israel's future and therefore duty-bound to resolve the recent deadlock in that country's domestic politics.

The year 1988 further exposed the relationship's potential for dividing Israeli and non-Israeli Jews unless both sides show greater sensitivity for each other's position and needs. As part of the coalition bargaining immediately following the 1 November elections to the Knesset, the three ultrareligious parties declared their intention to

Table 9. Largest Centers of World Jewry, 1986

			Percentage of Total Jewish Population	
			In the Diaspora	In the World
Rank	Country	Jewish Population	Percent	Percent
1	United States	5,700,000	60.6	43.9
2	Israel	3,562,500	—	27.5
3	Soviet Union	1,515,000	16.1	11.7
4	France	530,000	5.6	4.1
5	Great Britain	326,000	3.5	2.5
6	Canada	310,000	3.3	2.4
7	Argentina	224,000	2.4	1.7
8	South Africa	115,000	1.2	0.9
9	Brazil	100,000	1.1	0.8

Source: American Jewish Year Book 1988 (New York: The American Jewish Committee, 1988), p. 427.

table legislation (not for the first time) redefining who is a Jew according to the Orthodox interpretation. This aroused such a firestorm of opposition from Jewish communal leaders outside Israel, and especially from Conservative and Reform Jews in America, that even veteran Israeli politicians were taken aback and sought to put out the fire with as little damage as possible.

The present trend in Israel-Diaspora relations is clear. Appealing to Jewish solidarity is no longer sufficient. A basic gap has been in the making comprised of one part ideology, one part geography. Its existence is represented at the start of the nineties by what are generally accepted by Israeli and Jewish leaders to be the two deepest and most contentious issues. The first is the prickly "Who is a Jew?" question, and the second, the Palestinian question. Emphasizing different ideas of what constitutes safety and security for the Jewish people at the end of this century, together these two issues hold the key to possible Israeli futures internally and in links to the disaggregated Jewish hinterland watching and waiting in the Diaspora.

Given this new state of Jewish affairs, the onus of Israeli statecraft becomes, above all, to avoid confrontation with Jewish leaders and communities; to reduce differences and close Jewish ranks around shared concerns. In short, the goal is to maintain and, where possible, to revitalize this vital partnership with the one permanent ally, the Jewish people.

HOLDING THE LINE

What we have been considering here are Israel's vital international interests and objectives. These have not changed one iota; indeed, they are immutable. Without them there could be no viable state and certainly no Jewish commonwealth. But this does not mean they have been impervious to major developments over the decades, only that the changes are reshuffled priorities and emphases.

The pattern of aspiration vs. achievement in each of the seven major foreign policy areas indicates that Israeli diplomacy, for all of its labors and not insignificant accomplishments, nevertheless, has lost its early forward momentum. Where a young and enthusiastic Israel once set its sights too high, a harder, chastened Israel risks going to the other extreme of setting its sights too low. So much of the diplomatic struggle in the twenty years or more since the 1967 crisis has had to be directed at containing threats as they arise rather than pushing ahead with strategic initiatives.

"Things could have been worse." This is a standard government line of defense. And one that goes over surprisingly well with an Israeli public conditioned by now to the politics of national defense and its corollary: a diplomacy of defensiveness. In keeping with this thinking, success or failure oftentimes tends to be measured more by what greater damage was averted than by how much was achieved. Thus, at the time of the war in Lebanon in 1982 Egypt showed its displeasure merely by recalling its ambassador from Tel Aviv instead of abrogating its treaty of peace with Israel. "No small accomplishment for our side!" was the consensus opinion among relieved policy makers in Jerusalem. After all, things could have been worse.

For the moment, this observation is presented less in criticism than as a statement of reality, because such defensiveness traces more to resignation and caution than to any false sense of complacency. Whatever else its faults, Israel before 1967 and since 1973 is not a complacent state/actor model.

That the main thrust of policy is preventive can be seen in Israel lowering its sights, from maximizing the national interest to what the British and students of public policy call "muddling through" and the Israelis *lehachazik maamad* (to hold the line). The movement has been from receiving universal acceptance to staving off delegitimization; from attaining a genuine peace accompanied by secure, recognized boundaries to making the best of a tense truce along exposed lines; from having absolute security to living with a sense of absolute insecurity bordering on paranoia. On the international diplomatic front, as well, as late as 1989 an enormous amount of effort was being expended—for the time being successfully—in what can only be judged as a rear-guard action. With U.S. understanding, Israeli foreign policy labored at frustrating the PLO's applications for membership and full admission to such UN bodies as the World Health Organization, the International Labor Organization, the Food and Agriculture Organization, and UNESCO, where it already had obtained nonvoting, observer status.

The same is true in the remaining cluster of national goals. Instead of enjoying free trade, at this late date Israel still finds itself combating economic obstructionism, coming up against many doors closed to Israeli salespeople and products. Its foreign reputation, judging from media commentary, has gone from positive to blurred, to highly controversial if not negative. In the meantime, Israeli diplomats also have their hands full preventing the country from being labeled a detriment to world peace—a far cry from the desire to see itself, and to be seen by others, as a positive force. Nor have the government in Jerusalem and its representatives been entirely successful on the Jewish front, where different perspectives and viewpoints are no longer easily papered over or resolved.

If each issue-area has undergone profound internal change, so, too, have the core national interests in terms of their relative weight for policy makers and the priority assigned them. Bowing to situational verities, national security needs govern policy. The overriding necessity of assuring the physical safety of the state explains how and why the other six objectives have been subordinated: some (like being "a light unto the nations") temporarily shelved, others compromised and impaired. Preoccupation with national security was best underlined by the late General Moshe Dayan in 1975, who felt that, in lieu of a separate foreign policy, small Israel has only a defense policy into which international considerations are factored. Two years later, Dayan accepted appointment as Israel's foreign minister!

In the latter half of the 1980s, there were certain encouraging signs that Israel's troubled and defensive foreign policy might be turning the corner. At decade's end some definite inroads had been made: in projecting a more moderate and compromising peace stand, in improving the balance of trade, in restoring relations with more than a half-dozen countries. For the present, however, and in the absence of peace and security, Israeli foreign relations continue to be more evasionary than visionary.

CHAPTER 2

THE WORLD AS VIEWED FROM JERUSALEM

It was a generation that yearned for peace. . . . The closer we came to it, the higher towered the obstacles.

—Former Ambassador Gideon Rafael, *Destination Peace*, 1980

ISRAEL AMONG THE NATIONS

Time, war, and the burdens of small-state sovereignty have cut deeply into earlier Israeli reserves of idealism and goodwill, possibly even exhausting both.

"When the Iraqis killed 5,000 Kurds with gas bombs, I did not see anything in the world media comparable to the reaction to Israel's using sticks against Palestinians. The world's response was totally out of proportion to Israel's actions," said Defense Minister Yitzchak Rabin in April 1988 when the West Bank and Gaza *intifada* disturbances were in their fifth month with no end in sight and the conflict in the nearby Persian Gulf was nearing its violent climax.

In Rabin's comment one finds precisely the sort of Israeli defensiveness brought out in the previous chapter. But notice, too, the strong undertone of anger and resentment in his words that we believe express broad Israeli thinking and that consequently provide a useful starting point for understanding not only what national goals are of most concern to Israel but, equally important, how Israelis and their leaders look at international affairs. Pursuit of the national interest, like the conduct of relations with other countries, originates at home, beginning with elite perceptions and public attitudes.

This is especially true of an open society like Israel whose citizens are known to be highly politicized and definitely opinionated. "A country with one figurehead president and over four million prime ministers" is one way of describing the country, or two Israelis, three political parties. Also, on foreign policy issues Israelis tend to reflect a basic but complex belief system. Most, for instance, believe that the rest of the world really does apply an unfair double standard wherever and whenever their country is concerned. Such fundamental beliefs and images in turn directly affect the way in which Israel now plays the "game of nations" as opposed to how it did say thirty or forty years ago. These beliefs also affect the Jewish state's place (a) in world history and (b) in current Middle East and world politics.

Consider by way of illustration two vivid moments in Israeli diplomatic history. The first scene took place on 12 May 1949 outside the UN headquarters building in New York. An elated Israeli delegation headed by Foreign Minister Moshe Sharett himself proudly hoisted the blue-and-white flag of Israel, newly admitted to the world organization. The second scene was recorded a quarter-century later, on 10 November 1975. From the rostrum of the same United Nations, an indignant Ambassador Chaim Herzog demonstratively tore to shreds the draft text of the infamous General Assembly resolution pronouncing Zionism an anathema and Israel a racist state.

The contrast between the two scenes could hardly be greater. If the first exuded confidence, identification, and global commitment, the second tells of alienation and defiance. Abba Eban, Israel's first United Nation representative and future foreign minister, later recalled the flag-raising ceremony to have been "a moving symbol of a nation's return to the mainstream of world history after centuries of absence." But when his successor, Ambassador Herzog, rose to speak in 1975 the tone was entirely different. Straining to check his anger and at the same time to minimize the ignominy of the anti-Zionism attack, he announced that "for us, the Jewish people, this resolution based on hatred, falsehood, and arrogance is devoid of any moral or legal value." To Israel, he insisted, this "shameful exhibition" would be only a passing episode, whereas the world body was on the way to becoming the "world center of anti-Zionism."

More than forty years of political maturation have profoundly altered Israeli conceptions of what foreign policy and international relations are all about. Israelis have had to redefine for themselves such basic principles of world politics as "sovereignty," "power," "diplomacy," "international justice," "the rule of law," "peace," and "security." Another consequence is the disordering and blurring of the Israeli worldview.

UN endorsement of the Zionist claim to self-determination in November 1947 followed shortly thereafter by independent statehood in May 1948 imbued the 650,000 members of the Jewish community (*yishuv*) then in Palestine with an optimism verging on euphoria. From that initial peak of exuberance, however, the Israeli national outlook has long since shifted in the opposite direction. The mood is somber, down-to-earth, hard-nosed. Israel looks at the world more in relative resignation than in anticipation.

This change of attitude is not often remarked upon. Yet its influence on the conduct of Israeli foreign policy is great. Resentment is deep at how Israel fares in world public opinion and in international forums such as the United Nations. Cynicism prevails toward the role of morality or, for that matter, international legal codes in relations between states. Most Israelis discount professional diplomacy's ability to contribute in any serious way to strengthening the country. One often hears strong doubts voiced about realistic prospects for a genuine peace and reconciliation with the Arabs. The world beyond Israel's borders is often perceived of, in short, as distinctly inhospitable—a dangerous and challenging place.

THREE COMPETING IMAGES

How Israelis see themselves in terms of the world is framed today by three alternative worldviews. While radically different in orientation and implications for foreign policy, all three are rooted in traditional Judaism and inspired by scriptural chapter and verse. Each finds further confirmation in Jewish philosophy and in the collective Jewish historical experience. And each figured in the ideological-political debate over the Zionist solution to the "Jewish problem" that preceded formal statehood. Since 1948 they act, often at the subconscious level, as the filter or "attitudinal prism" through which Israeli policy makers relate to the external environment. The three competing schools of thought are these: idealist, pessimist, realist.

The "Idealist-Internationalist" Image

The first model adopts a positive approach to Israel among the nations. Resting on the Old Testament concept of Israel as *ohr la goyim*, "a light unto the nations" (Isaiah 49:6), it presents the Jewish people and Israel as charged with a special role in human and world affairs. Inspiration comes from the religious texts that speak of "the law that shall go forth from Zion" (Micah 4:2; Isaiah 2:3) and of the Jews as "a dominion of priests and a holy people" (Exodus 19:6). The notion of Israel as "the chosen people" is employed not in the sense of privilege but in terms of commitments and responsibility toward mankind. The entire spirit here is one of internationalism, since carrying out this lofty mission is only possible through close and direct involvement with the international community. This linkage is nicely captured in George Eliot's *Daniel Deronda*: "The world will gain as Israel gains . . . a land set for a halting-place of enmities."

Modern Zionist thinkers returned to this theme. In advocating Jewish nationalism as an act of both political and spiritual redemption, they argued that the Jews, as a people inspired by the universalism of their prophets, even when stateless had always been concerned with the world's problems. How much more so once reconstituted in their own homeland. Rather than motivated solely by considerations of narrow self-interest, they would insist on exercising a constructive influence in the cause of global peace, security, and understanding.

This is the kind of sentiment expressed by Israel's first foreign minister, Moshe Sharett, when on 15 June 1949 in the Knesset he described as a deeply moving event his invitation on 11 May to lead the first delegation of the Jewish state to its seats in the UN General Assembly hall. For Sharett and those of his generation admission to the UN was nothing less than the crowning act of recognition. It brought Israel back into the community of nations. It conferred upon the Jewish people equal rights with all free nations. And it closed the dark chapter of persecution, degradation, and discrimination.

According to this integrationist model, not only is Israel part of the international system, but it is ordained to act in a leadership capacity. The whole thrust of this positive worldview is upbeat. It presumes receptivity toward Israel and its mission on the part of other international actors. It assumes a condition of amity. It looks out upon the world and sees opportunities.

The "Pessimist-Nationalist" Image

The second model prescribes disengagement instead of diplomatic engagement. Where the idealist image touches on exultation, this one addresses Israel among the nations in grim terms of estrangement and alienation, citing the passage in the Bible that assigns Israel to being an eternal *am levadad yishkon*: "Lo, a people that dwelleth alone . . . and shall not be reckoned among the nations" (Numbers 23:9). Here the Jewish people, and by extension the Jewish state, appear as the quintessential outsider cast in the role of perpetual scapegoat, an international outcast positioned "beyond the pale."

Jewish history over the last two thousand years is offered by way of proof, the main themes being those of exile, persecution, discrimination, and pogroms climaxed by the extermination of six million Jews in Europe. Nothing, not even statehood, has sufficed to change this basic condition; anti-Semitic prejudice against the individual or the Jews as a whole merely transfers by extension to the Jewish state, with anti-Zionism serving as a convenient screen.

In seeking to explain to themselves the concentration of hostility, a great many Israelis perceive attacks by foreigners on Zionism and Israel as deriving from a fundamental hostility to a Jewish presence in the Jews' own ancient homeland. Witness, so the argument goes, such evidence in Israel's own more recent international experience as the long string of one-sided UN resolutions condemning Israel; the scandalous General Assembly equation, in 1975, of Zionism with racism; or repeated obstacles to Israel's inclusion in various world cultural and sporting events. In June 1982, as Prime Minister Menachem Begin rose to address the UN plenum, 102 of the 157 delegations walked out.

The foreign policy implications for Israel of this negative worldview are clear. In the fall of 1988, when a panel of five international arbitrators awarded the Taba enclave to Egypt, Premier Shamir exploded: "The UN, the world court, international arbitration, or international conference—it's always against us." Given the futility of reaching out, the aim becomes the exact opposite: to turn inward, to detach the country as much as possible from the external setting and to concentrate instead on Jewish self-reliance by harnessing inner resources—in Israel and within world Jewry—to the fullest extent possible. When adopted, whether consciously or not, this particular mind-set promotes introversion. It perpetuates the ancient themes of threat and persecution. It pictures Israel as alone and as friendless, with the possible exception of fellow Jews. And even they cannot be depended upon unconditionally. Israel, hungry for Jews, regards Soviet Jews who obtain exit permits by professing their love of Zion only to settle in America as cheating. In much the same way, they view South African Jews migrating to Australia, Britain, or Canada as giving up the challenge of Jewish nation-building for the easy life. Totally incomprehensible was the sight of El Al planes returning almost empty from Teheran in 1978, at the height of the Khomeini revolution, when Iranian Jewry failed to read the writing on the wall and to leave the country while the opportunity existed. Such an attitude is xenophobic, cautioning suspicion of foreigners and basic mistrust toward the international environment.

This pessimism also affects how Israelis relate to the core Arab–Israeli conflict. For many there is simply no political solution, while for others the problem is not that there is no solution but that no good solution exists for Israel in the late eighties. In such a state of mind the only choice is between bad and worse, with the search limited to choosing the lesser of possible evils. And, above all, it discounts diplomatic effort and public relations campaigns out of the conviction that the familiar double standard works against Israel: one standard for Israel and a completely different, less critical one for other countries. How else to explain why the Holy See persists in not recognizing the Jewish state of Israel? How else to account for anti-Semitic undercurrents in a Japanese society virtually without previous Jewish contacts and lacking a Jewish resident community to speak of? If there is no Israel-China border dispute, why should Beijing be so resistant to normalized ties? The second model, in short, caters to a latent separatist impulse among Israeli Jews.

Images 1 and 2, though polar opposites in that one is outgoing and the other introverted, nevertheless, share basic similarities. Both insist on viewing Israel as somehow set apart. It may be exceptional in either a positive (image 1) or a negative (image 2) sense—but always distinctive. Both are deterministic as well, insisting Israel's international position is preassigned. And both, as a consequence, in effect make Israeli foreign policy a prisoner of Jewish history.

The "Realist-Internationalist" Image

Yet there is a third, intermediate model that draws a line between the past and the emergence of a state of Israel in 1948. Rejecting in toto the concept of Israel as special, proponents of this view see everything in terms of *Realpolitik*. What governs Israeli behavior is not the Jewishness of the state but the very fact of its being a sovereign nation-state . . . and a small one at that. As such, it is subject to exactly the same political forces as others, bound by the same restraints, judged by identical standards, and entitled to the same privileges. Just as nothing should be taken for granted, so are all doors open before Israel. There are neither permanent friends no permanent enemies. History offers no legacy: neither of optimism nor of pessimism. The Jewish past is regarded as something of an embarrassment, holding back Israel's obligation to accommodate itself to the contemporary world. Similarly, the wish is to avoid being singled out either for special praise or for inordinate censure.

Status, image, security—everything depends on the degree of political astuteness Israeli leaders can show in planning and making their moves on the chessboard of interstate politics. Such thinking, for example, informs the policy of Israeli arms exporters. Weapons sales are a business; Israel is no different from, or morally superior to, Britain, France, the United States, or any other military exporting country.

The essence of this self-image traces back to Deuteronomy 7:14, where the assimilationist principle is given expression: "Appoint for us a king like all the nations around us." The theme is carried into the present by the declaration of statehood in May 1948 that asserts the right of the Jewish people "to be masters of their own fate, like all other nations, in their own sovereign state."

At present no single image dominates Israeli attitudes toward foreign policy and international politics. Already during the earlier, prestate era, Zionist writings combined and used all three themes in promoting the cause of political Zionism in the twentieth century. Idealism was at the heart of the belief that the Jews had reentered history and were quite capable of imposing themselves on world consciousness by political activism. But then, what, if not pessimism, acknowledged the non-Jewish world's enduring dislike for the Jews, thus dictating a nationalist solution to the Jewish problem? Dr. Chaim Weizmann, Zionism's leader in the interwar years, in turn was reflecting the realist ethic in claiming that the Jewish people were asking for nothing more than to be allowed to build in Palestine a nationality that would be "as Jewish as the French nation was French and the British nation British." Still, in this combination of perceptions the first and the third, with their cosmopolitan message of bounded optimism, enjoyed the greatest currency among Zionists up to and including the first years of independence.

Contemporary Israeli political debate indicates a change in outlook, however. The heroic period of the state-in-the-making capped by 1948 constituted the lofty peak during which there was an observable sense of high purpose. Since then, as traced in the first chapter, the idealist school has faded. Gone is any romanticism or generosity of spirit. With Zionism no longer in vogue even in the Zionist state, Israelis cannot exactly be accused of an excess of ideology. We are no longer speaking of the founders and their children as much as the grandchildren. Few Israelis of any age pay much more than lip service to the summons to act as standard-bearer for the world. On the threshold of the nineties a new, worrisome consensus has been forged. Public sentiment, especially among the younger generation, leans toward an austere and rather cheerless interpretation of Israel among the nations.

Opinion surveys conducted in the late 1980s pointed this up in sampling the Israeli public's position on the burning political issues of the day. On the pivotal question of peace for territory, even allowing for some movement, there remained a hard core of opponents in principle to a major territorial withdrawal.

Another poll, done for Tel Aviv University's Jaffee Center for Strategic Studies (JCSS) and released in 1989, revealed a number of further interesting responses that even if not absolutely and scientifically indicative of the trend in public thinking and in the national mood, are certainly instructive (see Table10).Consider the following ratios among the respondents:

- *2:1* against negotiating with the PLO unless it changed its basic position;
- *2:1* in favor of encouraging Arab emigration;
- *2.5:1* believed that Arab aspirations in the final analysis are aimed at conquering Israel and annihilating a large part of the Jewish population;
- *4:1* opposed a Palestinian state in the West Bank and Gaza;
- *4:1* in principle supported the death sentence for convicted Arab terrorists;
- *5:1* felt government handling of security matters in the territories to be too soft or just about right;
- *6:1* objected to returning the entire strategic Golan Heights to Syria even in exchange for a peace treaty; and
- *7:1* were convinced that harboring hatred for Jews was a reason for Arab opposition to Israel.

When confronted with the two alternatives of either giving up or annexing the disputed territories, a greater percentage of Israelis reached by the JCSS survey favored the latter (53 percent) to the former option (endorsed by 47 percent).

The apparent immediate effect of the 1987 *intifada* challenge to Israeli authority and residency in the West Bank was to make hardliners even more steadfast to the point of stoicism, while those who had previously been concessionary showed even greater impatience for a peace settlement to be reached with the Arabs whatever the cost. Also significant, however, was the pronounced softening of views by those huddled in the center who were undecided and wavering. Here the trend by 1989 was toward greater willingness, for example, to engage in a direct dialogue with the Palestinians. In a poll conducted by Mina Zemach and published in the *Yediot Achronot* daily on 10 February 1989, a full 53 percent of those questioned favored negoti-

Table 10. Israel Public Opinion on Yielding Portions of Judea and Samaria

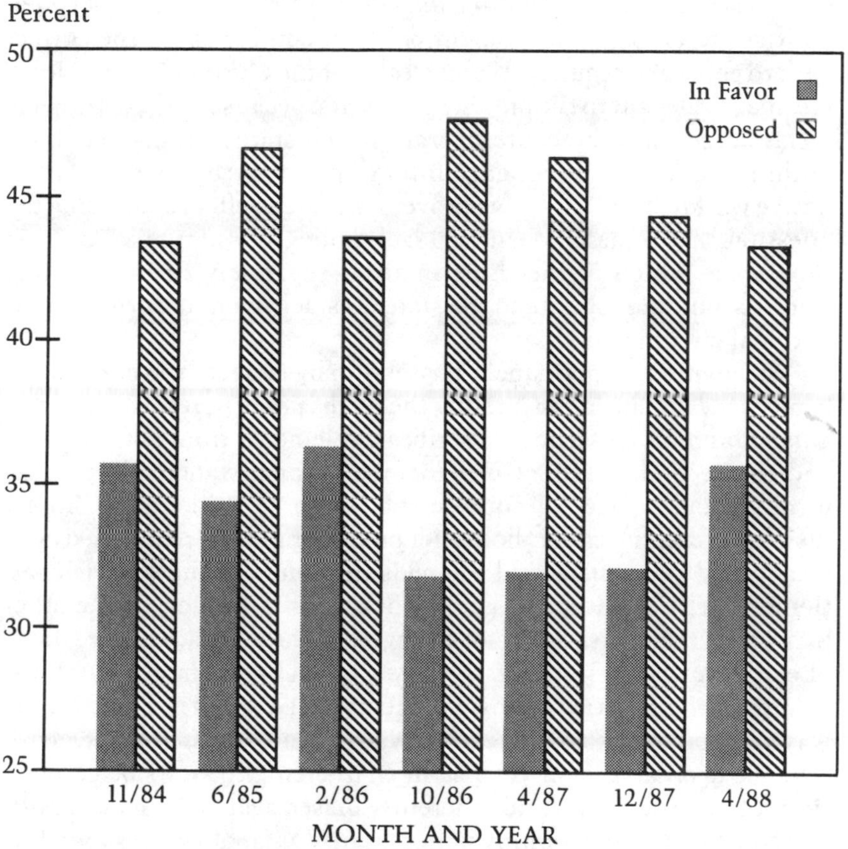

Source: Maariv, 21 June 1988, based on a Modiin Ezrachi survey.

ation with the PLO on the condition that it recognized Israel and put a stop to terrorism.

The needle on the barometer of foreign policy attitudes oscillates between fatalism and cold realism. There is certainly nothing like the erratic pattern Gabriel Almond and other students of American political behavior purport to discern in the United States, with sharp swings in the national mood and basic perceptions from one extreme to another. In Israel there is not so much a *crisis* of identity as an ongoing effort at achieving greater clarity, precision, and focus.

A regular part of extraparliamentary life in Israel of late has been the clash between two ideological movements, *Gush Emunim* (Bloc of the Faithful) and *Shalom Achshav* (Peace Now). Students of Israeli politics present this as a straight political contest about the correct path to peace and security. We suggest that the *Gush* vs "Peace Now" is directly relevant to the present discussion because both parties take us far deeper into the contemporary Israeli state of mind. Theirs is nothing less than a direct encounter of basic perceptions and alternative worldviews. These two movements are in effect addressing the question that remains open of Israel among the nations. Together they argue which of the three images—separately or in combination—is most appropriate to the state of Israel given its current international circumstances.

In arguing for permanent possession by Israel of the entire west bank of the Jordan and in offering the Arabs peace in return for peace, *Gush Emunim* in essence subscribes to elements from both the first and the second images. *Gush* members, for instance, cling to an idealism and a fixity of purpose that to some students of Zionist history is reminiscent of the earlier pioneering ethos that defied both established convention and the odds in promoting new Jewish settlement, self-sacrifice, and a policy of activism. Critics, on the other hand, discern in *Gush* behavior a dangerous throwback to the zealotry of earlier Jewish history, marked by a lack of realism and total disregard for the realities of power. The message of *Gush Emunim*, by way of rejoinder, is to argue for Jewish assertiveness together with reliance upon divine providence in challenging the outside conventions of a non-Jewish world inherently biased against Israel. In short, the spirit of *Gush Emunim* is necessarily unapologetic as well as confrontational in being ready to take on the rest of the world.

Shalom Achshav, in contradistinction, adopts a more conciliatory approach. It, too, retains a trace of idealism in the sense of still believing wholeheartedly in the attainability of peace. Where its adherents differ fundamentally is in the price that realizing peace requires. To the *Gush*'s call for peace through strength and by standing firm, they posit peace through flexibility, sacrifice, and a willingness to compromise. This is a formula dismissed by opponents as surely no less unrealistic, naive, and full of mortal risk for Israel than that proposed by the rival camp. Still, the motivation is to break the chain of senseless violence and hostility by human, political effort to the point of relinquishing territory in return for an end to the conflict.

Neither side has persuaded the other. The debate within Israeli society and in the mind of each Israeli citizen continues unresolved. But it does not rage in an empty vacuum. Now one image, now the other takes hold in response to changing conditions in Israel's external environment.

When times are bad for Israel internationally, as they were immediately after 1973 and again in the early eighties, the self-perception becomes one of having been abandoned by the world community. No less a personage than President Chaim Herzog, known for his urbanity and worldly experience, felt moved in June 1988 to blame "the irrational attitude of the Western world toward Jews, Judaism and, in our case, the Jewish State" as the determining factor in shaping the image of Israel in the world. Shortly thereafter, in February 1989, the U.S. State Department published a 1,600-page survey of human rights abuses worldwide, although the American media chose to focus most of their attention on twelve pages dealing with Israel's behavior in the administered territories. Herzog saw this as "a classic example of the problem that we as a Jewish state face," and alarming as well. His conclusion? "We have suffered from this obsessive prejudice as a Jewish people over the ages and apparently nothing very much has changed in this selective attitude, even though we have achieved statehood." At better moments Israelis simply accept the need to soldier on, to continue pressing their claim to normalcy despite what they insist are the seemingly endless obstacles thrown in their path.

FORCES MOLDING THE NATIONAL SELF-IMAGE

A new generation of post-1967 Israelis has drastically lowered its expectations as to both where Israel fits into international affairs and what can be gained from foreign relations. That much seems beyond question. The trend is confirmed by statistics on recent national voting patterns. Beginning with 1977 but continuing in the successive 1981, 1984, and 1988 Knesset elections, the strength and representation of the conservative right-wing bloc (the so-called "national camp") has increased significantly at the expense of the centrist and leftist parties (see Table 11).

More important is to ask what explains the dramatic shift away from the idealism characterizing Israel's founders only four decades ago. This lowering of expectations traces to the combined impact of four factors. These are (1) the weight of Jewish history; (2) lessons learned in prestate Zionist diplomacy; (3) international political realities; and (4) Arab enmity. National power deficiencies only further accentuate the implications of these four inputs.

The Weight of Jewish History

Within minutes of the dramatic UN roll call endorsing partition and Jewish statehood in November 1947 the Jews of Palestine joyously

Table 11. Left-Right Tendencies (1962–84)
(Percentages)

	1962	1969	1973	1977	1981	1984
Left–Right Label						
Left	31	6	3	4	4	4.7
Moderate Left		19	19	14	13	18.4
Center	23	26	33	29	39	21.0
Moderate Right						23.2
Right	8	16	23	28	32	15.3
Religious	5	6	7	6	6	2.1
No interest in politics; No answer	33	27	15	19	6	15.3
Economy						
Capitalist	7	10		11	10	6.6
More Capitalist	19	24	[not	18	25	28.1
More Socialist	39	38		31	40	50.2
Socialist	15	19	asked]	25	20	6.3
No Answer	20	9		15	5	8.8
Return the Territories						
None		38	31	41	50	41.1
A small part		52	52	43	42	21.4
Some part	[not					21.6
Most		5	10	7	4	5.9
All	asked]	1	2	7	3	8.2
No Answer		4	5	2	1	1.7
Sample Size:	1,170	1,314	1,939	1,372	1,249	1,259

Source: Asher Arian and Michal Shamir, "The Primarily Political Functions of the Left–Right Continuum," *Comparative Politics* 15, no. 2 (January 1983): 146.

took to the streets and danced until the early hours of the morning. There was a genuine outburst of optimism in those heady days of 1947–48 about Israel's international prospects. But this proved to be wishful thinking and short lived. In retrospect, it was only a brief departure from the customary reading of Jewish and world history that Paul Johnson calls the viewpoint of "a learned and intelligent victim."

Ben-Gurion sought to reshape the Israeli national character by glossing over that entire part of the Jewish past associated with dispersion and Diaspora but he failed. It has proven easier to get the Jews physically out of the ghetto than to get the ghetto psychologically out of Israeli Jews. Former Premier Menachem Begin, by contrast, no matter what the occasion, however gala and festive, would invariably make strong reference in his remarks to what were for him and many countrymen the two single most instructive recent world events: the Munich pact appeasement in 1938 and the Holocaust. For Israeli survivors of the Nazi gas chambers and their children, the move toward chemical and gas warfare at the start of the present decade evokes powerful memories and the deepest anxiety. At the level of attitudes and perceptions, nineteen centuries from Massada to Maidanek still profoundly influence Israeli international conduct.

Israelis retain a high degree of historical consciousness, similar, for example, to China and Chinese foreign policy. This weight of Jewish history lies heavily on both leaders and public. It is one of the primary sources for Israel's underlying insecurity and perceived isolation. The sense of aloneness comes almost as second nature to Israelis and probably figures in the opposition of people like Yitzchak Shamir to holding a large Middle East peace conference. The objection is not solely that multilateral peacemaking by nature is complicated and unwieldy, but that in the course of the conference proceedings Israel would find itself standing alone. These anxieties about an imposed isolation—of an *am levadad yishkon* even in the twentieth-century international system—came to the surface yet once more at the end of 1988, prompted by the unilateral U.S. decision to begin open dialogue with the PLO. For those Israelis still capable of being shocked by the changing fortunes of world politics, this was tantamount to watching your best friend talk to your worst enemy. If one wished, the American action could serve as a modern parable for the age-old moral that for the Jew no outsider could really be trusted.

Each new draftee into the Israeli army is taken to three specific historical sites as part of the induction process. He or she climbs to the top of the ancient fortress of Massada overlooking the Dead Sea, where the last 960 Jewish defenders against Roman imperium carried out a suicide pact in 73 C.E., ending Judean independence. The military recruits also pass quietly through the darkened exhibition rooms of Yad Va-Shem memorializing the 6 million Jewish martyrs. They are then formally sworn in at a ceremony held near the Western (Wailing) Wall in Jerusalem, location of the destroyed first and second temples.

The purpose behind these exercises goes beyond the merely symbolic. These sites and memories retain their evocative power. The consciousness of all Israelis, even those choosing to distance themselves from the Jewish tradition, remains deeply influenced by the collective Jewish experience, with its overriding message about the terrible costs of political impotence.

The Jewish past speaks of homelessness, of statelessness, of powerlessness. Present small-state insecurities only make these themes that such more poignant for Israeli leaders who avow: "Never again!" This consciousness helps explain Israeli thinking on a nuclear option, for example. In the opinion of politicians, strategists, and scientists who have advocated building the bomb, only the development by Israel of its own independent nuclear capability offers the ultimate deterrent to all-out Arab onslaught against the Jewish state and twentieth-century repetition of the Massada tragedy. No matter how vigorous their denials, or their surface appearance of nonchalance, even the youngest and the most worldly of Israelis have ingrained in their thinking the psychology of vulnerability. Speaking in angry reaction to the visit by President Ronald Reagan to the German military cemetery at Bitburg in May 1985, Defense Minister Yitzchak Rabin commented bitterly, "Let it be said that we, the members of the Jewish people, have taken an oath: 'To remember, and to forget nothing.' " That Rabin was not especially noted (as Begin had been) for evoking past Jewish themes when articulating his political views only gave his words greater weight.

Today's Israelis, in short, contend with the contemporary world through the prism of history. But they also accuse others of doing the same. In keynoting a conference in June 1988 on "Covering Israel on World Television," for example, Israel's President Chaim Herzog felt moved to attribute Israel's battered image at least in part to "that deep-rooted irrationality, that historic inability to relate normally to Jews and Israel, that prevents objective appraisal" of events and achievements in Israel.

Lessons Derived from Zionist Diplomacy

Most of the new states created after 1945 owe their freedom to armed liberation struggles waged against a foreign presence in the former colonized territory itself. It was only following independence that they were thrust, largely unprepared, into the international arena and had to begin engaging in foreign relations. Israel's experience is altogether different. Statehood was won by a political struggle on two fronts: in Palestine, against both the Arabs and the British mandatory power; but also internationally, in enlisting foreign support.

The idea that diplomacy was essential to Zionism's success had been driven home already at the close of the previous century by the founder of modern political Zionism, Dr. Theodor Herzl. His blueprint for political action stressed enlisting international support as an indispensable supplement to efforts by Zionist emissaries at mobilizing Jewry in the nationalist cause. Herzl himself made a number of important personal diplomatic approaches to the leading powers of the day in the final years prior to his premature death in 1904 at the age of forty-four. Successors like Nachum Sokolow and Chaim Weizmann expanded on this network of diplomatic contacts, so that only one year into statehood Foreign Minister Sharett was justified in saying, "Israel was a young nation, but an ancient people." "Though beginners in the art of statecraft," he noted, the Israelis had the privilege and responsibility of "being able to draw upon a rich and varied stock of universal experience."

A full half-century of exposure to the intricacies and pitfalls of world politics thus preceded formal Israeli sovereign statecraft. This in itself makes Israel something of an exception when compared to other new states. Independence usually finds such new states with serious shortcomings in organization, personnel, and records. Not so Israel. May 1948 found it already possessing all these plus a wealth of accumulated experience.

In those prestate years future Israeli leaders and statemen were witness to a string of historic events and therefore received an invaluable schooling in the realities of foreign policy. Some of the lessons included

- the unreliability of collective security and the steady erosion of international institutions as applied to the League of Nations during the interwar period;
- the sacrificing of a small state, Czechoslovakia, in the name of global peace and stability in 1938;

- the fact that the allegiance of great powers should never be taken for granted or held as above suspicion, a lesson taught by Great Britain's exercise in expediency in 1939, when it released itself from the Balfour Declaration commitment to support Zionism;
- the pluses, but also the minuses, of allowing and perhaps even encouraging the struggle for Palestine to be mediated in a wider, regional context once the neighboring Arab countries had begun to intervene politically in Palestine in the years 1936 to 1939; and
- the cynicism of world leaders in not doing more to prevent the systematic extermination of European Jewry once the full extent of the Nazi "final solution" became known during the Second World War.

Two encouraging insights derived from the pre-1948 experience were

- securing the Balfour Declaration in 1917. This early diplomatic victory taught how weakness by a smaller actor sometimes can be converted into strength through adeptness in exploiting momentary openings and the insecurities of others, just as Great Britain's wartime plight had made it receptive to overtures by the Zionists and as Israel succeeded in doing later in forging a close military pact with the French during the fifties.
- the timely reorientation in Zionist strategy and shift of focus from Great Britain to the United States in 1944 to 1946, offering guidance into the impermanence of power and its flow from one power center to another. Global power transitions require of others the ability to identify broad trends and to adapt one's self accordingly, as Israel did in the late fifties and early sixties with respect to the emerging Afro-Asian nations.

A further great insight comes from the historic 1947 General Assembly vote in favor of Jewish statehood. Obtained through intense Zionist lobbying, tactical maneuver, and persuasion, this singular success on the eve of independence confirmed that ultimately what matters in interstate relations is neither altruism nor goodwill but self-interest and political considerations.

These early mixed experiences must have dampened some of the initial ardor of Zionist representatives. Still, it was an important education that prepared Israeli foreign policy to cope more realistically with the international and regional problems that were to lie ahead.

To the extent that Likud leaders, as a subgroup, can be accused of acting less realistically than some of their Labour counterparts, this may not owe entirely to ideology. Worth remembering is that the Likud and its precursors, the Revisionists and then the Herut party, never really shared in this schooling. First, in the thirties, the Revisionists had broken away from the Zionist organization, removing themselves from its various political campaigns. Second, in the forties, they concentrated efforts in resisting the British inside Palestine. Then, from 1948 until 1967, Begin and his followers were relegated to the opposition benches and precluded from obtaining ambassadorial and diplomatic assignments. Consequently, when suddenly finding themselves in power, they were woefully unprepared and unschooled in foreign affairs. Indeed, this realization may have led Begin, for lack of any comparable candidate, to turn to Labour's Moshe Dayan and offer him the Foreign Ministry post. As proof of practical diplomatic experience fostering greater realism even in the nationalist Likud ranks was the emergence by 1988 of several qualified, pragmatic younger cabinet ministers. People like Moshe Arens, Binyamin Netanyahu, Ehud Olmert, and Dan Meridor brought to office recent exposure to the complexities and subtleties of statecraft.

Cold War Realities

Israel's rebirth did not occur in a vacuum but in a very specific context of time and place. The time, 1948, was one of profound global change: from war to peace, as well as the intensification of Soviet–American rivalry. A new set of rules and systemic conditions came into being that were then—and that remain now—beyond the capacity of Israel to control. These act as yet a third formidable influence upon Israel thinking.

Among the international forces shaping Israel's external environment and breeding further distrust on its part, five seem particularly noteworthy. The first is the superpower contest itself that, beginning in the 1950s, increasingly extended into the Middle East, linking the Arab-Israeli dispute to the larger cold war struggle and pressuring Israel to take sides. A second force is the scientific and technological revolution, which has produced the double threat of the nuclear "balance of terror" for the entire world and an unprecedented era of militarization and conventional arms races for the Middle East region. A third global trend is the wave of nationalism that has multiplied the number of state actors, increased areas of tension in the developing countries, redefined the global agenda, and inspired the concept of Third World nonalignment. Fourth, and related, is the growing reality of economic interdependence, with its implications for a range of issues from North-South relations, global resource allocation, and development strategies to world banking and trade patterns.

A fifth and final trend affecting all members of the expanded world community, including Israel, is the less than inspiring performance of the United Nations. When the use of poison gas evokes no prompt or effective response by the international community, what sanctions does any irresponsible or "crazy state" have to fear by breaking with international convention? In general, the absence of a powerful international authority capable of enforcement is felt, especially by the smaller and more threatened countries. International law and organization on the whole have been a disappointment in Israeli eyes in the key function of guaranteeing the security of small states and in the task of solving basic conflict as opposed to simply controlling interstate or regional tensions. It is one of the main explanations for why Israel has not favored multilateral diplomatic frameworks or conferences, for example.

Other worrisome trends could be mentioned, like the influence of fanaticism and ideology, secular as well as religious, on state behavior. Yet the point is that global conditions in the past forty years for the most part have affected Israel negatively in at least two senses. One is that international developments largely represent constraints; they place limits on Israel's independence of action, its diplomatic maneuverability, and the number of options open to it. The other impact has been for postwar events in general and Israel's international affairs in particular to reinforce some of those earlier Jewish and Zionist theses, whether as to politics among nations or Israel among the nations.

Arab Enmity

For Israel, time (the last half of the twentieth century) is reinforced by place (the contemporary Middle East). There are those who relate to Israel as an idea, a vision, a mission, a prophecy. Whatever else, though, Israel is a terrestrial, flesh-and-blood geopolitical entity subject to the enduring laws and forces of world politics. In this connection, if the international scene is more often than not a source of disappointment and concern for Jerusalem, then the immediate Middle East region is nothing short of menacing. The best way of putting it is that the Zionist utopian dream came to earth in a place of maximum inconvenience and danger.

This broad geographic expanse of great fascination, profound social contrast, and rapid political change, nevertheless, poses an exceptional security threat. If deficiencies in the existing international order toward the end of this century counsel still the wisdom of self-reliance, the dynamics of the Arab-Israeli conflict make this the closest thing to an imperative for Israel.

Arab world hostility toward the Zionist state has challenged not only the country's material resources but its reserves of hope and confidence as well. The prolonged struggle touches and influences every aspect of Israeli life. On the fourth day of the Hebrew month of *Iyar*, which in 1989 corresponded to 9 May, Israel solemnly marked the annual memorial day for its fallen soldiers. The entire nation paused as one to honor the 16,740 who have died since 1948 while defending the right of Jewish statehood and who represent the greatest cost of independence.

Nor have foreign policy attitudes been exempt; indeed, they are a chief casualty. Israel's founders, understandably flushed with success at working themselves up from a supplicant national movement to a full-fledged state in 1947–48, soon awoke however to the new realities. Peace might not be close at hand. The Arabs would not quickly reconcile themselves to the state's existence. It was excluded from regional economic and political frameworks. And all the while the Arab regimes were sanctioning acts of terror against Israeli targets and making war preparations.

In this psychological setting of living under constant strain, it is unrealistic to expect Israeli reactions to have been very much different from what they were. Various estimates indicate Israel was a direct participant in no less than eighteen foreign-policy crises from mid-May 1948, when it attained independence, until the end of 1979. Indeed, its entire history reads like one long chronology of local skirmishes, military alerts, sporadic outbursts of low-intensity violence, and large-scale combat (1948, 1956, 1967, 1973, 1982).

Such a pattern of unrelieved tension therefore deeply colors Israelis' view of themselves and of others. It is reflected in Israel's collective self-image as politically isolated and militarily encircled. Survival simply has taken on a different order of magnitude, pushing aside other more idealistic goals, skewing national priorities, and distorting value preferences. It also has consistently produced tension in the still undefined relationship of diplomacy vis-à-vis military force in the daily pursuit of national security.

The Middle East security situation, more than any other factor, accounts for the change in Israel's image from enlightened, liberal, and humanitarian to defiant. Perceiving Arab enmity as enduring and real permits little room for generosity, few illusions, and absolutely no major mistakes on Israel's part. In the long run, faith, trust, and self-assurance have been eroded and replaced by mistrust, by apprehension, and by a certain rigidity that foreigners often find disagreeable about Israeli negotiators. Thus it is that Israel's military approach to the dilemma of physical security and to regional politics is often diagnosed by outside commentators as a siege mentality, or "Massada complex."

Israeli attitudes toward the 1977 Sadat initiative and 1979 Israel-Egypt peace treaty are interesting in this particular regard. Seized upon at the time as inspiring, a decade later these "breakthroughs" are viewed by most Israelis, including many originally avid supporters, as disappointments. Instead of encouraging or reviving earlier, positive foreign policy expectations, the unsatisfactory and unfulfilled state of relations with Egypt—a "cold peace" and certainly a far cry from anticipated normalization—has only further reinforced Israeli anxieties.

On the other hand, Sadat's journey to Jerusalem and warm reception by the broad Israeli public are instructive in another, positive sense. That Israelis could welcome the Arab leader as bold and courageous instead of as the perpetrator of the Yom Kippur attack, with its terrible list of 2,378 Israeli causalties, also tells something of the Israeli makeup. The country has something of a "show me" attitude in needing to be assured about the sincerity of others' intentions. Once persuaded, Israel may be as forthcoming as any other state, as happened when all of Sinai was returned peacefully by none other than a right-wing government in return for an Egyptian pledge of peace. Quite conceivably it could happen again on the disputed eastern border, but only if and when a working political majority of Israelis, understandably concerned about their country's security and survival, have been convinced to take still further tangible and territorial risks for peace by a Palestinian leader of Sadat's stature.

Israeli insecurities are heightened by figures showing increased Arab military expenditure, by the purchase of intermediate- and long-range ballistic missiles, by the development of chemical weaponry, and by international apathy toward atrocities committed in the Iran-Iraq regional war. Israel repeatedly has demonstrated its faith not in others' professions of intent but, instead, in facts that might provide that extra, slight margin of immediate safety. This motivation can be seen, for example, in the prompt, unilateral annexation of east Jerusalem and its environs in June 1967, despite a chorus of outside protest, to frustrate any international initiatives to restore the status quo ante of a divided city. The same reasoning governs prevailing resistance to convening an international framework, for a UN presence in the West Bank and Gaza during a transitional period, or for international guarantees of Israel's security in any final peace settlement. In this sense we can say that current Middle Eastern geopolitical realities merely reinforce the three previous layers of Jewish–Zionist–small-state caution.

Correlates of Power

The drain on Israel's reserves of national will and power is a final factor in hardening the basic approach of the public and its leaders. The country is at a serious disadvantage in what is known as the "ends-means equation," signifying the amount of physical and material power a state needs to achieve its foreign policy objectives. In the case of Israel, its temporal means are inversely proportional to the magnitude of the threats it faces.

This imbalance may sound slightly disingenuous to some readers because Israel leaves many outsiders with the impression of strength and resolve. The foreign press is especially fond of depicting Israel as larger than life: as perhaps the world's fourth strongest military power, the dominant actor in the Middle East, a leading international arms trader, a favored ally of the United States, and almost certainly a member of the exclusive nuclear club. It isn't that this impression is entirely false; but it suffers from exaggeration and is incomplete.

For the sake of balance, and closer to the truth, are the following observations:

- Israel's strength lies mostly in the narrow physical-military sense of power.
- Even this force capability is limited to a defensive and deterrent role, since Israel would never be able to achieve a decisive military victory over its Arab neighbors.
- In virtually every other index of power Israel suffers from major deficiencies, all the way from land and population size to capital sources, energy supply, and raw materials.
- This weak power base cannot meet the security challenge, necessitating dependence upon the United States, world Jewry, and others.

- This weak power base is also conspicuous in comparative terms since the Arab coalition enjoys an overwhelming quantitative advantage (see Table 12).
- Even the slim qualitative edge enjoyed by Israel in such categories as human resources and scientific skills has been narrowing as Arab opponents in recent years have overcome some of their own initial shortcomings, whether one talks of the Arab lobby in the U.S. or military fighting strength.

Taken together, these Middle Eastern power realities remain a source of preoccupation for Israelis, whose concerns tend to focus (a) on how to get the immediate job of defense and security done and (b) on the question of the Jewish state's long-term staying power.

Jewish history, religion, and culture followed by a prestate introduction to world affairs in the twentieth century are to Israel's psychological environment as the contemporary global and regional setting are to its strategic environment. This confluence of four elements—Jewish history, Zionist diplomacy, international politics, and Arab enmity—largely determines Israeli values while serving as the backdrop for what will soon be the first fifty years of a renewed Jewish international presence. Nevertheless, if one were forced to choose from among the four in explaining Israel's changed political perceptions, it would have to be the regional factor of Arab enmity, especially when this enmity is viewed in relation to Israel's own precious few assets.

Table 12. Middle East Power Correlates

Country	Population (in millions)	Area (sq. km.)	Per capita GNP	Military Expenditure per capita
Israel	4,404	20,325	$5,370	$1,604
Egypt	49,610	1,000,258	$700	$61
Iran	44,210	1,647,240	$2,000	$236
Iraq	16,450	438,446	$1,222	$918
Jordan	2,794	99,700	$1,640	$226
Lebanon	3,100	10,452	$1,131	$133
Saudi Arabia	8,500	2,331,000	$12,230	$2,091
Syria	10,610	185,680	$1,760	$274

Sources: Jaffee Center for Strategic Studies, *The Middle East Military Balance 1978–1988* (Tel Aviv: The Jerusalem Post and Westview Press, 1988); Ruth Leger Sivard, *World Military & Social Expenditures 1987–1988* (Leesburg, VA: World Priorities, 1988).

Even if the Arab-Israeli conflict were resolved, there is no guarantee Israeli foreign relations would be problem free and unexceptional; witness the abiding institutional and doctrinal resistance of the Catholic Church in Rome to restored Jewish nationhood. Still, were it not for the salience of the conflict, the severity of the threat, and Israel's concentration on national security above all else, Israel's international position would be significantly less prominent, far healthier, and much closer to normalization.

❑

What can we conclude therefore about the view of the world from Jerusalem? Much like the Israeli national character, after undergoing dramatic change in the first years of independence it is now becoming more stable and consistent. Whether for good or bad, Israelis have reconsidered and redefined their place in the world. From their standpoint, Israel is here—in the Middle East, in the global arena—to stay. It certainly does not intend to commit national suicide, as Czechoslovakia did in the thirties. But in the process of making this pledge stick, some fundamental adjustments in perception and attitude have had to be made in the national psyche, matching those made in redefining the national interest. From a sense of responsibility and an awareness of mission, the recent tendency among the vast majority of Israelis is toward a narrow focus, featuring a self-preoccupation with Israel's own direct and most pressing needs in the face of the unknown. When Israelis feel themselves alone in a cold world (which was most of the time in the seventies and eighties), they have been known to grit their teeth and dig in.

To be sure, one can lament this backsliding from a posture of trust to distrust. But it also does indicate, on the other hand, a political realism and maturity on Israel's part at age forty. As a state actor it has come to terms with the world, dealing not with what ought to be, or what Israelis and Jews would wish international affairs to be, but rather with what is, with objective political realities.

The Israeli worldview is also contingent on reactions and actions by others. Israelis are forever testing the waters, gauging the intentions of outsiders, from Arabs to Americans. They are looking for clues that might help to clarify their own worldview and that might even permit restoring a sense of hope for a balance between blanket disapproval and reassurance by the outside world. As outspoken former Defense Minister Ezer Weizman pithily summed up his countrymen's state of mind late in the eighties: "There is too much disbelief in peace, a feeling that everyone is out to screw us."

It is this lack of confidence that must be overcome if Israel is to engage constructively in international diplomacy.

As part of this revised approach to external affairs, in peering out at their political environment and at the world at large, Israeli government officials profess to see few viable policy alternatives open to them or to Israel. National memory (the Jewish and Zionist experience) combines with the geopolitical contest (systemic and regional conditions) and with the limitations of power to foster a sense of *ein brera* (no choice) in diplomacy as well as in defense. It is in this frame of mind, and without illusions, that Israel undertakes to promote its national interests and to produce the most liveable results. For if the goal of foreign policy of late concentrates primarily on merely holding the line, then foreign policy attitudes in Israel are entirely consistent. They suggest a hardening of the line.

CHAPTER 3

THE DIPLOMATIC RECORD

Small nations do not have a foreign policy. They have a defense policy.

Moshe Dayan, 1975

Introspection comes close to being an Israeli national pastime. If, as we have seen, Israelis are critical of outsiders, they can also be unsparing in criticizing themselves.

By any reasonable standard Israel easily qualifies among the most progressive and successful of all the new states created since 1945. Yet public discourse seems to delight in dwelling on the shortcomings, past and present. This is especially so when the object of censure is foreign policy performance. Typical is a scholarly evaluation of Israel at twenty by the Hebrew University's Professor Michael Brecher. Dramatic accomplishments were admitted in the vital areas of nation-building, commitment to democracy, and social integration, only to have the study conclude sourly: "But those achievements have not been matched in the sphere of foreign policy."

Was this conclusion warranted in 1968? Is it valid twenty years later? To answer, and at the same time to fill in some of the diplomatic background, this chapter attempts a brief overview of the history of Israeli foreign relations since 1948.

CRITICS AND CRITIQUES

If Israelis are hard on themselves and unsparing of their leaders, they certainly do not lack for critics abroad who are also down on Israeli diplomacy. One often has the feeling of playing to a critical global audience. Every act—whether of omission or of commission—is subjected to inspection under a microscope. To some, Israel is a reproach; to others it is simply unintelligible.

Certainly the gallery of critics is a diverse one, starting with those bitter enemies for whom the single commendable act Israel might be capable of would be to self-destruct or, at minimum, to shed its Jewish and Zionist identity.

Less easily dismissed are the legions of well-wishers offering free counsel in an attempt to save Israel in spite of itself. Such authoritative voices usually divide along two lines: critics of Israeli strategy or critics of Israeli tactics. Some express reservations about the substance of Israeli foreign policy, its definition of the national interest and prioritization of goals, and the moral content and working premises of the general policy or of specific decisions. Others disapprove of Israel's international conduct, including the entire style and tone of Israel's diplomacy. As for example, an American weekly described Israel's political leaders in 1988 as "dispiritingly small—visionless and timid, working the world from a defensive crouch." Many Europeans, nearly all Arabs, and all official Soviet writers argue the opposite: that Israel is overconfident, not insecure. That it is too strong. And that its leaders see no need to compromise.

Israel's leaders are asked in effect to achieve the politically impossible: to be tough but also magnanimous, principled yet pragmatic. In the cross-fire of criticism Israel ends up being charged with both forms of hyperbehavior—aggressiveness and complacency—and faulted for being alternatively too assertive and too passive in its foreign relations.

Perhaps the most effective group of critics, and the one armed with the best credentials, arises from within the academic community. Specialists in comparative foreign policy display rare agreement in drawing a less than flattering profile of Israel as an international actor. Culled from a number of scholarly writings this critique presents Israel as essentially conservative and status quo oriented. Lacking in foresight and in rational, long-range planning, it is moved by impulse or by crisis exigencies into pursuing basically a formalistic and reactive diplomacy rather than one showing initiative. Such a posture of equivocation, devoid of imaginativeness and originality, thus accounts, in the eyes of the scholarly community, for how and why Israel has no one but itself to blame for the long and depressing string of so-called missed opportunities that if seized upon at any given moment, might have permitted the realization of such cherished goals as normalcy and Middle East peace. This critique is effectively summarized in the words of an American scholar, Professor Morton Kaplan: "A nation and society that came to power in 1947 as innovative and inspired by justice by 1967 had become tired, defensive, and repetitive in its strategy."

There is a good deal of truth in this composite critical assessment. But there are also important qualifications, including the following:

1. *What might have happened.* In the real world of small-state diplomacy effective statecraft must also include steps directed at *averting* political crises and worst-case scenarios that, even though timely and successful, by their very nature go unacknowledged.
2. *What did happen that we do not know about.* Similarly, in Israel's case much of the diplomatic record covering the first forty years remains classified, particularly those diplomatic interventions (both initiatory and preventive) conducted under tight secrecy and that, if publicized, might fundamentally alter the above impression.
3. *The half-filled glass.* Due weight ought to be given, in fairness, to instances of mixed (i.e., limited or partial) successes, such as Israel's associate membership status with the European Economic Community (EEC).
4. *Uneven performance.* Scholarly generalizations about policy conservatism and openings allowed to slip away may apply to a certain policy area (lack of boldness on the Arab-Israeli conflict issue, for instance) but not to others (American and non–Middle Eastern ties, trade contacts, informal diplomatic exchanges, and the like).
5. *There is no finality in foreign policy.* "Success" and "failure," we must always remind ourselves, are relative and subjective terms influenced, among other things, not only by the preferences of academic analysts (a moral Israeli foreign policy, liberal territorial concessions, etc.) but by the time frame used for passing judgment. What at one moment appears to be a setback, later may be seen to have had positive consequences, and vice versa. Was the 1956 Sinai campaign wise or folly? Was the Six-Day War a glorious military triumph or a political disaster? Does the 1970 policy of standing behind King Hussein in the Jordan crisis qualify as a missed opportunity if a Palestinian takeover in Amman might have reframed the Arab-Israeli struggle? Could the costly 1973 war have planted the seeds for an Israeli-Egyptian reconciliation?
6. *There is also no clear departure point.* Sweeping, across-the-board judgments leave us confused as to exactly how long this alleged state of foreign policy paralysis has been going on.

Are critics talking about a comparatively recent phenomenon, an outgrowth in 1984 of the defective national unity government power-sharing framework? Are we to believe that lack of movement derives even earlier from the retarding influence on national policy of Menachem Begin and the Likud conservatives after 1977? Perhaps the loss of diplomatic momentum really began in the aftermath of the 1967 victory that encouraged a misplaced sense of complacency and of exaggerated self-confidence? Or is cautious foreign policy on the part of Israel something far more structural and enduring, possibly going as far back as 1949? For it was then that the full enormity of the challenges facing Israel first made itself felt on the nation's leaders and on Israel's collective psyche.

In approaching Israel's diplomatic record critically, we admit to believing that cautious foreign policy is structural and deeply ingrained. Israel's retreat into siege diplomacy comes closely upon the heels of its greatest diplomatic achievement: restored nationhood in 1948. From a broader historical perspective, 1967, 1977, and 1984 only pushed Israel deeper into its defensive shell. With these reservations in mind we proceed to survey the highlights of Israeli foreign relations not so much chronologically as on the basis of successive governments and premierships.

THE FIRST FORTY YEARS: A SURVEY

The close tie between personality and situation stands out in Israel's diplomatic history. Due to the immediacy of *chutz u'bitachon*—foreign affairs and security—policy making in Jerusalem is elitist. Concentrating authority in the hands of a single individual, or several people at most, means that personal leadership counts for a great deal: in defining political situations as acute or not and in responding to sudden, unanticipated, or threatening challenges from the external environment.

Ben-Gurion and the Policy of Pragmatism (May 1948–December 1953)

Even now one has difficulty assessing David Ben-Gurion's true, lasting impact on Israeli foreign relations, so dominant has been his person and legacy in power, in opposition, in death. As the country's first prime minister, Ben-Gurion was instrumental in establishing a number of precedents together with firm policy guidelines. His shadow, like that of DeGaulle for the French Fifth Republic or of

Washington in his famous farewell address, still looms large, with each of Ben-Gurion's seven successors in one way or another having to measure himself (or herself) against the Old Man and his record.

For Ben-Gurion the permanent foreign policy foundations for Israel were embodied in the May 1948 declaration of independence. Three clauses in particular: (a) an appeal to the United Nations to assist the Jewish people in the building up of its state and to receive Israel into the comity of nations; (b) an offer of peace and good neighborliness to the Arab people and states; (c) an appeal to the Jewish people throughout the Diaspora to rally around the Jews in Israel and to stand by them "in the great struggle for the realization of the age-old dream," the redemption of Israel. Already identifiable here is the three-dimensional construct for all of Israel's future external interventions: Jewish affairs, Middle East regional politics, and the global arena even further afield.

The Ben-Gurion government lost no time in operationalizing this conception, moving with considerable vigor on each of the three diplomatic fronts. The impetus derived from the urgency of the two paramount tasks on its agenda: to terminate the 1948 war of independence and consolidate political and territorial gains; and to begin coping with the awesome responsibilities of nation-building dramatized, above all, by opening wide the gates of Zion to a massive influx of Jewish refugees from the Arab countries as well as survivors from the European concentration camps.

Regionally, Ben-Gurion pressed for armistice accords at the Rhodes talks while pursuing secret treaty negotiations with Transjordan's King Abdullah. Once the peace momentum was lost, however, owing to the absence of compelling incentives for either side, his Middle East stance changed. In the face of Arab intransigence, Ben-Gurion indicated less willingness to be conciliatory and gave greater weight instead to Israel's security component. This expressed itself in strengthening of the Israel Defense Forces (*Tsahal*), enforcement of a retaliatory policy aimed at punishing Arab armistice violations, plus a declaratory (*casus belli*) policy of explicit warnings meant to deter Arab aggression.

This shift in political (as distinct from military) strategy away from the Middle East subsystem was matched by strenuous efforts at the third, or international, level. The United Nations was for a while a major focus of Israeli diplomacy. The eloquent voice of Israel's head of mission, Abba Eban, resonated in General Assembly debates, and Israel studiously set before the organization its grievances: enforced closure by Egypt of the Suez Canal and the seizure of cargo, as well as flagrant border infractions by Egypt, Jordan, and Syria. Once its case fell on deaf ears, however, and a pattern of automatic bloc voting began to produce not so much sterile recommendations as mischievous, biased UN resolutions, Israel soon lost enthusiasm for multilateral diplomacy. In keeping with Ben-Gurion's preference for flexible responses to unfolding problems, political efforts were redirected toward fostering a series of new bilateral relations.

To achieve this end Ben-Gurion was prepared to give up the cold war principle of strict nonidentification. In an essay on "Israel among the Nations" written especially for the *Israel Government Year Book* in 1952, the prime minister repeated his government's duty to promote relations of friendship and reciprocity with every peace-loving country "without prying into its internal constitution"—an explicit signal of evenhandedness directed toward both the West and the Soviet Union. Yet in practice this neutralist stance was no longer feasible by 1952. For as early as 2 July 1950 Israel's cabinet had decided to endorse the UN Security Council resolution called for by the United States in labeling as aggression the June invasion of South Korea by the Communist North backed by the USSR.

Thereafter, Israeli foreign policy under Ben-Gurion consciously sought to open an avenue to Western Europe, the major powers, and the United States. Accomplishments in that direction were the repairing of strained relations with Great Britain and the start of a French connection. Less rewarding as yet were ties with Washington. Easily the most dramatic foreign policy decision during Ben-Gurion's first term occurred on 3 January 1951 and involved participation by Israel in a negotiating process with the Federal Republic of Germany, successor to Hitler's Third Reich only a few years after the annihilation of European Jewry. Following the stormiest session in Knesset history (7–9 January 1952), the government—led resolutely by Ben-Gurion—pursued direct talks with Bonn authorities and eventually ratified the German reparations agreement in March 1953. Shortly afterwards, complaining of fatigue, Ben-Gurion took a temporary leave of absence in July and then formally resigned in December.

Sharett and the Policy of Accommodation (December 1953–November 1955)

As foreign minister since 1948, Moshe Sharett championed if not an entirely different approach to foreign relations then at least different nuances. In particular, he talked (fought would be too strong a word) against Ben-Gurion's more hard-line stand toward the Arabs. Sharett questioned the efficacy of military reprisals, for example, and emphasized their negative international repercussions for Israel. He also advocated conciliatory gestures aimed at accommodations with the Arab world only to find himself repeatedly outmaneuvered by Ben-Gurion in Mapai party consultations and in cabinet deliberations.

Succeeding Ben-Gurion provided Sharett with the opportunity at last to pursue his own thinking and to seek a fresh course. But by the end of 1953 it may already have been too late for such a major policy departure. Ben-Gurion, it turned out, had managed to lay firm policy foundations. Cold war nonalignment, for instance, was no longer realistic; that February Moscow had recalled its ambassador from Tel Aviv. Neither was the Palestinian option for a Middle East settlement previously entertained by Sharett feasible given the partition regime with Jordan that had come into being since 1949. A second factor working against Sharett, an experienced statesman, was his own personal makeup. Because he was not a political infighter, Sharett failed in the key leadership role of premier. During his brief term in office the influence of the intelligence service and the defense establishment on policy making became dominant; this came at the expense of the Foreign Ministry, which Sharett himself continued to lead.

Sharett's loss of control provides a good deal of the explanation for the embarrassing 1954 security mishap (*esek bish*, or Lavon affair). Poorly conceived and executed in Egypt, the plan sought to work through a secret ring of Egyptian Jews to strain Cairo-Washington relations. Third and last, the political situation prevailing at the time hardly conduced to a foreign policy of moderation. Despite having opted for the pro-Western orientation, Israel saw itself as isolated and insecure in the face of increased hostility by the Arab nations. Overtaken by events Sharett's policy produced little of substance; against the backdrop of a deteriorating general security situation and renewed Middle East arms race, Sharett had little recourse but to accept Ben-Gurion's return to the post of defense minister and then, in November 1955, to the office of prime minister.

Ben-Gurion and the Policy of Confrontation (November 1955–1963)

In returning to power, the 68-year-old leader cast aside the policy of restraint. Convinced of the need for a strong military response to the mounting border tension, Ben-Gurion proceeded to undertake two interrelated decisions that best illustrate his combined diplomatic-military strategy. The first decision, a prerequisite for the second, was to redouble Israel's quest via Paris for the backing of at least one Western power. Cooperation between France and Israel was made possible by shared concern at Nasserist Egypt's incitement of Arab radicalism directed against European colonialism, on the one hand, and against the Zionist state on the other. Assured of this vital outside support, Ben-Gurion was encouraged into ordering military plans for implementing the second decision to strike preemptively against Egypt.

From Israel's standpoint the 1956 Sinai campaign and Suez crisis produced mixed results at best. Like the 1948 war, military success brought diplomatic complications. Certainly the Israeli initiative fell considerably short of Ben-Gurion's own far-reaching "grand design." During the clandestine tripartite (Anglo-French-Israeli) preparatory conference at Sèvres on 30 September–1 October, according to Michael Bar-Zohar, Ben-Gurion's biographer, the premier had spelled out the details of his ambitious plan. If carried out, Egypt's charismatic President Nasser would have been ousted, the Suez Canal returned to international control, *fedayeen* terrorist operations ended from bases in Gaza and the Sinai desert, and Lebanon's political structure and borders rearranged, culminating in a division of East and West Bank Jordan between Israel and Britain's client, Iraq.

Instead, the armed confrontation accomplished the minimum objective of providing a breathing space before the next round. Direct diplomatic costs included strengthening Nasser's regional sway over Arab politics for more than a decade; a global projection of Israel in collusion with Western imperialism; subjection to international criticism, including an American ultimatum and another from Moscow; and, ultimately, the embarrassment of having to accept a unilateral troop withdrawal from the Sinai Peninsula and Gaza Strip without even the most minimal international security safeguards demanded by Ben-Gurion against remilitarization of the areas by Egypt.

Despite this far less than satisfactory denouement to the 1956 crisis, the subsequent period, corresponding to Ben-Gurion's last hurrah, is no less instructive for understanding his principal legacy to Israeli statecraft. For he demonstrated tactical flexibility, always in the dedicated pursuit of bedrock national and security interests. During his last years in power the elder statesman departed in one sense from previous form. Aside from the Suez affair Ben-Gurion throughout the years had not taken a direct part in policy initiatives (in the many secret conversations with King Abdullah, for example), always preferring to rely on special emissaries. Toward the end, by contrast, we find him surprisingly active in personal diplomacy, undertaking official visits abroad. He held important meetings with four prominent world leaders: President Dwight D. Eisenhower (March 1960) and his successor, John F. Kennedy (May 1961); German

Chancellor Konrad Adenauer (in New York, March 1960); French President Charles DeGaulle (June 1961). In July 1961 he visited France, Belgium, and Holland, and the following year he traveled to Canada, the United States, and France. As important as these missions were in promoting closer ties with the West—the meeting with JFK led to the first important American sale of military equipment (the Hawk missile) to Israel in 1962—after Ben-Gurion's retirement from office in 1963, Israel was in essentially the same international position as before: still in a state of war regionally, isolated and defensive globally.

Eshkol and the Policy of Indecision (June 1963–February 1969)

Decision making under Ben-Gurion, although not always successful or necessarily open, did suggest Israel to be a resolute state actor, an impression reconfirmed by the bold capture of Nazi war criminal Adolf Eichmann on Argentine soil and his abduction to Jerusalem for trial in May 1960. Whatever else, attempts had been made, like in 1956, to change the small country's external environment. The following period, in comparison, suggests a good deal of the same temporizing and indecisiveness found in Sharett's time.

In this regard there are at least two ironies about Levi Eshkol and his foreign policy. The first is that the Eshkol era brought a profound change in Israel's larger geopolitical position because of the 1967 Six-Day War—but a change neither initiated nor sought by Israel. A second irony is that while himself wishing to be Israel's "pilot of the calm" (to use Walter Bagehot's classic distinction), Levi Eshkol was forced by events into the unfamiliar role of "pilot of the storm"; it is as a crisis leader that he led the country to victory in the 1967 war.

Although a warm and engaging personality, Eshkol was hampered in the foreign policy sphere by two particularly serious drawbacks. He had to operate in the shadow of Ben-Gurion who, from retirement in Sde Boker, frequently criticized the new government's conduct of national and foreign affairs. And he was inexperienced in foreign affairs, having been chosen mostly for his domestic competence and managerial skills. Consequently, after an uninspiring national radio address on 28 May 1967 as the Middle East crisis escalated, the prime minister came under pressure from the public and from the military command and was virtually forced to turn over the defense portfolio to the former chief of staff, Moshe Dayan.

Popular impressions aside, the precrisis years of Eshkol's term in office, 1963–67, indicated definite gains for Israel in foreign relations. This was the time of greatest success in the ambitious program of economic and technical assistance to the Third World. As part of this drive Eshkol himself made a tour in May 1966 of six African countries: Liberia, Senegal, Congo (Kinshasa), Madagascar, Uganda, and Kenya. Further afield, Eshkol stressed the need for an ongoing dialogue with European heads of government. He visited Paris for political discussions in June 1964 and London in March 1965. In May 1965 he proceeded to establish diplomatic relations between Israel and West Germany. Most impressive, however, was the distinct improvement in the attitude of the United States toward Israel, in which Eshkol had a personal hand, as testified by his cordial reception in Washington in June 1964—the first official visit by an Israeli prime minister to the United States. Here, and again while a guest at the LBJ ranch in Texas in January 1968, the premier enjoyed excellent rapport with President Lyndon Johnson. This personal chemistry smoothed the way for administration approval in December of purchase by Israel of fifty F-4 Phantom aircraft.

These diplomatic inroads are impressive. Yet there are strong traces of indecision in the Eshkol government's handling of foreign relations. Using the 1967 war as a reference point, a sense of drift accompanies successive phases from precrisis to crisis and then post-crisis.

The period preceding the 1967 military confrontation reveals little Israeli initiative or movement toward resolving the Middle East dispute. But it was not alone. The entire decade 1957 to 1967 is hardly noted in the annals of the Arab-Israeli conflict as a time of bold peacemaking proposals by international parties or by the Arab states either. The Eshkol government, like those before it, had a hard enough time preserving the status quo against disruptions such as the controversy over diverting the headwaters of the Jordan River and repeated border incursions from Syria and Jordan.

In the crisis phase, extending from mid-May to 5 June, Israel faced its most grave security threat. Eshkol and his cabinet were wracked by hesitancy, torn between taking no action and relying on international pressures to defuse the situation initiated by Egypt, Syria, and Jordan or going to war. This span of twenty-two days is appropriately referred to in Hebrew as the period of *konenut* (preparedness) or, still better, of *hamtana* (standing by), which conveys the sense of anxiety and indecision then prevailing in Israel. Last-minute diplomatic efforts aimed at averting war and mobilizing international support failed abjectly. Foreign Minister Abba Eban returned empty-handed from a hasty mission to London, Paris, and Washington at the end of May. So, too, did urgent appeals to King Hussein of Jordan not to commit his army against Israel fall on deaf ears. In the end, Israel was left with only the military option, which, when finally executed on 5 June, resulted in a stunning battlefield victory for Israel.

The extent of the military feat took even the country's political elite by surprise. By 12 June Israeli troops controlled the Golan Heights to the north, the entire Sinai up to the Suez Canal on the southern front, and all of the West Bank. Caught off guard, and seized like everyone else by a sense of relief and euphoria, the crisis government was slow to react politically to this entirely new and fluid situation. The initial tendency was to treat the occupied territories as an invaluable bargaining chip to be used in bringing the defeated Arab countries once and for all to the negotiating table. With each passing week, however, the twin arguments of security-in-depth and of an "integral Israel" (*Eretz Yisrael hashlayma*) closer to its biblical dimensions in the Holy Land gained broader public support. The numbers of those wishing to see the post-June borders as permanent swelled appreciably, spawning a movement for erecting settlements in Sinai, on the Golan, and in Judea and Samaria. What strengthened this view as much as anything else was the proclamation on 1 September by the Arab summit conference in Khartoum of a policy of no peace, no recognition, and no negotiations with Israel. The unity government, itself deeply divided, was incapable of making up its own collective mind between total withdrawal or unilateral annexation. This was the state of nondecision (itself a kind of decision!) prevailing on 26 February 1969, when Prime Minister Eshkol died suddenly.

Meir and the Policy of Steadfastness (March 1969–April 1974)

The five years in which Golda Meir served as prime minister of Israel offer a lesson against freely passing out grades on Israeli foreign policy. Her contribution in this area at a minimum requires great respect for the caveat mentioned earlier in this chapter about uneven performance (i.e., adept in one sphere while inept in another). Two broad areas must be distinguished: (a) the Arab Middle East and (b) the rest of the world, since Mrs. Meir was inclined to show less flexibility toward the former than toward the latter.

Possessor of a well-defined political *Weltanschauung* and iron-willed, Mrs. Meir held to fixed positions on the issue of peace and war in the Arab-Israeli zone. Specifically, she insisted on nothing less than signed peace treaties and refused to entertain one-sided concessions by Israel as a precondition for negotiations. She fought outside diplomatic initiatives (the Rogers plan, the Jarring mission) that she saw as inimical to Israel's interests. She sought to contain Soviet advances in the Middle East. Supported by Defense Minister Dayan, she authorized strong military ripostes against Egypt during the Suez Canal war of attrition (September 1968–August 1970) and against PLO-sponsored international terrorism and air hijackings. She took a dim view of the prospects for a peace settlement based on territorial compromise; nor did she place much hope on King Hussein of Jordan as Israel's peace partner. Finally, Prime Minister Meir dismissed all Palestinian claims to political and national status, insisting upon seeing the plight of the Arab refugees in limited, humanitarian terms only.

Showing the same steadfastness and singlemindedness of purpose, Golda Meir was more successful/adept in effectively strengthening Israel's position internationally through closer collaboration with the United States. Convinced of the vital need for Israel to win over American support, and given her insight into the American mind and United States political system deriving from her youth in Milwaukee, she assumed direct, personal charge of this key policy area. Bypassing the Foreign Ministry, and often working outside bureaucratic channels, she relied heavily on her hand-chosen ambassadorial appointee in Washington, Simcha Dinitz. Also, while Israelis laugh at stories of Golda flying off to the States with her shopping list of economic and military aid requests, she was singularly effective in cutting through White House, State Department, and Pentagon red tape. She enjoyed immense popularity with the American press, Congress, and American Jewry. A frequent visitor to the United States, she met personally with President Richard Nixon on four separate occasions between September 1970 and October 1973.

These two dates, however, represent both the high water mark and low point in the United States–Israel relationship at that time, as well as intimating some of the good and bad implications in what was already becoming a growing dependency on the United States as superpower patron. In September 1970, Mrs. Meir exploited the Jordan crisis, impressing the American public and policy makers alike with the thesis of Israel as the only dependable United States ally in the volatile Middle East region. In October 1973, however, she tragically wavered in her customary resolve for the sake of the United States–Israeli relationship. Belatedly apprised of an imminent Egyptian-Syrian attack, instead of following the traditional doctrine of preemption, she chose instead to wait, in part because of American warnings not to be the first to initiate fighting, thereby precipitating the traumatic Yom Kippur War. Even though Israel absorbed the blow and sufficiently recovered to assume the offensive, Mrs. Meir's confidence was badly damaged. Still, she led a demoralized country in the next stage of renewed international diplomatic activity, capped by the Geneva conference (December 1973) and the first Israel-Egypt separation of forces agreement (January 1974). Following national elections, Mrs. Meir resigned in April 1974.

Rabin and the Policy of Disengagement (June 1974–April 1977)

Former chief of staff Yitzchak Rabin was selected by the ruling Labour Party to replace the exhausted "Iron Lady" as premier. Despite this vote of confidence he entered office with several disadvantages. For one thing, Rabin assumed power at the most difficult time in Israel's history. The nation was still licking it wounds from the Yom Kippur War, having suffered over 2,500 casualties—or something like one percent of the population! It was also only beginning to come to grips with the many social, economic, and strategic implications of the recent fighting. As part of learning the lessons from the war a major military and intelligence reorganization was also under way. Furthermore, Rabin had little experience in domestic affairs, and although good at rational problem-solving, he was uninspiring in public appearances; in addition, he had to contend with personality clashes and infighting within his own Labour Alignment coalition.

The Rabin government failed to serve out a full four-year term, falling prey to internal politics, but it was involved in some of the most intense diplomatic activity yet experienced by Israel. These years 1974 to 1976 coincide of course with the period of "shuttle diplomacy" associated with U.S. Secretary of State Henry Kissinger. The 1973 crisis had thrust the Middle East conflict even closer to the forefront of the international agenda both as a threat to world peace and as the central theater for Soviet-American confrontation. For Israelis the crisis and its immediate aftermath signified the interconnectedness of the regional and global arenas.

Kissinger's Middle East strategy was unambiguous. It called for applying American influence and pressure to exploit the military standoff among Israel, Egypt, and Syria to achieve political gains. With Kissinger's help, and under his constant prodding, Israel became a party to two important diplomatic accords: an Israeli-Syrian disengagement reached in May 1974 that was followed in September 1975 by a second Egypt-Israel agreement (Sinai II). Actually, there was a third accord; as part of the trilateral negotiations and in assuaging Israeli fears at yielding tangible assets in the Sinai (withdrawal from the Gidi and Mitla passes, yielding the Abu Rudeis oil fields), Israel was able to win from the United States a memorandum of agreement providing unprecedented American assurances and undertakings to help meet its economic, military, strategic, and diplomatic needs.

These achievements did not come easily, or without heavy cost. Preoccupation with disengaging Israel on both the southern (Egypt) and northern (Syria) fronts meant giving less priority to reaching an understanding on the eastern frontier with Jordan. Many observers would later feel this was a missed opportunity. Less attention was shown by the Rabin government to areas further removed from the Arab-Israeli conflict zone, although the prime minister himself was later revealed to have made secret visits to Morocco and Iran, for example, in promoting Israeli interests. Nevertheless, Soviet bloc estrangement continued unabated; the United Nations forum became openly hostile; relations with the Western European countries also remained strained (in the previous October crisis only Portugal had cooperated in the U.S. arms airlift to Israel); and everywhere Israel turned it encountered the Arab oil factor wielded as a political weapon against third-country ties with Israel. One rare bright moment was the sensational Entebbe rescue operation in July 1976. Although more military than diplomatic, nevertheless it brought home to the world Israel's determination to lead in the fight against international terrorism.

It is perhaps indicative of the general tenor of Israel's external defensiveness in the mid-1970s that even the crucial U.S.-Israel bilateral relationship did not escape erosion. Already during the Nixon-Ford administration, generally regarded as sympathetic, Israel came under heavy pressure. The so-called reassessment by Washington of its Mideast interests from March to December 1975 carried with it implied sanctions against Israel should it refuse to cooperate with America's mediation efforts toward achieving Sinai II. Matters only got worse with the transition to a new, Democratic administration under Jimmy Carter in January 1977.

Yitzchak Rabin's last months in power saw further strains in the Washington-Jerusalem axis. This may have been partially due to personality differences; during Rabin's visit to the White House in March he and the president reportedly did not get along well. Far more serious though were the fundamental changes introduced by Carter and his advisers into U.S. policy toward Israel and the Middle East that centered essentially on repudiating the entire formula of "step-by-step" diplomacy crafted by Kissinger and subscribed to by Israel. This abrupt policy reversal extended to each and every one of the key "modalities": the goal, the process, the sponsors, and the central participants.

Where Kissinger and Israel had set their sights on phased interim accords, the objective now became a comprehensive peace. Where both favored separate talks, the Carter policy called for reconvening the multilateral Geneva conference framework. The previous consensus elevated the United States to the role of sole broker, whereas the new administration consciously encouraged active Soviet patronage. Similarly, Kissinger and Rabin saw eye-to-eye on Egypt and the Arab moderates as essential partners, while the architects of the Carter approach argued for winning over Syria and the extremist Arab rejectionist front. Lastly, and most ominous: Kissinger and previous Washington officials had embraced the Labour view of Jordan as Israel's indispensable peace partner; now Israelis read statements by President Carter about a homeland for the Palestinians that although not precluding the Jordanian option certainly complicated it.

There is the likelihood this gap between policy views and leaders in the two countries might have widened into a full-fledged diplomatic confrontation had the political situation in the late spring of 1977 continued. What averted such a crisis, however, were two unforeseen developments—the surprise Labour party defeat by its Likud rival in the May general elections and the electrifying Sadat initiative of October 1977 that entirely upset the Carter policy opposed by Israel.

Begin and the Policy of Revisionism (June 1977–September 1984)

The Begin-Likud era really consists of three distinct periods: the first Begin government (June 1977–August 1981); the second Begin government (August 1981–September 1983); and Yitzchak Shamir's caretaker government (October 1983–September 1984). So much about Menachem Begin, his public career, political philosophy, and meaning for Israel are of abiding interest and controversy. It is the wisest course, therefore, to eschew any larger interpretation and to confine the discussion to a factual account of Israeli foreign relations in those years, seeking to fit them into the broader context of policy success and failure.

One general observation is inescapable, however. As argued here, leaving aside the special dimension of Diaspora relations, all Israeli prime ministers from Ben-Gurion on have operated within a split vision: there is the Arab subsystem and then there is the rest of the world, including a heavy emphasis on ties with the United States. Some of Begin's predecessors distinguished themselves in one area but not the other. Eshkol's record, for example, like that of Golda

Meir's, was better in extraregional than in regional affairs; Sharett failed to gain distinction in either policy sphere.

Had the period been restricted only to 1977–81 Begin might have gone down in history as singularly successful in both areas, whether because of astuteness, good fortune, or both. Under his leadership, Israel reached a peace agreement with Egypt and a closer understanding with the United States. But the following years almost negated these earlier gains. The second Begin government was marked by the war in Lebanon, failure to move beyond the narrow Egypt-Israel peace, a regression to the role of international outcast, and the most strident tones yet heard in the Israeli-American dialogue. This curve pattern in the rise and descent of Likud foreign policy is summarized by three major events: the 1979 peace with Egypt, the historic journey of President Anwar Sadat to Israel—a definite diplomatic plus for Israel—in comparison to Operation Peace for Galilee in June 1982, and the Reagan initiative *contretemps* in September of that year.

After twenty-nine years in the political wilderness as opposition leader, once the Likud coalition government had been formed, Menachem Begin concentrated heavily on security and foreign affairs. Already in July 1977 he conferred in Washington with President Carter and then visited Bucharest in August for important talks with Romanian President Ceausescu to explore the possibility of a meeting with Sadat. At the same time Begin authorized Foreign Minister Moshe Dayan to hold secret conversations in Morocco with an emissary from Cairo.

Once the bold peace initiative intensified and became public, Prime Minister Begin followed a pragmatic course. In the protracted negotiations with Egypt that led from Jerusalem to Camp David and ultimately to the lawn of the White House for the treaty-signing ceremony on 29 March 1979 by way of Ismailiya, Cairo, Aswan, Salzberg, Leeds castle, Blair House, and Brussels, Begin in effect matched Sadat (and Carter) move for move in the classic chess game of world politics that earned for both Middle Eastern statesmen the 1978 Nobel peace prize. At home Begin also had to play astute domestic politics in steering the Camp David frameworks and then the final draft peace treaty terms through the three successive phases of cabinet, Knesset, and public debate. After an emotional marathon session, the Israeli parliament on 27 September 1978 approved the Camp David accords by a vote of 84 in favor, 19 opposed, and 17 abstentions. The treaty itself encountered even less resistance on 22 March 1979: 95 for, 18 against, and only 2 abstentions.

Begin's exact role remains subject to conflicting evaluations with critics variously accusing him of being overly compromising and not forthcoming enough. Still, Begin clearly demonstrated a strong sense of realism in grasping the magnitude of the opportunity presented by Sadat's bold initiative. It offered Israel a chance in one fell swoop

1. to break the tradition of conflict;
2. to establish instead a precedent for both Arab-Israeli direct negotiation and peacemaking;
3. to revise the Middle East military balance by detaching Egypt from the Arab war coalition;
4. to recast Israel's international image by showing it was not wedded to territorial conquest;
5. to convince friends in the United States and elsewhere of Israeli sincerity in waging peace; and
6. above all, to reap the benefits of peace at home.

All of this without compromising Israel's vital interests, security or the Jewish right, which Begin considered immutable, to be in the West Bank territories of Judea and Samaria. If diplomacy is the art of the possible and the ability to achieve by negotiation and compromise one's maximum gain with minimal risk or loss, then the 1979 treaty has to qualify as a benchmark in Israeli foreign relations.

The treaty also stands as the high point in Likud foreign policy. It would be exaggerated to present the first and second Begin governments as totally different. The use of force in the 1982 military intervention in Lebanon, for example, was preceded by Operation Litani in March 1978, also into southern Lebanon. Still, there is a distinct difference in style and tone between 1977–80 and 1981–84. Precisely what caused this *volte face*, if such it was, will remain a matter of speculation. Most likely it owed to a combination of negative influences. In his second term Begin often appeared distracted, listless, and in declining spirits, as well as in poor health. The composition and makeup of his closest advisers on security and foreign policy matters also changed with the departure of Defense Minister Ezer Weizman and Foreign Minister Dayan. And not to be overlooked is the fact that once the Sinai was no longer a contentious issue, both the peace process itself and American pressure came to rest on the status of the West Bank, which for Begin had a special ideological and emotional significance that made compromising on Israeli settlement and territorial rights almost impossible for him.

The last Begin years in power suggest greater testiness and irascibility in external affairs. Stung by world condemnation of Israel's indirect complicity in the September 1982 killing of Palestinian refugees in Beirut by Christian militia, the prime minister snapped back: "*Goyim* kill *Goyim* [non-Jews], and they immediately come to hang the Jews." In December 1981 Begin responded to American pressure by delivering an unprecedented tongue-lashing to the U.S. ambassador, Samuel Lewis, reportedly saying: "What kind of talk is this of punishing Israel? Are we a vassal state of yours? Are we a banana republic? You will not frighten us with punishments." He added, for good measure, "The people of Israel have lived 3,700 years without a memorandum of understanding with America—and they will continue to live without one for another 3,700."

This bellicosity can be witnessed in deeds as well—and not only by the siege of Beirut or events in the Sabra and Shatila refugee camps. An earlier air strike against PLO headquarters in Beirut in 1981 precipitated the U.S. decision to suspend delivery of F-16 planes. Then there was the destruction of the Iraqi Osirak nuclear reactor in June 1981. Knesset legislation the following December extending Israeli law and jurisdiction to the Golan resulted in suspension of the recently concluded U.S.-Israeli memorandum of understanding on strategic cooperation. Thus, whatever his motives, Begin's immediate rejection of the Reagan peace proposals in September 1982, along with other differences straining relations with the United States and deriving from the strategic decision to enter Lebanon by force in 1982, effectively conveys the troubled state of Israeli external affairs when a year later the dispirited Likud leader suddenly announced his resignation from office and retirement from public life.

Foreign Minister Yitzchak Shamir had to deal with this declining state of affairs when he succeeded Begin as prime minister in October 1983. In fairness, however, Shamir's term in office was too short to yield any clear picture or pattern of success and failure. His major preoccupations were with the inflationary economy and with trying to extricate Israel from its Lebanese misadventure. To his credit, after having earlier fought the Sinai concessions to Egypt, once in office Shamir openly defended the peace settlement. On the debit side, though, he was conspicuously unsuccessful in March 1984 in preventing Lebanon from abrogating its normalization agreement negotiated with Israel eleven months earlier. In effect, Shamir's was but a caretaker government. Knesset elections were held in July 1984, resulting in a government of national unity in September that is discussed in the next chapter.

In the final analysis, Menachem Begin dominated the foreign policy process after 1977, acting out of an operational code based on his youth in Poland and adult affiliation with the Zionist revisionist movement of Vladimir Jabotinsky. His years in power underscore this theme of "revisionism" but not in the orthodox Herut sense. Begin succeeded initially in revising and strengthening Israel's international standing; the country's geopolitical situation also took a considerable turn for the better. Unfortunately Begin then turned around and permitted a further revision in Israeli regional and global relations, this time to Israel's disfavor, through his consent in principle to the disastrous war in Lebanon.

This closing remark about diplomatic opportunities—those missed and those seized—serves as a prefatory comment in turning next to the matter of a recurrent, distinctive Israeli diplomatic style. The coming chapter suggests a number of basic continuities that run through Israel's foreign relations from the early Ben-Gurion era of firm direction to the contemporary stage of divided leadership under two successive governments of national unity.

CHAPTER 4

CONTINUITY AND CHANGE

This is perhaps our historical destiny to swim against the tide. But we keep on swimming. We have not drowned yet.

Prime Minister Yitzchak Shamir, 1979

Researchers like to address foreign relations by Israel not as a linear procession—a steady stream, an even flow—but more like a series of disruptions. As a state actor Israel comes across to many outsiders as a nerve-racking, unsettling player. Its behavior is unpredictable and explosive; its policy disjointed, moving by fits and starts; its diplomacy marked by breaks in political relationships. In a word, discontinuity is the dominant impression. This chapter speaks, however, to the constancy in Israel's approach to world politics.

Those convinced of Israel's inconsistency sometimes blame personality or ideological differences for Israel's erratic performance. What could the foreign policies of two individuals so completely unalike as Ben-Gurion and Begin possibly have in common when one was the supreme realist, the other so dogmatic? Or, for that matter, such opposites as Shimon Peres and Yitzchak Shamir who alternated as premier in the 1984–88 national unity government?

Other observers trace Israel's purported inconsistency to the situational variable, arguing it is unfair to expect regularity and predictability from a state that has had far more than its share of fast-breaking events. Crises and wars by definition force unplanned, spontaneous reactions. They also cause disequilibrium by transforming the preexisting situation almost beyond recognition. Look at the contrast in Israel's international position before and after the 1967 Six-Day War.

Diplomatic historians, in applying the tool of periodization, contribute to this impression of discontinuity. In striving for clarity by working within neat time frames, they identify for Israel a number of policy departures, but certainly no less than four "great divides":

1948: the shift from supplicant to sovereign statecraft;
1967: possession of the administered/occupied West Bank territories that compounded the search for an Arab peace and for international acceptability;
1973: the year of the Yom Kippur trauma, which is referred to in Hebrew as nothing short of a *reidat adama* (a tremorous earthquake);
1977: remembered for Sadat's strategic diplomatic surprise, but even more for the *mahapach*: the political upheaval in Israeli politics caused by the Likud party's replacement of Labour after twenty-nine uninterrupted years in power.

The last event has given rise to a school of thought that insists on treating what transpired because of the 1977 elections in epochal terms. Begin, representing something labeled "new Zionism" or "neo-Revisionism," imposed a "new" belief system while violating traditional diplomatic strictures. The Likud leadership proceeded, so we are told, to restructure the modus operandi of Israel's foreign policy system, thus bringing about, for example, the aberrant 1982 Lebanon invasion.

Such contrasts, suggesting radical swings of the foreign policy pendulum, are overdrawn. Not that there have not been important changes in various aspects of Israeli external affairs in the first forty years, many of them traced in the earlier chapters, due to the interplay of personality and situational factors. Nevertheless, these changes have been more of degree than of kind, and of style rather than substance. Moreover, this preoccupation with change is unfortunate in that it overlooks essential similarities in the sense of permanent features, recurrent patterns, or themes, and ongoing processes as well as policy orientations. The argument of this chapter is that Israeli foreign relations, when viewed from a forty-year retrospective, really feature an intermix of continuity and change.

PERMANENT FEATURES IN THE CONDUCT OF FOREIGN RELATIONS

Consistency immediately presents itself in the foundations of policy. In the continued absence of peace, universal recognition, and security, the core goals described previously remain constant for all Israeli governments to date. So, too, did their concentration on security stay narrowly defined. Foreign policy, in short, suggests fixed national purpose. It is this anchor, for example, that made power-sharing under the national unity government possible after 1984. Also, the view of the world and of Israel's place in it has not oscillated from government to government. Where governments differ is not in defining the national interest but in fitting together the clusters of objectives and then in selecting the most appropriate means available at a given moment for their pursuit.

Prudence

Another strand of continuity comes under the heading of prudence. Being Jewish and Zionist, Israel could easily have succumbed to the two rigid postures of either moralist absolutism or a blind nationalism. Instead, there has always been a strong trace of pragmatism in handling complex, threatening external situations.

The essence of prudence lies in realism and caution. In entrusting power to government, all that states, societies, and individuals can really ask of their leaders is the detachment necessary for distinguishing between the normative (what ought to be) and reality (what is). Such realism is a quality particularly to be sought when policy makers must define a political situation, determine what capabilities are needed or available to pursue a certain set of goals, and then decide, in the event of a deficiency of power, whether to forgo that objective or to supplement power from an outside source. Prudence in the form of caution is a necessary commodity for small states like Israel for whom survival depends on never exaggerating their status or depleting their weak power base. Looking at the brighter side, the psychological and material costs of Lebanon in 1982 may have reinforced this lesson, serving as a preventive against the misplaced application of power and prestige beyond the country's direct security borders.

Of course, such caution and realism also have their drawbacks. In the Israeli case prudence has dictated settling for security over peace; relying on force over diplomacy; emphasizing substantive even if partial gains over public relations and image-building and short-term over long-range strategic planning; and, not least, preferring surety to risk-taking. This prudent approach leads to zig-zags that students too easily misinterpret and take for inconsistency.

Flexibility and pragmatism at decisive moments extend well back into the prestate period. They are featured, for example, in a Zionist decision as early as 1937 to endorse the twin principles of political accommodation and of partitioning Palestine as an historical necessity to achieve statehood. In retrospect, the 1937 stand on partition was like crossing the Rubicon for Zionist statesmen. It involved a shift from dogmatism to a diplomatic mode premised on bargaining and compromise. Incidentally, it is this crucial stage of transition from ideology to realism that had been absent in the Palestinian position from the thirties through the eighties.

Pragmatism is what later led Ben-Gurion from 1951 to 1953 to negotiate the reparations agreement with Bonn. He was also one of the first world leaders to appreciate China as a rising power. In 1956 pragmatism prompted him to go to war against Egypt only to turn around in March 1957, when, bowing to American and Soviet pressure, he ordered unilateral withdrawal by Israeli forces from the Sinai and Gaza. Again, prudence—in the sense of recognizing objective limits to the possible—explains Eshkol's acceptance in 1967 of UN Resolution 242, Meir's participation in Kissinger's early shuttle diplomacy, and the Rabin government's reluctant consent to the Sinai II undertaking in 1975. Finally, and of special significance in the context of the argument for continuity over discontinuity, there is Begin's encouragement of the Sadat initiative and, even more, his signing of the Camp David frameworks. Both acts surely stand in the tradition of Israeli *Realpolitik* and guarded pragmatism.

One weak spot in Israeli pragmatism comes in knowing when to bend and be concessionary. In world politics timing may not be everything, but it certainly counts for something. Some theorists of small-state behavior would advise holding out until the last possible moment to extract better terms from the negotiating process. This worked for Israel in 1975, as an example, when in return for accepting the second disengagement pact with Egypt, Israel received an American pledge of political and military support. But for the most part, not moving early in bowing to the inevitable, perhaps even attributing concessions to Israel's own initiative, has only exposed it to greater pressure and embarrassment. This happened with the 1957 Sinai withdrawal. Years later the same thing happened when, in April 1988, Jerusalem finally agreed to conditions insisted on for a long time by the European Economic Community regarding the right of Arab citrus growers in Gaza to market their produce directly and outside of Israeli export controls. So, too, in the protracted and at times acrimonious negotiations over Taba that, in any case, Israel eventually yielded to Egypt in 1989. In each instance a good deal of recrimination and bad will might have been avoided by earlier assent.

Elitism

Foreign affairs and security policy making in Israel has always been elitist, from Ben-Gurion's time to the present. The only question each time is exactly how many people might be direct participants in a particular decision, from a single individual to at most, a handful of officials.

This emphasis on personalism within a select group of high policy elites may be necessary in Israel, given the dictates of an exceptional threat situation. But it is also hazardous. From the standpoint of democratic government, concentrating power and authority so exclusively discourages accountability; and, in terms of national security, it encourages error by dispensing with such safeguards as full policy debate, review, and multiple advocacy. Had policy making been more open in the weeks before June 1982, Israel's overextension in Lebanon might have been averted, for example. Given Israel's commitment to democracy together with the unacceptable costs of a strategic blunder, prudent conduct by Israeli leaders at the top so far compensates for centralized responsibility and power. Indeed, it is a sine qua non for survival.

Once again, the pattern was established considerably before 1948. The diaries of Theodor Herzl reveal how, unassisted, he negotiated with the rulers, statesmen, and financiers of Europe and the Near East at the turn of the century. By far the most adept practitioner of such "lone wolf" diplomacy was Chaim Weizmann. A consummate diplomat, he made important friends for the Zionist cause in the interwar years and had a direct hand in the two greatest achievements of prestate political efforts: the 1917 Balfour Declaration and American support in 1947–48 following Weizmann's personal eleventh-hour appeals to President Truman.

One might have assumed then, in 1948, that such freewheeling and individualized diplomacy would end with statehood, its place taken by institutionalized policy making. Instead, this early stress on the personal and interpersonal side of foreign relations has continued throughout, becoming yet another constant. Ben-Gurion's own involvement in the final stages of the secret 1956 negotiations with France has already been mentioned; so, too, the Eshkol-LBJ rapport, Meir's hold on Nixon, and Rabin's success with both Nixon and Ford but not with Carter. Personal diplomacy in the grand manner in a sense came full circle with Begin and his clear preference for making decisions himself and for holding direct contacts at the highest level. One reason peace feelers by President Sadat in the fall of 1977 met a warm reception in Jerusalem is because the offer fit in so perfectly with an Israeli diplomatic style that regards core issues like peace and security best handled by heads of government free of bureaucratic interference and red tape. The best case in point, of course, is the trilateral negotiations at Camp David in September 1978 among Begin, Sadat, and Carter.

It has been noted that bureaucracy, among its functions, liberates decision making from the accident of personalities. Nevertheless, the student of Israeli decision making is advised to pay greater attention to the biographies of national leaders than to formal organizational charts.

Limited Options

The foreign policy agenda, with it emphasis on security, unites all Israeli leaders regardless of ideological belief, operating style, or personal idiosyncrasy. They also share the limited choices in meeting the country's challenges.

Historical forces like Arab nationalism or the US-USSR rivalry are well beyond the capacity of Israeli statesmen to eliminate or to direct—merely to encourage or to moderate slightly. Every government is forced, therefore, to operate within narrow margins as it seeks to avoid the twin perils of humiliation or holocaust. Options are rarely appealing. If they make sense they may not be politically practicable. Thus, few Israelis relish the country's reputation for conventional weapons transfers, yet neither do they regard the government as having much choice but to continue promoting the longstanding and nonpartisan policy of arms sales. Indeed, in some senses, like the successful nonmilitary aid program to the Afro-Asian nations in the sixties, Israel has been impressive in creating fresh options and in making so little go a long way.

Still, poor diplomatic alternatives have been a constant source of frustration. This may help explain how and why a certain mind-set gradually took root among civilian as well as army leaders who argued for Israel using military force to impose its will on defiant adversaries. Ostensibly defensive at first, this power school of problem solving disparaged the value of conciliatory gestures, eventually arriving at the exaggerated conclusion that even complex political problems might lend themselves to a military solution. A deeper collective bias implanted itself against the efficacy of noncoercive means and accommodation with the Arab enemy and in favor of force. This predisposition, rather than forced distinctions between Labour party moderation and a bellicose Likud stand, is what really underlay the 1982 march on Beirut. The Lebanese intervention thus represented a logical, if unfortunate, culmination to the simplistic notion about military power's utility and effectiveness.

Since 1982 Israelis—public and leaders alike—have been absorbing the lesson that force has definite limits. Any new thinking on foreign policy must rest on the proposition that diplomatic persuasion has got to be the independent variable and military coercion the dependent variable. Appreciation for diplomatic subtlety and initiative as more effective in the long run than blunt physical force would be a desirable conclusion to this national learning process.

Middle East Aloofness

Israel's relationship to the surrounding Arab regional subsystem serves as another durable foreign policy feature. Essentially a corollary to the power school, aloofness suggests that whatever influence Israel may have had on Arab society and politics has been limited, indirect, and restricted almost exclusively to the battlefield. This policy of noninterference has a touch of Greek tragedy to it, since to adopt a clear position and take sides on inter-Arab issues would expose Jerusalem to charges of "divide and rule": exploiting centrifugal forces in the Arab world to keep the Arab people weak and disunited. Arab propagandists then turn this around, citing aloofness by Israel as proof of the Jewish state being a foreign body imposed on the Arabs by force and therefore alien to the region, politically destabilizing, and insensitive to its rhythms, its passions, and its concerns.

The prestate period witnessed any number of attempts at overcoming local Arab opposition to Jewish nationalism. Finding the Palestinian Arab leadership uncompromising, Weizmann, Ben-Gurion, Sharett, and others sought to sidestep this obstacle by seeking moderate Arab partners in the adjacent Arab countries. Efforts such as the 1919 Weizmann-Faisal agreement were of no avail, however. They only negatively prejudiced Zionists' attitudes toward the region and toward the Arabs as a whole. Thus, impatience with the intricacies of Arab bazaar politics and with Arab politicians who disappointed merely reinforced the cultural affinity Weizmann and his colleagues felt toward Europe.

Developments during 1948 and after further strengthened this pattern of estrangement. Unabated Arab enmity denied Israel all possibility of taking any leadership role in Middle East affairs. The longer this unnatural state endured the more prone Israelis became to taking refuge in rigid policy assumptions. Conventional wisdom came to see the Arab world largely in monochromatic terms: a solid bloc of hostility from the Euphrates to the Maghreb; Arab unity as a direct threat to Israel that must be prevented; regional instability and domestic turmoil serving Israel's immediate purposes, and therefore to be encouraged; Arab leaders as impervious to peace overtures; and the Arabs as only understanding force.

There have been several notable exceptions in which Israel has to one degree or another been a party to Arab political alignments. Four such instances are

first, its open identification with Jordan in the 1970 double crisis that found the Hashemite throne threatened simultaneously by a civil war and by a military invasion from Syria;

second, defense of the Maronite Christian community in Lebanon, which predates the 1982 war;

third, the peace with Egypt, which at least theoretically has opened up the possibility for Israel's direct participation in various regional coalitions centering on economic collaboration as well as regional security; and

fourth, the working relationship with the Hashemite monarchy that embraces the east and west banks of the Jordan River and has taken on the character of a tacit understanding.

These four cases are exceptions to the general rule of Israel's regional exclusion. Nevertheless, they offer encouragement for imaginative Israeli diplomacy by hinting at the prospects for Israel as an integral and accepted part of Middle Eastern affairs in the future.

Great Power Support

For the present, meanwhile, Israeli foreign policy suggests an overwhelming preoccupation with securing a patron from among the leading international state actors. This "one great power" doctrine has persisted in Israeli thinking for more than forty years.

The strains of its isolation from the Arab states meant Israel had to look elsewhere. As a result, the previous quest by Zionist diplomats for ties of friendship and support outside the Arab Middle East in the arena of European world politics in essence repeated itself after 1948. Efforts by Israel at leaping beyond the wall of official Arab hostility and military encirclement during the 1950s saw the country active in at least two secondary spheres of Middle East politics. One of these was known as the "minorities policy" and consisted of backing for other threatened ethnic, religious, and political opposition groups: the Druze, the Maronites, the Kurds. The second thrust was the "periphery policy," which encouraged meaningful contacts with the several non-Arab countries of the eastern Mediterranean–Red Sea–Persian Gulf axis: modernizing Iran and Turkey, Christian Ethiopia, and even Cyprus.

As important as such contacts were for Israel in avoiding total Middle East ostracism, the main thrust of policy was to enlist the aid of the great powers. From this perspective Ben-Gurion's brief attempt at nonidentification between East and West must be seen as a departure from the pattern established in the twenties and reverted to in the fifties—and by Ben-Gurion himself. Herzl and the early Zionists had understood almost instinctively that for Jewish nationalism any minimum winning coalition meant the moral as well as political backing of a least one world power. This was the thinking behind Weizmann's "British connection" during the formative years 1917–39; it also governed his reorientation away from Britain and toward the United States from 1944 onward.

Once estrangement from the communist bloc precluded the Soviet option and made nonalignment meaningless for Israel, Ben-Gurion was astute enough to realize the need to forsake nonidentification in favor of alignment with the Western powers. The question reduced itself to which of the Western nations might be amenable to closer ties with the Jewish state. The truth is that in the 1950s and 1960s none of them was prepared for a permanent relationship with Israel. Instead, Israeli leaders settled for partial or short-term political marriages of convenience with West Germany, Great Britain and, most successfully, France.

However, by the mid- and late sixties, application of the one great power strategy increasingly came to focus on the United States. True, there had been earlier disappointments. Ben-Gurion, for all of his talk about independence and self-reliance, had sought a mutual defense treaty with Washington only to be rebuffed; similar requests for formal security guarantees in 1957 were turned down. During the 1967 crisis the United States failed to honor its commitment to freedom of navigation. Even so, the subsequent governments of Eshkol, Meir, Rabin, and Begin assigned an absolute top priority to widening and strengthening the special relationship with Washington.

It would be almost impossible to overestimate what success in this superpower orientation has meant for Israel and for Israeli national interests. While not freeing the country from the attendant danger of dependence on a foreign power, even so, ties with the United States in truth have vindicated each of the premises behind the great power strategy initially conceived of nearly a hundred years ago by Herzl. The benefits of American friendship are direct, tangible, and meaningful whether viewed in terms of enhanced defense capability and economic viability ($3 billion in fiscal year 1989) or in terms of moral and diplomatic support expressed through the U.S. veto of anti-Israel resolutions in the UN Security Council.

For all of these reasons the doctrine of maintaining close working relations with the West in general and the United States in particular will continue to serve as an accurate guide to Israeli foreign policy. Any leader or government in power in Jerusalem will be pledged to work at preserving the gains from this final illustration of diplomatic continuity. The American connection has remained Israel's number one international concern through the third and fourth decades. It, like the single-minded pursuit of national security by a policy elite of pragmatists with limited room for maneuver in the Middle East or elsewhere, is documented in the four-year record of the first national unity government.

PERES-SHAMIR AND THE POLICY OF CONTINUITY (SEPTEMBER 1984–NOVEMBER 1988)

History will show that the national unity government (NUG) was a misnomer. It often seemed motivated more by factional than by national interest. It suggested greater disunity than unity. And it failed to provide what Israel needed most: resolute government and effective leadership. Nevertheless, this NUG would contain several surprises. Not only did it confound all the political experts by serving out its full term, but the Labour-Likud coalition achieved some important gains on both the domestic and external fronts, actually doing better on the latter. Certainly this NUG confirmed as well as contributed to the pattern of stability and consistency in the basic components of ongoing Israeli foreign policy, which is the main argument of this chapter.

That the national unity government was lacking in both enthusiasm and favorable prospects could be sensed already at its inception on 13 September 1984 and confirmation by the Knesset. This swearing-in ceremony followed an unsettling period for Israel resulting from the inconclusive election results for the eleventh Knesset. The voting on 23 July showed that neither of the two dominant parties—the left-of-center Labour Alignment and the right-of-center Likud bloc—had earned the confidence of the electorate. Weeks of exhausting consultation, soundings, and interparty bargaining left no viable option other than for these two traditional rivals to bow to public pressure and consent to a unique power-sharing arrangement.

As finally negotiated, the Labour-Likud pact provided for a twenty-five member cabinet headed on a rotation basis for two years each by Labour's Shimon Peres and then by Yitzchak Shamir of the Likud. Thus, to end the political impasse the two men agreed to alternate in the two key positions of prime minister and foreign minister. Noteworthy to the theme of continuity and of undisputed primacy ever since 1948 of national security, the NUG's accord stipulated that Labour's respected Yitzchak Rabin would hold the defense portfolio during both halves of the administration.

No less problematic in the NUG's formation was the search for some kind of consensus on substantive policy guidelines that would address the country's pressing needs but that also would be politically acceptable from the standpoint of the two parties' respective platforms. This quest for the middle road and for the lowest common denominator resulted in a pledge to concentrate the new government's efforts on six primary objectives. At the domestic level the two most immediate priorities were, first, to improve the political climate in the country and avert any further dangerous polarization; second, to reassert effective control over a stagnating economy plagued by rampant inflation, depleted foreign currency reserves, crises in the banking system and on the stock exchange, and low capital investment. Foreign relations would have to take second place while these pressing internal issues were attended to.

Still, this did not imply total inattention to the external front by the two-headed NUG. Nor would the outside environment permit such detachment. In acknowledging this reality, the government's statement of aims listed at least four foreign policy goals. Extricating IDF forces from Lebanon as quickly and as expeditiously as possible was assigned the highest priority. Keeping to its pledge and to a strict timetable, the NUG successfully carried out an almost total withdrawal from southern Lebanon by June 1985. Beside this effort, the government undertook to normalize relations with Egypt, to repair the country's image and network of relations abroad, and to breathe new life into the wider Mideast peace process.

As expected, the NUG failed to produce any major foreign relations breakthroughs. Yet to its credit it managed to hold together and even to hold the line diplomatically—no small accomplishment given the combined external-domestic challenges it faced, the complexity of the problems, and the sharp differences of both personality and political viewpoints between the two reluctant government partners. This national unity government's overall performance is best analyzed by considering briefly its fidelity to each of the permanent features of foreign policy.

The first constant, aside from the enduring cluster of security and other goal priorities taken for granted by now, has been the realism of successive governments. The NUG certainly did not stray from the pattern of its predecessors in this regard. Under both Peres and Shamir the government proceeded with extreme caution. Critics viewed this with consternation and called for greater boldness, although it is not at all sure they would applaud two outstanding foreign policy occasions when discretion apparently was set aside: the Pollard spy affair and the arms-for-Iran episode! On the other hand, the argument for slow deliberation could just as easily have provided the rationale for diplomatic immobilism and for doing almost nothing. But it didn't; instead, the NUG foreign policy reflects a degree of activism and of solid accomplishment wholly out of keeping with its negative popular image.

Realism where Israel is concerned signifies slow, persistent, painstaking labors with the hope of realizing limited and partial gains rather than bold action on behalf of dramatic political breakthroughs. With this in mind, consider the following inventory of diplomatic accomplishments recorded during the 1984–88 troubled period of the NUG:

- inaugurating formal relations with Spain;
- restoring ties with Cameroon, the Ivory Coast, Togo, and Poland;
- encouraging a diplomatic thaw with the Soviet Union, Hungary, and the other Warsaw Pact countries of Eastern Europe;
- preserving the "cold peace" with Egypt, indicated by a decision in January 1986 to enter into international arbitration proceedings over the Taba question as part of normalizing relations, and resulting in the Peres-Mubarak summit in Alexandria that September as well as other discussions through normal diplomatic channels;
- opening more direct lines of communication to other Arab leaders: the televised meeting of then Premier Shimon Peres at Ifrane, Morocco, with King Hassan II in July 1986 and the so-called London agreement on the terms of reference for a Middle East peace conference worked out between Peres and Jordan's King Hussein secretly in April 1987;

- strengthening association with members of the European Economic Community, highlighted by Britain's Prime Minister Margaret Thatcher's official visit to Israel in May 1986;
- a cabinet policy announcement in March 1987 reviewing ties with the Republic of South Africa and ordering restricted commercial relations;
- the quiet upgrading and cultivation of improved relations with a range of other countries previously reserved in their attitude to Israel, including Greece, Turkey, India, and the People's Republic of China; industrializing nations in the Far East and Oceania toured by Israel's President Chaim Herzog in 1987; and Japan, whose foreign minister visited Israel in June 1988 for the first time; and
- utilizing the United Nations both as a neutral meeting place and as a forum for presenting Israel's position on regional as well as global affairs, exemplified by the speech before the General Assembly in October 1985 by Prime Minister Peres offering a reasonable blueprint for peace and by Prime Minister Shamir's address in May 1988 to a special UN conference on disarmament in which he advocated a nuclear-free zone in the Middle East and a decelerated conventional arms race.

The overall impression at decade's end, therefore, was of renewed diplomatic engagement in international affairs by Israel through cautious probings and undertakings.

Much the same is true for the continuing presence of elitism in the handling and execution of foreign relations during the NUG. Here two features stand out. The first is that the very fact the government was deeply divided, in addition to being too large and unwieldy, only encouraged an even greater propensity for centralization. Little could be done unless first approved by those at the top. Second, since personality is weighted heavily in Israel's foreign policy process, then it was weighted twice as heavily in a situation of shared responsibility, so that much depended, of necessity, upon Peres's and Shamir's leadership styles and their feelings toward each other.

The question of collective government responsibility (as opposed to that of individual ministers) has long plagued Israeli decision making. The NUG, unusual in its composition to begin with, was even more distinctive for experimenting with various policy-making arrangements and structures. Unable to settle on any single formula, Peres and Shamir resorted to four different formats, with a clear preference for smaller and less formal groupings.

Although too cumbersome for effective action, the full twenty-five–member cabinet continued to be used in weekly sessions for general policy debate. In recognition of its own shortcomings, a proposal was adopted in May 1985 for creation of an inner cabinet to be set up under the first NUG (1984–88) that would have the final say on matters of defense, foreign affairs, and settlement. The fact that this fine-tuned, delicately balanced body of ten ministers (five Labour Alignment and five Likud members with an additional member from each party added in 1988) tended to become deadlocked resulted in yet a third practice. The more serious issues often were handled by Peres, Shamir, and Defense Minister Rabin in what came to be known as the "forum of the three premiers," Rabin having served as prime minister in 1974–77. In other instances, however, any one of the three men might have chosen to act independently, without gaining prior consent of his two colleagues, let alone of the inner cabinet or of the coalition as a whole, as in the case of Peres's 1987 understanding with Jordan's monarch. This happened again, for example, in May 1988, when Rabin by himself authorized an IDF search-and-destroy operation in substantial numbers against terrorists in southern Lebanon, which he vindicated as coming under his jurisdiction and consistent with Israel's standing security policy.

This gravitation toward extra-institutional initiatives largely stemmed from inevitable personal and policy differences arising from the abnormal Peres-Shamir and Labour-Likud forced cohabitation. Although the two leaders did strive, especially in the early part of the NUG, to maintain a correct working relationship, they could not for long paper over suspicion and rivalry further fueled by a series of misunderstandings, private initiatives, and personal slights.

It was bad enough in terms of Israeli foreign relations that this impossible mixed state of competition-collaboration violated standards of good government and conduced to policy paralysis on anything but a few points of consensus or minor matters. On several occasions Israel paid a heavy price in policy disarray and also in international embarrassment for this absence of closer coordination. The Pollard affair, involving a "rogue" intelligence operation in the United States, was one instance; Israel's part in Irangate being another. In neither case was it entirely clear where the source of authorization originally lay; what does seem obvious is that perhaps neither (but especially the Pollard case) would have been approved had the decision been made in a larger ministerial forum and after fuller deliberation on relative cost benefit.

Israel increasingly gave the impression of working at cross-purposes. Especially in its last two years and following the Peres-Shamir rotation, the first NUG often seemed to be pursuing two foreign policies. The institutional arrangement of shared authority may have strengthened the two principal decision makers at home, but it certainly weakened their international bargaining position . . . and Israel's.

Peres lauded his April 1987 London agreement with King Hussein; Shamir made light of it. Peres fought for convening an international Middle East peace conference and for endorsing the 1988 Shultz plan; Shamir as prime minister fought against them. In September 1988 Labour and Likud accused each other of having sold out Taba (700 meters of seashore, less than 1 square kilometer of land, one hotel, and one tourist village) when an international arbitration body ruled against Israel and recognized the Egyptian claim.

Further straining what at times verged on an impossible situation were such negative phenomena of policy making as a steady stream of leaked confidential material (one of the worst coming in January 1985 confirming a secret airlift of Ethiopian Jews still in progress and leaving thousands behind) and independent political initiatives on behalf of Peres and Shamir involving trusted staff members from within either the Prime Minister's Office or the Ministry for Foreign Affairs.

Part of the problem, as elitist theory teaches, stemmed from differences of character and style between the two men. On the most basic substantive policy issues Peres and Shamir were not all that far apart. For example, they agreed on the need to foster U.S. ties, on rejection of the PLO as a negotiating partner and opposition to a Palestine state on the West Bank, on northern border security, and on dealing forcefully with the *intifada* uprisings on the West Bank after December 1987. Also, in the selection of options Peres and Shamir could not be described as polar opposites. Each leader accepted the use of force as witnessed by their support for active defense along the Lebanese border, counterterrorist strikes abroad, and although unconfirmed, the daring attack against the PLO's operations chief Abu Jihad in Tunisia in April 1988. Similarly, each appreciated the value for Israel of promoting economic trade relations in North America, with Western Europe, and increasingly, with the Far East. Nor, finally, was there much difference between the two as regards the discreet use of overseas arms sales by Israel as an effective instrument on behalf of national policy objectives, diplomatic as well as strategic.

Even in terms of their approach to national office the two leaders possessed at least a few strikingly similar traits. Both men were respected as dedicated, hard-working, down-to-earth, and pragmatic problem-solvers, albeit with different ideas of what constituted realism and what represented folly. Neither Peres nor Shamir was viewed as charismatic, but rather as even-tempered and self-restrained. Understandably, both capable individuals, having emerged from under the shadow of a strong political figure (Ben-Gurion for Peres, Begin for Shamir), felt cheated as well as constrained by the national unity framework imposed on them. Lastly, in performing their duties, Peres, like Shamir, may not always have been best served by his own party colleagues or by the advice of two competing sets of staff members.

Yet, in the end, they presented two contrasting foreign policy styles, with Peres far better at public relations, projecting an image of himself as a statesman and of Israel as a rational, moderate state actor genuinely interested in peace. Also, at least on the surface, Peres gave the impression of being more of an activist than Shamir, utilizing many different channels, including secret ones, for increasing diplomatic contacts. To the extent that these differences mattered, they merely reconfirm the importance of personality in Israeli policy making.

This leaves us with a final strand of uniformity between the first national unity government and coalitions that had come before it. In the actual content or thrust of foreign affairs, Peres, Shamir, and the NUG upheld the traditional course of asymmetry in Israel's Middle East–great power relationship, doing better in the latter half than in the former. As of 1988 Israel could not claim to have made any progress in its quest for admission into the Arab and regional political configuration. Here a policy of cautiously holding the line revealed that every one of the familiar, long-standing barriers remained in place. Peace with Egypt, absolutely pivotal for Israel's wider peace prospects, still did not convey much more than the absence of armed tension—itself a desirable although minimal goal. Despite courtship of Hussein by Peres in particular, Israeli-Jordanian relations remained tacit, something akin to unpeaceful coexistence.

Meanwhile, the regional arms race spiraled out of effective control, marked by the advent of chemical warfare, surface ballistic missiles, and China as an aggressive weapons supplier. Like previous governments, the NUG watched with concern Syria's leadership role in the armed struggle against Israel and, just across the northern frontier, the continuing civil war in Lebanon, while awaiting the outcome, if any, of the Iran-Iraq war of mutual attrition. Likewise, on the core Palestinian problem it was not at all clear whether the Labour-Likud combination of dovish and hawkish opinions had even begun to undertake an overdue reassessment of the basic Israeli position toward the Palestinian national movement.

On the other side of the equation, both halves of the NUG could claim to have used the Reagan era in American foreign policy to strengthen bilateral cooperation with the U.S. superpower in a whole range of areas. Not that this meant relations with Washington were in any way idyllic. Actually, a good amount of time and effort went into smoothing ruffled feathers, reducing policy divergencies between the two countries, and, in general, averting confrontation. The potential for misunderstanding still existed, what with Israel's enlisting of an American Jew, Jonathan Pollard, for purposes of espionage; recrimination over who inspired the Iranian secret arms-for-hostages operation and who then proceeded to mismanage it; and, for added measure, the Pentagon's effective blocking of the Lavi fighter project. At the close of the eighties, U.S. insistence on the international conference format and recognition of the PLO, accompanied by official criticism of Israeli military policies in the Gaza and West Bank territories, highlighted other legitimate points of difference that seem inevitable in such patron-client relationships.

The net result of national unity foreign policy, while ambiguous and less than a ringing success, nevertheless, on balance deserves a positive evaluation. In terms of the core Middle East–superpower orientations, 1984 to 1988 clearly did not bring any breakthrough. To the contrary, the lowering of the curtain on the first NUG found Israel at once more dependent than ever on a single foreign supporter, the United States, and no closer to ending estrangement from those very Palestinians who held the key to peace between Israel and the neighboring Arab world.

Yet in foreign policy, success is never measured in absolutes, only in relative terms and on the basis of small inroads and gains. Accordingly, NUG representatives in looking back could credit diplomatic efforts in 1984–88 with having brought the traditional one great power doctrine to its greatest realization. American assistance was converted from credits to outright grants. A U.S.-Israeli free-trade agreement, reached in 1984, went into operation. Israel was invited to participate in the Strategic Defense Initiative, capping expanded joint U.S.-Israeli military and intelligence cooperation in the security field. America continued its backing for Israel at the United Nations and with Third World countries, identifying with Soviet Jewry and pledging to oppose any international initiative aimed at imposing peace terms prejudicial to Israel. That the overall trend in Israel's foreign relations in 1988 was seen as somewhat improved helped Ministers Peres, Rabin, and Shamir justify their consent to four more years of the same governing combination after another indecisive national election in 1988, thus preparing the way for national unity government II.

Continuity is the watchword that marked Israel in its transition from the first to the second unity coaltion, and from a fourth to a fifth foreign policy decade. Also, in closing this initial section devoted to interests, attitudes, and the facts on historical file, continuity predominates. It stands out more than any single instance of goal revision, above any identifiable shift in the country's mood, and beyond any particular leader, government, or diplomatic event—success or failure.

Foreign policy at the present continues to reflect the message of eternal hope enscrolled in Jewish history and religious tradition. The Zionist thesis of prudence in the face of political adversity is as valid in the 1990s as it was in the 1890s or in the 1920s; nothing basically has changed. Similarly, Israeli leaders cannot help but recognize the abiding need for realism in a superpower system and world of surprises, in the same manner that foreign policy premises continue to acknowledge the Middle East imperative for strength and eternal vigilance.

Continuity appears in the fundamentals of Israeli diplomacy. It is found in the outlook of Israelis toward the world. Finally, continuity reenters the discussion in the domestic procedures for making and conducting foreign policy, covered in part two.

PART TWO

DOMESTIC SOURCES

Foreign policy is Israel's middle ground, the point where its national and international politics meet, interact, and influence decision making in Jerusalem. These two independent political forces—one internal, the other external—converge from opposite directions and help to determine the course of Israeli policy.

It is conceivable that domestic and global considerations might together encourage Israeli foreign policy initiatives. Only on rare occasions have they actually done so, however, one instance being the way in which friendship and solidarity with the United States has made good political sense at home and also in the international context. Far more common is to find either set of political considerations acting as a check against policy departures, whether in synch with the other set of considerations or not. Suffice for a certain option to be seen as damaging for the government in terms of domestic or coalition politics to have it disqualified even though it might be advisable for Israel externally, or vice versa. A third possibility of mutual negative reinforcement is evident in the notion of an unilateral withdrawal from the West Bank. Regional conditions, such as constant Arab militarization and Palestinian non-cooperation, argue against such an option; but so does the presence of strong opposition within the Israeli public.

The previous discussion concentrated mostly on the external, international dimension: Israel among the nations. A sense of balance is restored in the following three chapters by integrating domestic and foreign affairs and by looking more closely at the impact of factors inside Israel upon foreign policy. Without understanding the domestic political scene we cannot possibly account for the behavior of Israel beyond its borders, now or in the future.

Consider the thesis of Israeli diplomacy as deadlocked to the point of paralysis. Leaving aside reservations about the validity of the thesis itself, we find its supporters divided as to the principal explanation for this policy conservatism. One tendency is to point to the external geopolitical environment as so hostile and threatening that it dictates Israeli leaders always proceed with utmost caution. A second explanation, while centering on the internal social and political scene, attributes foreign policy sclerosis to a breakdown of the national consensus, particularly following the Six-Day War.

Emphasis on the frayed national consensus is certainly warranted. Still, we suggest there are three domestic structural sources affecting Israeli foreign policy performance, and all three are connected to the policy-making process.

Policy, in the first instance, has to be formulated and clarified through authoritative bodies and individual leaders screening options. It is during this initial phase of the process that original ideas and possible diplomatic moves become subject in Israel to the influence of a multiplicity of political institutions and procedures. In the second stage a given policy must be coordinated. Here, however, it becomes exposed to bureaucratic politics involving rival, competitive government ministries, which further slows down a policy decision. Then, in a third and final stage, policy has to be implemented. Here the problem for a small state like Israel in carrying out its foreign relations consists of finding the appropriate means or policy instrument for getting the job done properly. Not infrequently a policy may be wise and advisable for Israel, but the means not always available or its political influence with a foreign country not always sufficient.

As part two is meant to illustrate, Israel does not lack innovative and theoretical schemes for improving its overseas relations. The trouble is that policy making thoroughness, teamwork, and abundant national power are not exactly strong points of Israeli foreign policy. Each of these will be analyzed in turn as part of the three phases: policy making, coordination, and implementation. Israeli statecraft is the story of politicians, bureaucrats, and diplomats.

CHAPTER 5

POLICY MAKING

A permanent ministerial committee, called the Inner Cabinet, will be established. It will have 12 members, six from each party. . . .
Should disagreements arise and the Inner Cabinet does not reach a decision on a certain issue, the matter will not be brought before the Cabinet without the joint agreement of the prime minister and the vice premier.

Coalition agreement between Likud
and the Labour Alignment, 1988

Israel's handling of foreign affairs is not identical to that of any other country, if only for the obvious reason that no single definition or prescription exists on how foreign policy ought to be or must be conducted. As a guide for understanding the Israeli model, neither the American political system familiar to many readers nor standard textbooks on government are sufficient. To start with only the most basic distinction, Israel is a practicing democracy, but it is a parliamentary democracy rather than a presidential or a federal one.

That Israel has a democratic form of government at all is in itself noteworthy. Constitutional theory holds that countries at war are justified in suspending democratic practices in favor of crisis government. Yet, in spite of the constant danger facing it and the official state of emergency still legally in effect since 1948, Israel has maintained its commitment to the democratic process. It is also true, however, that living under a permanent security threat has colored how foreign and defense policy is made. The result is an uneasy and not entirely satisfactory compromise between an open policy debate and the dictates of expediency and efficiency.

DEMOCRATIC POLICY MAKING, ISRAELI STYLE

Israel is not an ideal place for the careful planner or seeker after systematic policy making. Rather, the country's entire history suggests spontaneous improvisation. While this can be seen almost everywhere, nowhere is this quite so pronounced as in the realm of security and foreign affairs where much depends on the reactions, but even more so the initiatives, of others. A fluid external and security situation requires that Israeli leaders deal with concrete problems and pressing developments as they arise. To a large degree, therefore, decision making for Israel is crisis decision making under conditions of exceptional urgency and stress. We should not be led astray as many scholars have been, however, in confining research and analysis to Israel's crisis decisions in the first forty years. The impact on overall foreign policy of noncrisis, routine, low-level, and ongoing policy decisions is no less pronounced or any less worthy of attention.

The result is a confused and inconsistent pattern of policy making. Depending on such variables as the nature of a given issue and the priority assigned it, the Israeli model has features common to an open, democratic society, but also many elements of centralism. In formal terms the process gives the impression of being highly structured, yet it can also be surprisingly unstructured and free of institutional restraints. Ample room exists for the interplay of individual preferences, for political manipulation, and for operating outside prescribed channels. In short, the foreign policy "system" of Israel is, in reality, anything but neat and systematic.

A better approach is to insist that any policy-making process, if it is to qualify as both democratic and effective, should reflect the following: broad participation, the airing of different viewpoints, open policy debate, accountability, and policy review. Although Israel does well on some counts, it does not pass this fivefold test with flying colors.

The reason is that appearances are misleading. At first glance it would seem there are a great many participants involved in shaping Israeli foreign policy. The list begins with the four million self-appointed Israeli premiers, each of whom is convinced he or she knows best. From there the list extends to the media, nearly a dozen different political parties, special interest groups, the full 120-member Knesset and its subcommittees, the government (or the full cabinet), and a score of individual cabinet ministries.

Reality, by contrast, shows the devolution of authority and its consolidation by a rather narrow ruling circle. Power, according to this pattern, tends to flow steadily upward from the people, so that actual responsibility has come to reside in fewer and fewer public institutions and individual political leaders. This process can be traced by looking briefly at each of the above potential participants within the Israeli political system. Our principal finding is that the inability of these groups to vitally or consistently affect foreign policy decisions is matched by an expansion of authority in the hands of a few, self-reliant policy elites. A glimpse into this contraction or narrowing of the field of would-be decisional actors was provided in the previous chapter's description of foreign policy under the first national unity government.

NARROWING THE FIELD

On the night of 25 September 1982 several hundred thousand Israelis descended on Tel Aviv's Malchei Yisrael Square to take part in what has been the largest protest demonstration ever held in the country's history. Called to demonstrate mass public displeasure over deepening military involvement in Lebanon, it helped force the government into reversing its position and agreeing to set up a full and independent inquiry panel. Here was participatory democracy in action, making it possible for citizens to have a real say on vital issues of the day, to reach and influence their chosen leaders directly without any of the intervening layers or institutions of government. But this is not how things usually work in the Israeli political scene, beginning with the public's marginal role in the normal handling of foreign affairs.

The General Public

The Israeli electorate may be sovereign, but its impact on major government policy tends to be secondary. Public dissent or support becomes a more serious consideration usually only as part of the election cycle, either every four years or when early elections are called. Political leaders pay closer attention to shifts in public sentiment when seeking voter support and a broad mandate to govern. Otherwise, for a variety of practical reasons it is difficult for the public as such to influence foreign policy directions in between elections, let alone affect a specific decision.

The streamlining of Israel's policy-making machinery owes little to rational choice and even less to antidemocratic sentiment, but it owes a great deal to the cumulative national experience with repeated wars and crises. Structural changes and redesigns engineered over the years have geared the country for dealing at any moment with immediate high-risk security situations, yet they do not allow for close involvement by an interested and concerned public except perhaps for when the threat has passed. What happened in 1982 was possible only because the conflict in Lebanon gave indications of dragging on indefinitely, thus giving citizens an opportunity to express themselves. Still, the rule holds: when time and discretion are essential, the public is unlikely to be consulted, nor will it be a direct participant in the policy process.

Lack of access to complete information limits the public. Often Israelis are not fully informed. And because of the system of proportional representation wherein voting is for a party list rather than for individual candidates, Israelis also usually lack direct access to their leaders. Moreover, although they may be opinionated and articulate on each and every political issue, Israelis are not known for being doers or joiners. Most people prefer to give the government a free hand in dealing with national strategy and high policy matters while they engage in individual, private pursuits. Whatever political mobilization, recruitment, and structured debate that is found generally is confined to party membership and institutions. One interesting recent development were initiatives taken by individual Israeli citizens in testing the law that forbade contacts with the PLO by participating overseas in meetings with Palestinians known for their affiliation to the PLO. Here was an instance of private citizens to some extent taking the lead in shaping new foreign policy directions. In May 1989, residents of Ashdod and Ashkelon took to the streets to express outrage at Arab acts of violence, especially the brutal murder of an Israeli soldier home on leave. Their call for a ban on Arab workers from Gaza might have provided another instance of shaping policy had it led to a groundswell of public protest and spread to other cities.

Nor does it help the cause of dispassionate, rational discourse that until fairly recently no framework comparable to the Council on Foreign Relations or the Council on World Affairs in the United States or the Royal Institute of International Affairs in Great Britain existed in Israel for holding a wide-ranging review of Israeli relations or bipartisan debate on foreign policy issues outside of the usual party forums. In December 1988, a new international affairs study group, the Israel Council on Foreign Relations, held its inaugural meeting in Tel Aviv. In scheduling a program of guest speakers, the council set forth its larger objective of acquainting Israelis with developments in the outside world and, in the words of its president, former Foreign Ministry Director-General David Kimche, in that way "perhaps to reduce our provincialism." Still, the notion of "the Israeli public" remains all but meaningless in practical political terms and in daily foreign policy decisions.

Moreover, public opinion outside of the election cycle is remarkably pliable and subject to political manipulations. Peace-related questions do arouse controversy. But otherwise Israelis are inclined to confirm decisions already taken and to lend support for announced government policy, especially when few alternatives suggest themselves, like in avoiding dependence on the United States or on reaching a genuine peace in the absence of a credible Arab peace partner. *Aliya* is not an issue. Neither is the wisdom of encouraging rapprochement with the Soviets and Eastern Europeans. South Africa is not a contentious domestic issue. Nor is the practice of marketing arms and military expertise. Dissent is thus restricted to the fringes.

Public pressure is really the exception rather than the rule. Notable exceptions include calls for installing Dayan in the Defense Ministry in May–June 1967, contrasted with demands for his ouster in 1973, and calls for Sharon's resignation as defense minister in 1982. Yet they were more *ad hominem* than substantive, and over security rather than external policy.

An additional shortcoming is that in so pluralistic and politically charged a society as Israel, public participation easily can produce a countervailing effect, with different sectors negating each other's influence, thus unintentionally encouraging policy paralysis. This was brought out well in the case of the 1984 and 1988 elections that led to NUG I and NUG II. In short, only to the extent that the Israeli public places outside limits on what policy alternatives it is prepared to accept can it be said in any way to help shape foreign policy.

Ordinarily, the pattern works in the reverse. Opinions and attitudes held by the public are formed by foreign policy actions as well as by how situations and choices are presented to it. In this sense, a policy has got to be politically acceptable to a majority of the public. Actually, such flexibility on the part of the public gives Israeli leaders enormous leverage should they in fact wish to lead. This is still a far cry, however, from direct public participation in policy making.

The Public Media

Public participation is essentially indirect, expressing itself through the three agencies of the media, voluntary associations, and political parties. Of these, the first has gained most in influence and prominence.

Since the time of the prestate Jewish *yishuv* (community) in

Palestine, the nation's press has provided an important link between government and public. The Israeli population, numbering 4,425,000 by 1988, consistently registers one of the world's highest literacy rates and per capita ratios of newspaper circulation. The media help frame discussion of current affairs by offering hourly radio news and broadcast coverage and providing background material as well as in-depth analysis to a national evening TV audience. And by enabling an exchange of views they are involved in setting choices before the public.

On the other hand, the media's role, like that of the public at large, has definite limitations and is often circumscribed. Censorship, for example, remains in force formally and informally. All news items and details are subject to prior authorization by the military censor. No less significant, the Press Council has accepted voluntary self-censorship in the wish not to jeopardize national security. Objectivity is also a problem. Some of the daily press is affiliated with political parties or, if independent, tends to take a predictable editorial position. *Haaretz* and the English-language *Jerusalem Post,* for example, are known for their consistent anti-Likud and antireligious stand. Radio and television are under government control as well.

The inevitable tension in the media-government relationship is aggravated further by the recurrent and increasingly prevalent phenomenon of press leaks. That the problem exists at all owes to the behavior of government officials and laxity in enforcing the law, but it is also due in part to a major development in the newspaper profession in Israel. No longer content with mere news reporting, during the eighties the press has moved into investigative journalism. Consequently, instances of government mismanagement, foreign policy improprieties, or even secret diplomatic contacts once easily covered up are today more promptly exposed and discussed, the censorship codes notwithstanding. Given the difficulty of the Knesset in performing its role as parliamentary watchdog over the executive, the media fulfills a vital function by encouraging a higher level of democratic debate on the part of an informed citizenry. Censorship currently is one of the main domestic battlegrounds in Israel. The outcome is certain to influence the level of public interest, familiarity, and influence on foreign matters of state as well as national defense policy.

Interest Groups

Public opinion in a democracy also can influence government through the lobbying of small segments of society. The best example, of course, is the United States, where pluralism has inspired a plethora of special interest groups and associations actively engaged in promoting a certain policy preference or course on the basis of ethnicity, religious affiliation, trade or profession, economic and social class, or even regionalism—the "Eastern Establishment" and West Coast on foreign trade policy. In Israel one finds nothing so extensive, so organized, or so effective. Group advocacy plays little if any role in foreign policy formulation; indeed, such special interests are a rarity.

There are ample reasons why. As noted previously, Israelis are not inclined toward political activism and are not easily aroused to take to the streets on other than bread-and-butter economic issues. Their political association pretty much begins and ends with party membership, if that. In fact, it may be that Israel's multiparty system is a substitute for pressure groups; special interests like those of the Orthodox community are advanced by the several religious parties. Actually, special constituencies do exist, but they focus mostly on domestic issues: higher compensation for disabled war veterans, tax privileges for development town residents, etc.

Two instances of effective lobbying, which also illustrate how easily accessible and receptive national leaders can be to well-directed pressure in a small country, are, first, insistence by heads of the northern border towns and farm settlements in 1981–82 that the government use strong military measures to prevent what was becoming an exodus of residents because of repeated Katyusha rocket shellings by the PLO from Lebanese soil; and second, government consent in May 1985 to a prisoner-of-war exchange involving 1,150 Palestinians for three Israeli soldiers following sustained pressure by relatives on key cabinet members. Yet, strictly speaking, both instances involved internal security and personal lobbying rather than nationwide mobilization of a cross section of Israelis on a purely external, diplomatic issue.

When they do arise, partisan foreign policy interest groups tend to be comparatively short lived. Ad hoc floating formations may arise at a given moment to contest a specific issue or policy only to disband once a decision has been taken either way, without becoming permanently institutionalized. This was seen after the 1973 war in the mushrooming of individual and group protest over government-military responsibility for the Arab surprise attack. Or the group may proceed to reorganize itself into becoming a full-fledged political party.

Given these qualifications, the record of foreign policy lobbying in Israel is unsurprisingly brief. For several decades the outstanding example of public protest was the bitter struggle in 1952 against

German reparations waged by concentration camp survivors and opponents of reconciliation; this did not alter the fixed course of government policy set by Ben-Gurion. After 1967 *Ha-tenua limaan eretz Yisrael ha-shlema* ("the movement for an integral land of Israel" and not "greater" land of Israel as usually mistranslated) arose to advocate retention of the captured territories. It was joined in 1974 by the *Gush Emunim* (bloc of the faithful) activist settler movement, opposed in turn since 1978 by followers of *Shalom Achshav* (Peace Now) committed to relinquishing control of the contested land in exchange for peace. But even these three are borderline cases as to whether their orientation is more toward external or internal affairs. In a sense they straddle both categories, arguing as much over budget priorities, security, and the future of Israeli society and democracy as over the attainability of peace with the Arabs through diplomacy. This larger, ongoing debate since 1967 over the linkage between domestic-foreign policies has been rekindled on several particular occasions: by the 1977–79 negotiations with Egypt, by the 1982 Lebanese war, and again in response to the unrest in the West Bank and Gaza after December 1987.

Arguably the most powerful foreign policy lobby in Israel is the defense establishment, acting at two levels. The professional army and General Staff enter the policy process directly as formal participants and institutional actors represented by the Ministry of Defense. They are reserved for discussion in the following chapter on the bureaucratic process.

But a large number of former career officers continue to influence public and foreign policy making even after military retirement at a relatively young age. Many have become corporate executives, and in their management positions they use to advantage such assets as personal popularity, reputation, expertise, proximity to the centers of power, and contacts with bureaucrats, politicians, and ministers in promoting their particular viewpoints on the broad topic of security and foreign affairs.

This has been particularly true of the defense industries and corporations like the Israel Aircraft Industries (IAI) actively pressing for military exports. The company effectively lobbied, for example, on behalf of the Lavi fighter project in its early stages. Due in no small part to the unraveling of this strong military-industrial coalition, the government finally decided to cancel the program on 30 August 1987, at the same time removing a source of friction on the bilateral U.S.-Israeli agenda.

Two other identifiable subgroups within the Israeli society seem positioned to exert greater influence on foreign relations than they actually do. One is composed of the various immigrant associations that reflect Israel's tremendous ethnic pluralism, with people coming originally on *aliya* from so many different countries (see Table 13). Organizations like the South African Federation and the Association of Americans and Canadians in Israel (AACI) have a natural interest in promoting *aliya* from the West and in streamlining immigrant absorption. Their impact, however, has been marginal at most. Surprisingly, although unschooled in democracy, émigrés from the Soviet Union have been less reticent than those émigrés from the West and therefore much more effective in the rough-and-tumble of Israeli politics in promoting their cause and more vocal in mobilizing public support, both in Israel and abroad, on the question of Soviet Jewry. Similarly, too, Ethiopian immigrants banded together to form a Committee for Family Reunification to lobby for a public campaign on the part of the government and world Jewry to persuade the Ethiopian authorities to release the 15,000 to 20,000 Jews still stranded in Ethiopia.

Potentially important in this regard is the encouragement given world Jewish leaders and communities by some Israeli politicians to assert themselves on the argument over peace and the territories dividing Israelis. Bearing in mind that Israel does not permit absentee ballotting, this call to nonresident Jews goes beyond forgoing the old Zionist prerequisite of *aliya* and residence. If heeded, this would be tantamount to inviting an overseas constituency, Jews in the Diaspora, to function as a privileged pressure group and lobby determining domestic and national policy!

The second potential group with a disappointing record encompasses Israeli intellectuals and members of the academic community who might be expected to take a lead in molding public and official thinking as well as in articulating clear policy choices. Why don't they? Perhaps it is because Israeli academics do not agree with each other and are divided among themselves; they are far from presenting a united front. Also, many intellectuals, true to their calling, show a disdain for "dirty politics" and prefer not to get involved. In any event, like other Israelis, they, too, have a hard time coming up with practical alternatives that are policy-relevant to the country's complex security and diplomatic enigmas. Another explanation may be that ever since the Likud's surprising rise to power in 1977 many Israeli liberals and academics have been left behind by the public's swing to the right and to more nationalistic positions. Surely a deeper cause lies in traces of the "two cultures" marked by a poor regard for *eitzez-gibbers* (Yiddish for advisers) and the Jewish intelligentsia on the part of the country's earlier generation of pioneers and nation-

Table 13. Ethnic Constituencies—Immigration by Country of Birth

	Period of Immigration			Period of Immigration	
Country of Birth	1919–48	1948–88	Country of Birth	1919–48	1948–88
Iraq		129,530	United Kingdom	1,574	22,144
Iran	3,536	72,837	Germany	52,951	16,332
Turkey	8,277	60,494	Yugoslavia	1,944	8,509
Yemen	14,566	46,414	Netherlands	1,208	5,404
India, Pakistan, Sri Lanka		25,405	Austria	7,748	5,155
Syria		8,449	Italy	1,554	3,810
Yemen (Aden)	1,272	4,210	Greece	8,767	3,767
Afghanistan		4,112	Belgium		3,303
Lebanon		4,016	Scandinavian		
Other countries	13,125	2,438	countries		2,946
China		920	Switzerland		2,499
			Spain		1,263
ASIA TOTAL	40,776	358,825	Other countries	2,329	2,350
Morocco		265,825	EUROPE TOTAL	377,487	832,849
Tunisia		52,276			
Libya	873	35,800	USA	6,635	59,188
Egypt, Sudan		30,102	Argentina	238	35,961
Other countries	1,907	24,290	Brazil		6,763
			Canada	316	6,474

Table 13. (Continued)

Country of Birth	Period of Immigration 1919–48	1948–88
Algeria (including Morocco and Tunisia)	994	23,887
Republic of South Africa	259	13,669
AFRICA TOTAL	4,033	445,849
Romania	41,105	266,622
USSR	52,350	202,917
Poland	170,127	169,400
Bulgaria	7,057	39,926
Hungary	10,342	28,483
France	1,637	24,402
Czechoslovakia	16,794	23,617

Country of Birth	Period of Immigration 1919–48	1948–88
Uruguay		6,360
Chile		4,233
Australia, New Zealand	72	3,161
Mexico		2,670
Colombia		1,352
Venezuela		683
Paraguay, Guyana		387
Central America		301
Other countries	318	2,468
AMERICA AND OCEANIA TOTAL	7,579	130,001
NOT KNOWN	52,982	20,815

Source: Central Bureau of Statistics, *Israel Statistical Abstract*, no. 39 (1988), pp. 161–63.

builders. To the extent scholars and specialists have any real policy input, it is on an individual rather than an organized, institutional basis.

Before leaving the subject of Israeli pressure groups, it is interesting to follow the fortunes of *Ha Moetza l'Shalom u'-Bitachon* (the Council on Peace and Security), formed in 1988. Comprised primarily of former career army officers, its aims were to encourage a territorial compromise and to provide viable solutions for Israel's security needs on the West Bank other than by retaining physical control over the land and its people. From the outset, the council's credibility was questioned because many of its founding members and spokespeople were also associated with the Israel Labour party. Typically, within months it was challenged by a rival group, *Ktzinim v'Akademaim lemaan Bitachon v'Shalom* (Officers and Academics for Security and Peace), that argued the indispensable security value of the West Bank and its retention by Israel. Both groups took part in the national election campaign in 1988. Characteristically, immediately following the elections both dropped from public sight. Were either organization, or both of them, to lose credibility with the public as a result, or eventually to become incorporated by Labour and Likud respectively, this would confirm the tendency for prospective interest groups, lobbyists, and protest movements to be swallowed up by the dominant political party formations or to become themselves converted into political parties.

Political Parties and Foreign Policy

The overall pattern presented here of an increasingly centralized foreign policy-making process the further we go from the public is reinforced when the discussion extends to political parties. Their contribution can be argued any number of ways. For example, Israel's numerous parties perform a useful democratic function by mirroring policy divisions around the country as well as by brokering the clash of foreign policy interests. But if judged as central participants in the actual making of policy, then the parties and their rank-and-file membership need to be viewed in a restricted capacity.

Through a process of elimination many of the parties are ineligible or exclude themselves from any direct role. Some of them are not parties in the strict sense, being narrow in scope and essentially single-interest groups. The ethnic and religious parties, for instance, do not articulate a detailed, programmatic foreign policy agenda.

Others, like the Communist party, are so ideological and doctrinaire that they command little public attention or support from uncommitted voters seeking pragmatic solutions and alternatives. More to the point politically, we should keep in mind that political parties do not make foreign policy; governments do.

All governments in Israel have been coalition governments constructed around one of the dominant parties—Labour or Likud—reinforced by several junior partners who, as the price for inclusion, stand to lose their policy distinctiveness; once co-opted, they are bound by coalition discipline. Not to be part of the ruling government coalition means being relegated to the opposition seats in the Knesset. This status may provide a rostrum from which to deliver principled criticism against the government, to expound one's own party proposals or to table no-confidence resolutions. But being in the opposition does not bestow the right to share in decisions or even necessarily to be consulted; hence parties outside the coalition normally have no real input. In times of particular national stress (1967–70; 1984–88), the major opposition faction has even been included in governments of national unity premised on bipartisanship. On such occasions, for all intents and purposes the real focus of policy debate then shifts from the floor of the Knesset to the cabinet table where an agreed policy must be worked out jointly.

Moreover, when the system functions smoothly according to the rules of parliamentary and coalition politics, the result is automatic legislative approval for foreign policy decisions or actions presented to the Knesset by the ruling coalition. What counts in the final analysis is the ability to marshal a minimum of at least 61 votes (out of 120) in support of government policy or, in any case, not to lose on a motion of no-confidence.

Lastly, even though some twenty different movements and parties at one time or another have dotted the Israeli political landscape, the two that really matter foreign policy-wise are Labour and Likud. And yet, more recently, and other issues aside, when it comes to international relations their positions have been neither profoundly different nor unbridgeable; witness the ability of the first NUG to complete its full term. Barring a fundamental change in Israel's external-regional environment, as each bloc becomes larger, more diverse, and less ideological, this too will serve to blunt their remaining respective differences.

In closing out the eighties, Labour and Likud pretty much saw eye-to-eye on basic foreign policy guidelines. They agreed on the centrality of the U.S. relationship while seeking improved ties with the Soviet bloc. Both stressed the need for Israel to be more fully integrated into the international community but were reserved toward the United Nations. Both appreciated how important fostering trade relations and promoting exports were for the country's economic future. Labour was no less committed than Likud to practicing arms sales diplomacy. Each remained sensitive to the Jewish connection and to the status of world Jewry, was concerned at the unrelieved Middle East arms race, and was pledged to maintaining a strong defense posture as well as to combating international terrorism. Similarly, both recognized the obligation to enforce the peace treaty with Egypt. Thus, at the end of the decade the foundations remained for a consensual and bipartisan Labour-Likud foreign policy.

The single major exception to consensual, bipartisan Labour-Likud foreign policy is the Arab-Israeli conflict and its resolution. And even here the cutting edge between the two party protagonists shrinks once the debate moves from rhetoric and posturing to the specifics, substantive and procedural. There were some very definite conceptual differences, to be sure, on such questions as the necessity for Jewish settlement projects on the West Bank and their security value, repartitioning of the territories, and the wisdom of Israel's participation in an international conference. Nevertheless, closer examination of their party platforms and statements by party leaders in the 1988 election campaign revealed, for instance, that Labour joined Likud in a commitment to peace negotiations between Israel and the Arab states and to a peace settlement based on the principle of compromise; in dismissing total withdrawal from all the territories or relinquishing undivided control over Jerusalem; and in acknowledging the legitimate rights of the Palestinian Arabs to self-rule short of a Palestinian state on the West Bank while showing sensitivity to Jordan's stake in any eventual territorial rearrangement. Until an agreed final settlement can be reached both parties are on record as committed, at a minimum, to preserving law and order in Gaza and the West Bank.

In short, it may have been true in the era of Ben-Gurion and a dominant Mapai party (precursor of today's Labour Alignment), that party policy was national policy. As made famous by Golda Meir's "kitchen cabinet," informal consultation among top Mapai functionaries and government ministers (*sareinu v'chavereinu*) often constituted the abbreviated, actual policy making process. Now, due to the factors discussed here, the political parties have been eclipsed at both the intraparty and interparty levels.

THE KNESSET

The two institutions symbolizing Israeli sovereignty and national unity are the president of the state and the Knesset. Solely from the standpoint of their relevance for foreign affairs, although it may sound somewhat harsh, their role is essentially instrumental: they each complement the policy process, perhaps meaningfully at times, but they do not figure as independent actors or policy initiators.

The president enters the picture at various moments in a primarily representative and ceremonial capacity. As the official head of state, he or she is charged with such functions as accepting credentials of foreign envoys, officiating at state receptions, and undertaking visits abroad on behalf of Israel. Israel's first president, Dr. Chaim Weizmann, fought unsuccessfully with Ben-Gurion to concentrate greater authority in the presidency. Within these narrow prerogatives, however, much depends on the office holder's personality, definition of the position, and deftness in utilizing these limited powers to the maximum politically possible. The incumbent in the late 1980s, Chaim Herzog, for instance, traveled abroad extensively, proving quite effective as Israel's goodwill ambassador.

Restricted presidential power stands in sharp contrast to references about Knesset supremacy. According to Israeli constitutional theory the single-chamber parliament is the highest authority in the land, although its real power is less impressive, especially in matters of foreign policy. In formal terms the Knesset possesses considerable authority; its duties include debating government issues, passing legislation, reviewing treaties, holding hearings, and questioning civil servants, ministers, and ambassadors. Annual debate on government budget requests often is the occasion for a more wide-ranging review of the work of the Ministry for Foreign Affairs and of Israeli foreign relations in general. In addition, members of Knesset (MKs) on occasion are found engaging in public diplomacy as delegates to world congresses and interparliamentary unions, or by hosting foreign heads of state invited to address a session of the Knesset, as President Sadat did in 1977 and President Carter in 1979.

Nevertheless, the Israeli Knesset has fewer substantive powers in external affairs than some of its counterparts in other countries. By way of illustration, under the Basic Laws (which substitute for a written constitution) only the full cabinet is able to sign and ratify international agreements; regulations passed in 1963 and 1984 at most enable the Knesset to review any such accords in the context of a general political debate. Recent practice has been for the government to submit the document to the Knesset after the text has already been initialed but before final signature. In this, as in other areas of cabinet-Knesset relations, the outcome is almost always assured in advance based on the ruling coalition bloc's stamp of approval.

Insight into what underlies parliamentary ineffectiveness can also be had from the way the Knesset works, both in plenum and in committee. The Knesset plenary touches on foreign policy matters in one of two modes. One is through a full-dress debate; in 1978 an exhaustive debate took place well into the night when the Begin government tabled the Camp David frameworks negotiated with Egypt and the United States, and 118 out of 120 MKs rose to endorse or condemn the controversial pact. The other mode permits the members themselves to initiate discussion through parliamentary steps such as motions for the agenda, private members' questions to a specific minister, or proposed votes of no-confidence by opponents of the government or its specific policy.

However, there has been a pronounced tendency of late to emphasize committee work over plenary debate. This has meant greater prominence for the Foreign Affairs and Security Committee (FASC), traditionally regarded as the most prestigious of the Knesset's ten standing committees. This institutional shift within the Knesset also conforms to the larger policy making preference for the few over the many—although, rather ludicrously, not by all that much. Membership on the "select" Foreign Affairs and Security Committee had swelled in the mid-1980s to twenty-five, or more than one out of every five MKs!

One is justified in wondering why it is that membership on the committee should be so prized when it has so little statutory power and perhaps even less in practice. Being denied the tools to be a full partner in either the shaping or the implementation of foreign and defense policy is bad enough. But the committee's experience suggests it may very well be its own worst enemy.

The very size and composition of the FASC make it an unwieldy and fractious body, a miniplenum debating forum. Membership is keyed in proportion to the numerical weight of the various Knesset coalition and opposition factions; it has always been an unwritten law that the Communist party is barred from participation on security grounds. The selection of representatives on the FASC is therefore an internal matter for each of the parties entitled to one or more seats on the committee and thus invariably governed by party politics—itself a sign of the broader politicization of foreign policy by which the policy becomes hostage to domestic political considerations. Owing to this diffuse selection process, the committee of late has been packed with ex-military people who have entered politics.

This may be good for the parliamentary supervision of security affairs, but it also suggests an imbalance, since there are few former diplomats present to argue the sensitive diplomatic side of Israeli defense strategy. Equally apparent is the fact that other committee members have been chosen perhaps for their political clout within a given party or perhaps as a quid pro quo for joining—and hence making possible—the ruling coalition, not because they are experienced in, or necessarily conversant with, the complex issues involved in foreign affairs and security.

Party factionalism on the committee sets off a chain reaction. Discussion tends rather quickly to become partisan, with heated exchanges between government representatives and opposition critics. Another manifestation of the politicization even of something as sacrosanct as national security is the by now almost routine leaking of classified background material and sometimes verbatim minutes from closed FASC sessions to the media. This, in turn, has provided top military and government decision makers with a justification for not appearing before the committee even in *in camera* session or, should they consent to appear for not sharing privileged information because of the likelihood such material will be reported on the radio within hours and reprinted in the afternoon newspapers. The result is a serious decline in the value of such briefings. At most, government officials come to inform and to report before the committee—not to seek its advice or its consent.

Another result of leaks to the media and party factionalism is to further narrow the parliamentary in-group, those MKs "in the know." Devolution of Knesset participation in foreign relations first went from the full body to its Committee on Foreign Affairs and Security; now the main work of FASC tends to be carried out in smaller subcommittees. This restructuring was encouraged by two of the committee's recent chairmen, Moshe Arens of the Likud and Labour's Abba Eban, who saw the smaller format as both a more efficient procedure and as an attempt at regaining the FASC's lost influence and involvement. These subcommittees have concerned themselves in recent years with such specific foreign policy–related questions as intelligence operations, arms procurement, military exports, and future strategic doctrine. Again, however, such efforts unfortunately have been peripheral, their impact on actual policy-making inconsequential. The result is that for the present this senior committee, representing the Knesset and ultimately the entire nation, remains handcuffed. The bottom line shows that the Knesset has no real power of decision. As any detailed historical analysis would easily show, there have been few instances of major foreign policy decisions upon which the Knesset or its committees have had a demonstrable impact.

WHO REALLY DECIDES POLICY?

Consequently, the Knesset joins the Israeli public, representatives of the media, various peripheral interest groups, and the political parties on the policy sidelines. When the moment for decision comes, all of them are more like spectators than front-line participants. This leaves the government and the high policy elite, in theory at least, able to formulate a foreign policy on Israel's behalf virtually free of direct outside interference and without necessarily having to share either responsibility or power.

Such concentrated power makes it more difficult for Israel always to meet the four standards for a policy that is both effective *and* democratic: (1) an open foreign policy debate encouraging (2) consideration of all possible options, accompanied by (3) a mechanism for policy reassessment assuring (4) strict accountability. This should not be taken to mean, though, that any Israeli government has a free rein or can afford to ignore the public mood—only that the checks and balances of the Israeli political process are informal, rather than being constitutional and institutional.

After the 1982 Lebanon experience, no leader or cabinet would dare ignore deep-seated social opposition and commit Israel to another military adventure in a neighboring Arab country without first securing broad public backing. The concentration of power at the government level suggests, though, how the streamlined policy-making trend ("streamlined" in the sense of a progressive narrowing in both the number of size of participating bodies) applies even to the government (the *memshala*).

The workings of the Israeli cabinet system are a separate topic and beyond the scope of this book. Getting a sense of where the real locus of executive power lies requires that a key distinction be drawn. On the one hand, organizational flow charts can be obtained that show all those cabinet ministers and ministries who are positioned to be part of the decision making process neatly arranged in square blocks. On the other hand, though, there is the real "system": those few individuals who really determine policy and make the major decisions. Thus, note the custom adopted in the 1980s under the first and second national unity governments that saw the full cabinet of as many as twenty-six ministers cede its authority to a ten-member inner cabinet (enlarged to twelve in the 1988 NUG) that proceeded to defer major foreign policy and security decisions to an even smaller forum consisting of three former prime ministers. Nor are instances lacking then, or in earlier years when strategic decisions have been deferred by the cabinet to a single minister—and not necessarily the prime minister!

In principle, the cabinet is bound by the rule of collective responsibility. In practice, though, one will have a hard time distinguishing acts ascribed to the cabinet from those authorized by an individual minister or subgroup of ministers. Such disharmony and lack of coordination are by no means new. It is just that they have become more prevalent than ever before in the last years given the nature of the NUG model of government. Any government based on a coalition of several unlike-minded political parties should not be expected to speak in complete unison; how much less so when the two main opposing parties are thrown together against their wishes.

The second NUG came into being in November 1988, pledged to improve on its predecessor. For one thing, there would be no rotation this time. It was agreed that the government should speak with one voice, that voice belonging to the prime minister. But no sooner was the second NUG formed than individual ministers began expressing their personal views and initiating actions on their own. To cite but one example, in February 1989, the agriculture minister unilaterally suspended formal ties with Greece in reprisal for its pro-PLO stance. Israel's ambassador to Athens apologized to the Greek authorities for the rash decision but could not promise its immediate repeal.

At about the same time, Defense Minister Rabin was going public with his four-stage peace initiative to end the *intifada* and engage West Bank Palestinians in local elections and negotiating processes, except that there were mixed signals as to whether the plan had or had not first been tabled in the cabinet and did or did not have Prime Minister Shamir's endorsement! It was thus apparent that the reconstituted national unity government, whatever its longevity, would not set the standard for well-ordered policy making in Israel. Nor would it break with the long-pattern of divided counsel at the top, although a real effort at doing so was made in May 1989.

After seven hours of discussion by the cabinet, Prime Minister Shamir gained formal government approval for his two-stage peace plan and call for holding Palestinian actions. What made this noteworthy in terms of how policy is made were several exceptional things:

- the unusually long amount of time given to an agenda item, even one as critical as the peace process;
- the high degree of consensus among cabinet members, with twenty endorsing the plan and six voting against;
- the opponents divided across rather than along party lines, with two ministers from the left and four from the right; and
- as a result of the debate and vote, for the first time in many years, Israeli policy stood behind a specific, sufficiently defined set of peace guidelines that might then be put out for discussion with other governments and world leaders.

For Israeli policy making this was quite an accomplishment.

But at the same time the handling of the Shamir plan exposed the less commendable side of the institutionalized-personalized-politicized system. For example, in order to craft this minimal working consensus, the architects of the plan purposely failed to cross their t's and dot their i's, leaving unaddressed such key questions as whether the Palestinian balloting would be held under international supervision, whether a complete halt to the *intifada* would be insisted upon as a precondition to the peace plan, and whether the 140,000 Arab residents of east Jerusalem could be enfranchised. If this lack of specificity made initial consensus possible, it also assured later sharp differences of ministerial view and the prospect of a government crisis if and when Israel was called upon to provide specific answers to such sensitive and fateful questions.

Another complication posed by the existing system is that it discourages serious discussion of national strategic goals at the full cabinet level. At most the cabinet deals with broadest generalities or, at the opposite extreme, with small details and tactical, procedural aspects. Some critics would even go so far as to argue that 1978 was the last time long-term national objectives and strategies for ending the Middle East conflict were seriously aired by an Israeli government.

Reliance on subcabinet decision frameworks has no statutory basis whatsoever and yet seems to be a common practice. Individual ministers have always been given a high degree of freedom to take discretionary action, as in the statutory use of emergency powers going back to the British mandatory period for assuring order and the uninterrupted supply of goods, transport, and services at home. Also in foreign policy matters this tendency to create and operate from within smaller and smaller circles of decision through individual or ad hoc arrangements has a fairly long and honored tradition. It began with Ben-Gurion's habit of consulting his Mapai ministers (*sareinu*) to craft an agreed position before the weekly cabinet session, and includes, most significantly, his personal decision to go to war against Nasser in 1956 and the secret diplomatic pact he reached with the French without any prior cabinet authorization. Centralization continued after Ben-Gurion but took different forms: Golda's "kitchen cabinet" of course comes to mind, especially the decisions not to mobilize additional IDF reserve units and not to strike preemptively that were made at the beginning of the Yom Kippur War. During the war itself, the full cabinet and the General Staff returned to the center of policy formulation. During the Likud era, Menachem Begin drew upon the days of Levi Eshkol, reviving the subcabinet Ministerial Committee on Security and Defense as the principal decision making body.

Regardless of the specific form this streamlining takes at any given time, policy will rest as much on personal intuition as on institutional, bureaucratic analysis. Clearly, the smaller the group, the greater the impact of personality. We need to look always at the two-dimensional psychological factor: (a) the character and personality of individual leaders; (b) interpersonal relationships among the two or three people making foreign policy. This has made for any number of interesting combinations.

Three Decision Makers

Important decisions—if they are going to be made other than by the full cabinet—ought to involve at a minimum those three officials primarily responsible for national security and foreign relations: the prime minister and his foreign and defense ministers. For Israel this may have to represent the best compromise possible between the dictates of swift decision and of collective wisdom. Still, even this process depends on the specific participants and their particular working relationship. Two examples will suffice: 1969–74 (Meir-Eban-Dayan) and 1974–77 (Rabin-Allon-Peres).

The period between the 1967 and 1973 wars is dominated by Israel's military hero and defense minister, Moshe Dayan, whose opinions time and again helped determine government policy. Foreign Minister Abba Eban may have taken issue with Dayan's tough stand but was no match when it came to political infighting, while Prime Minister Golda Meir herself tended to defer to Dayan's sound military background, experience, and judgment. Consequently, Dayan left his mark on an entire series of crucial diplomatic security issues, from the "open bridges" policy and Jewish settlement in the territories to Israel's determined stand on Arab terrorism; from the war of attrition with Egypt to the Rogers and Jarring initiatives and later Sadat peace process; and from brinkmanship with the Soviet Union along the Suez Canal to crisis management in close collaboration with the U.S. at the height of the 1970 Jordanian civil war. By the same token, his failure to pick up on Arab military preparations in the fall of 1973, plus hesitancy in pushing for a last-minute preemptive air strike, played a major part in the Yom Kippur War surprise.

If Dayan's experience sheds insight on both the advantages and disadvantages of having one member of the ruling triumvirate predominate, the following period of 1974–77 suggests what could happen should no "first among equals" or *primus inter pares* emerge. That the team of Premier Rabin, Foreign Minister Yigal Allon, and Defense Minister Shimon Peres had the unenviable burden of coping with the military and diplomatic fallout from the Yom Yippur War–oil revolution was hard enough. Poor chemistry among the three leaders, documented by Rabin's bitter autobiographical reference about Peres's disloyalty toward him, only complicated the task of pursuing a united policy course. U.S. Secretary Kissinger for one used the situation in pressing the interim agreements upon Israel. Far more successful for a while was the Begin, Foreign Minister Dayan, and Defense Minister Ezer Weizman Likud troika, which appears to have functioned closely even if not smoothly in 1978 at Camp David.

Two Decision Makers

In Israel's loose system it is not absolutely necessary that all three top position holders be involved in a decision. Such a possibility arises whenever one person fills two of the three key posts—premier, defense, foreign affairs—at the same time. This has actually happened on at least five occasions: when Ben-Gurion was his own defense minister; when Sharett retained the Foreign Ministry; when Eshkol, modeling himself on Ben-Gurion, dealt with security affairs until the 1967 crisis; when Begin temporarily acted as defense chief in 1981; and when Yitzchak Shamir, called to succeed Begin, held on to his job at the Foreign Ministry as well. In such cases the presence of only two people at the top can go either way in terms of facilitating policy making. In Sharett's case it worked badly—even worse when Peres and Shamir had to act jointly, finding it hard to reach agreement even on diplomatic appointments, such as choosing a nominee for the ambassadorial post in Washington. When Mrs. Meir teamed up with Ben-Gurion, the two-player arrangement worked better, and it proved it could work well in 1983–84 when Defense Minister Moshe Arens complemented Shamir in coordinating policy efforts.

One Decision Maker

There have been a greater number of instances than is publicly acknowledged in which decisions were made by a single minister who, for one reason or another, did not seek the counsel of his two principal colleagues.

An early outstanding instance of a solitary crisis decision was Ben-Gurion's purposive strategy in 1956 to take Israel into war including secret collusion with France and then Great Britain. In the nonmilitary sphere probably the most costly error in the history of Israeli foreign relations came from a single-person decision in the early eighties. While in Washington for discussions with administration officials in 1981, then Prime Minister Begin waived an American offer to convert its aid from loans to direct grants without first consulting his own treasury advisers. Partly as a result, Israel ended up with an onerous debt of $5.5 billion, with a life span of thirty years at a cost of 12 to 14 percent per annum in debt servicing. Only after 1984 did U.S. foreign military support to Israel become outright grants.

Solitary decision making became especially fashionable in the period 1984 to 1988 as mounting strains within the national unity government threatened to sweep aside gentlemanly good form and the sense of national responsibility with which Ministers Peres, Rabin, and Shamir at least initially had entered the power-sharing arrangement.

By the time of the 1988 national elections, Shamir and Peres were trading accusations, charging each other with "murdering the peace" and "murdering the truth." Shamir was convinced that Peres had operated behind his back and against coalition principles by soliciting American and West European pressure, by making concessions to Egypt on Taba, by undercutting Israel's claim to be on the West Bank for security reasons, and in general, by conducting his own private, independent foreign policy. Most galling to Shamir were the circumstances behind the Peres-Hussein 1987 London accord and America's shift to support for a wide Mideast conference with Soviet participation. On this basis, in agreeing to renew the Labour-Likud format for another four years in 1988, Prime Minister-designate Shamir showed flexibility on most points while refusing to budge on his opposition to Peres as foreign minister. Instead, the latter entered the NUG II government as head of the Finance Ministry convinced that Shamir, for his part, was obstructionist and not entirely committed to finding a compromise solution to the Arab-Israeli conflict.

Israeli historians continue to argue over exactly how to classify decision making on Lebanon in 1982. Their interpretations, however, come down to two possibilities: either the strategy for marching to Beirut, engaging the Syrians, and restructuring Lebanon's politics was shared by Prime Minister Begin and Defense Minister Sharon only, or Sharon was the sole architect of what would become known as "Arik's war." But what everyone seems to agree on is that the intimate circle, possibly including Chief of Staff Rafael Eitan, was not much larger than this; the remaining cabinet ministers received only partial information and during the initial phases of the military operation were unaware of what policies they were being asked to approve. Arguably, had the war plans been more thoroughly debated and reviewed in a larger government forum, Israel could have been spared the costly extended entanglement in Lebanon.

Because of the informal, unsystematic, and perhaps even haphazard way by which Israeli foreign policy sometimes is made, the diplomatic record contains more than a few ill-conceived operations, security mishaps, and political setbacks—what historian Barbara Tuchman calls "folly" and Irving Janis "fiasco." Lebanon, the Pollard affair, and the Iran affair have at least one thing in common: they all are the product of streamlined policy making. Together they stand as an abject lesson against acting on personal impulse or in bureaucratic cabal at the expense of preparatory staff work, and they ought to confirm that at the end of such a curtailed process lies failure just as often as effectiveness and success.

In Israel, elite policy making poses the challenge of getting into the act and of getting the foreign policy act together. This takes us and the process to its next phase of policy coordination.

CHAPTER 6

POLICY COORDINATION

> *. . . the conscious determination not to know too much, the failure to exercise effective control over the bodies officially responsible to them and the propensity of bad judgment evinced by our top leaders [in the Pollard affair] was not a one-time affair but the catastrophic continuation of a long-term pattern.*
>
> —The *Jerusalem Post,* 1987

On 30 August 1987 months of public suspense and government indecision over the fate of Israel's Lavi fighter aircraft finally came to an end. Speaking for the government of Israel, the then ten member inner cabinet decided by a single vote to abort a project that had been under way for more than a decade and was about to go into production after successful test flights and the investment of over $1 billion. Media speculation as to the reasoning behind this dramatic reversal of policy was unofficially confirmed by cabinet ministers participating in the decision. The Lavi simply had become alternatively too expensive, too ambitious, too sensitive diplomatically—probably all three combined.

Left unsaid in most post-mortem analyses were indications of serious government mismanagement and bureaucratic rivalry. Plaguing the Lavi project from its inception, the absence of close policy coordination is a recurrent feature of Israeli foreign policy. And while any of a half-dozen or more celebrated cases of bureaucratic infighting can illustrate the harmful consequences for Israel internationally, the Lavi had been chosen as one of the best documented.

THE GROUNDING OF THE LAVI

Popular opinion inside Israel attributed the downing of the Lavi to external, U.S. pressure. It was no secret the Pentagon opposed a plan largely financed by the American taxpayer that, if completed as scheduled, might make Israel a serious competitor in the late 1990s in the lucrative world market for advanced, state-of-the-art jet fighters. An important corrective to this common view is provided by the findings published in Hebrew by Israel's state controller shortly before the fateful 1987 government decision. Stripped of its dry legalistic style, the report is unprecedented in Israeli terms both for its candor and its strong criticism of governmental and administrative bodies directly charged with promoting the Lavi's development. The special report confirms how in this instance the machinery of government—that warren of hierarchical organizations and anonymous officials responsible for administering government policies—was its own worst enemy (and the Lavi's).

The state controller charges that some of the most basic and standard operating procedures in public administration were consistently violated. On this list were

- individual decisions taken at the ministerial level without adequate preparation or discussion;
- policy makers being supplied with partial data, in both senses of the word—incomplete but also one-sided and self-serving—and without providing for alternative sources of information;
- failure to investigate thoroughly fundamental premises like export prospects for the Lavi, even though this had been an important consideration for going ahead with the project;
- neglecting to reconsider at each stage of a reversible process whether the Lavi continued to be cost effective against other alternatives (outright import of the F-16 or comparable aircraft, or coproduction with the United States);
- failure to anticipate or guard against cost overruns caused by modifications to the plane's design, mission assignments, engine, configuration, and payload that affected the unit cost of each Lavi and delivery timetables.

Finally, the report goes on to conclude: "There is no way to account for these features other than as suggesting an unwillingness to examine solutions except those meeting the views of the defense industry and various branches of the defense establishment." Students of public policy will recognize this as "groupthink."

One fault emphasized again and again by the state controller is how the Ministry of Finance was denied full participation in Lavi policy making. Its personnel and economic advisers were effectively squeezed out of the main decision process by Lavi enthusiasts in the military establishment in contravention of an explicit 1980 Ministerial Committee on Security and Defense directive calling for an ongoing joint study of economic variables by the Defense and Finance ministries. Instead, as the report explicitly states, there was a lack of cooperation between the two government agencies. Finance Ministry experts were denied access to cost estimates in the possession of defense sources—estimates that became the basis for recommendations submitted to the cabinet and approved by it without extensive discussion.

Thus, for example, a warning was given in April 1981 by the finance minister himself, and in May by his director-general, that no decision should be taken by the Ministry of Defense on an engine for the Lavi in the face of insufficient study. Both men went on record that any decision of this sort without their economic opinion would be regarded as precipitate and irresponsible. Still, on 8 May the defense minister chaired a discussion of the engine selection question without Finance Ministry experts being present. The ministry was invited to send representatives only for the closing briefing on 29 May. Again, in February 1982, in an apparent effort at closing the breach, an interdepartmental committee composed of the two estranged ministries and the Israel Defense Forces was set up as an advisory board. But it met only eight times over the next ten months; after 1982 it did not convene again.

Interagency cooperation might have identified and solved problems in the earlier stages of the ambitious Lavi undertaking. Because cooperation was missing, the economics of the Lavi received insufficient attention until it was too late. How could government leaders possibly determine the Lavi's cost effectiveness when they didn't know how much it was going to cost in the end or were fed unduly optimistic projections? By 1987 total estimated expenditures needed to make an otherwise impressive warplane airborne had become so prohibitive that the government's hand was forced in deciding against program completion.

THE ORGANIZATIONAL MAZE

While fascinating in itself, the Lavi has been recalled here with a specific purpose in mind. It helps introduce fundamental aspects of the organizational setting within which Israel functions during the critical intermediate phase between adoption of a foreign policy decision and full implementation. Easily forgotten is the possibility that a policy may be wisely chosen and still fail miserably because of how it was handled (or mishandled) by bureaucratic actors positioned deep within the middle and lower echelons of government.

The fate of the Lavi enterprise provides a sober reminder of the price a small and vulnerable Israel may be forced to pay when decision makers rest content with issuing policy directives on the principle that debate ends with a decision and that all energies are geared from that moment on to assuring its success. This is not an accurate guide to the real world of bureaucratic politics in Israel or probably anywhere else. Micromanagement is required to curb internal divisions and to insist that the respective agencies closely orchestrate their actions regarding an approved directive. When such micromanagement was not provided, the Lavi ballooned into a high-priced boondoggle that devoured an unconscionably large portion of Israel's limited defense budget. What happens, though, when Israeli vital international interests and physical security are at stake?

Bureaucratic struggles over foreign policy issues are certainly not new to Israel. They are as old and established a feature as the early collision in the mid-1950s between Ben-Gurion's military and Moshe Sharett's diplomats over the doctrine of "an eye for an eye" in reprisal for Arab incursions. The result was mutual estrangement, which left the Foreign Ministry uninvolved and often uninformed in what became essentially a military policy. Only following retaliatory actions by the army were the diplomats urgently called upon to defend Israel against condemnations at the United Nations and by foreign governments. By the same token, internal dissension and policy disarray are also as recent as the Lebanon, Irangate, and Pollard string of setbacks. Israel was also embarrassed by a genuine credibility gap in 1987–88 when authoritative yet competing agencies in Jerusalem expressed contradictory responses to the Shultz initiative, to the London understanding with Hussein, and to proposals for convening a Middle East peace conference.

So bad had interdepartmental and interpersonal relationships become at the beginning of 1988 that Prime Minister Shamir at one point openly attacked his foreign minister, Shimon Peres. "Everything he does is in the middle of the night," Shamir charged. "What I do he wants to know about so he can sabotage it." Nerves frayed by West Bank rioting and mounting U.S. and world pressure to negotiate with the Palestinians, Israel's leading foreign policy defenders came close to losing complete control over the process. Minister-without-Portfolio Moshe Arens admitted as much at the time in taking Shamir's side. According to him, "We have one government and one prime minister . . . but for the first time in our country's history—and for the first time in the history of democratic countries—there is a minister in the government, the foreign minister, who is conducting his own policy. Not that of the prime minister, but his own." Arens may have been exaggerating about the absence of precedent; still, his point was well taken in describing policy disunity.

How can such an intolerable state of affairs come about? What makes it go on for so long? More important: why isn't a stop put to this habit of Israeli leaders speaking for Israel in discordant voices? To a certain extent bureaucratic divisiveness is unavoidable. There is little use in looking for knaves, culprits, or individuals willfully sabotaging policy. Bureaucratic politics, as Professor Graham Allison in his study of the Cuban missile crisis reminds us, teaches that in government and diplomatic service where one stands very much depends on where one sits. Officials will fight for policies they genuinely perceive to be consistent with the national interest. The problem is that officials define the national interest from different departmental perspectives. Moreover, not only is this organizational rivalry inevitable, but—if kept within certain limits—it can have a healthy effect by presenting decision makers with alternative policy options.

Even allowing for all this, Israeli foreign policy must seem incomprehensible at times to an outsider. It helps therefore to see it as a response to several determinants: to the national and security interest, of course; to immediate, specific situations; and to the personal preferences of a Ben-Gurion or a Begin, a Peres, or a Shamir. Nevertheless, one always must consider an additional influence: the interplay of entrenched government agencies dependent *on* each other in some areas, autonomous *from* each other, and intensely competitive *with* each other at different points. So intense and at such cross-purposes that the student and outside observer have no choice but to draw from the dictionary of interstate conflict in describing such phenomena of the Israeli interdepartmental contest as subversive and delaying tactics, coalitions and counteralliances, negotiated compromises aimed at resolving tensions, threats and sanctions, outflanking movements, brinkmanship, breakdowns in communication, etc.

One of the earliest and best examples of bureaucratic politics in Israeli statecraft happened in 1950. In response to overtures by China's new Communist rulers the Ben-Gurion government considered the propriety of pursuing diplomatic relations with Beijing. The basis for discussion were two different viewpoints presented by Foreign Minister Sharett on behalf of experts within his own ministry. People like the ministry's director-general Walter Eytan argued in support of the initiative, among other things defending it on the grounds that avowedly pro-Western countries in Scandinavia had already set the precedent for recognizing the People's Republic of China; there was thus no reason why a nonaligned Israel couldn't or shouldn't proceed in a similar course. On the other hand, Abba Eban, Israeli ambassador in Washington, had dispatched cables strongly urging against the move because of prevailing cold war sentiments in the United States; powerful groups in Washington would not at all take kindly to such an independent and unfriendly act by the infant Jewish state. Sharett himself was indecisive in the face of such divided counsel. The cabinet ended up opting for greater caution, preferring the known (the United States and prospects for warmer relations) to the unknown. China would have to wait. Here was Israeli politics played out not so much between two separate agencies as within a single department, leaving the Ministry for Foreign Affairs incapable of crafting its own consensus.

Other contributing factors that encourage interdepartmental divisiveness are more specific to Israel. One point to remember is that cabinet posts often are seen as an opportunity for extending political influence. In former times, the most important ministries having a hand in Israel's external relations—Defense, Foreign Affairs, possibly Finance—were controlled by the dominant party of the governing coalition. This is no longer the case. Ben-Gurion and Sharett or, for that matter, the team of Meir, Dayan, and Eban, whatever their personal incompatibility, at least interacted with each other out of a shared political ideology and party platform.

Contrast this with more recent combinations. For instance, Rabin-Peres-Allon: three men for whom factional loyalties or identification merely compounded their personal and policy differences. Rabin represented mainstream Labour; Peres, the breakaway Rafi faction; Allon, the Achdut Ha-Avodah party. Suffice to note that having Labour's Shimon Peres in the prime minister's seat and Likud's Yitzchak Shamir at the head of the Ministry for Foreign Affairs (the two switched positions in midterm as stipulated by the conditions for their 1984 coalition agreement) made for a singularly unhealthy and strained decisional environment during the troubled existence of the first national unity government. NUG foreign policy in the period 1984 to 1988 will long endure as the outstanding example of the Israeli politicized—and also decentralized—bureaucratic model carried to an extreme, resulting upon occasion in near-anarchy.

In illustrating our point, absolutely nothing even comes close to equaling the 1988 Tamir expedition to Moscow. At the end of November, inquisitive reporters who noted the absence from his Foreign Ministry office of Co-Director-General Avraham Tamir and asked of his whereabouts had been informed he was on a routine but unofficial visit to Zaire and Mozambique. But then, in the middle of a cabinet session Foreign Minister Peres was handed a note telling him Tamir had phoned from The Hague and was about to fly to Moscow after receiving a visa for the Soviet Union. Peres reportedly instructed: "Stop him! Tell him to return immediately!" Disregarding Peres's explicit request to call off the visit, Tamir continued anyhow.

Reporting next from Moscow, Tamir claimed he was there solely for purposes of a technical inspection of the Israeli consular delegation working in the USSR and denied any official meetings with Soviet government authorities. Following a tour of the city he returned to Israel after a forty-eight hour visit. When some Foreign Ministry people expressed surprise and outrage at the whole affair, insisting the uncoordinated trip could only cause Israel embarrassment, an indignant Foreign Minister Peres insisted Tamir would be called to task. The press commented that Tamir at a minimum should be dismissed for his disobedience and severely reprimanded. Instead, nothing more came of the caper because either there was more to the Moscow mission than met the public eye, or the whole incident happened in the final days of the NUG in power and of Peres at the Foreign Ministry.

That the power and authority of an Israeli prime minister are poorly defined becomes another contributing factor for the impact of bureaucratic politics. He may speak for the government, represent it abroad, and should he choose, bring about its dissolution by forcing early elections. He has at his disposal a large staff in the Prime Minister's Office and directs the cabinet secretariat. He appoints ministers and may even prefer to wear two hats: on more than one occasion a prime minister has served as his own foreign minister or defense minister. He also has the right to be a party to actions by other ministers or, at a minimum, to be fully informed. He is, after all, the *prime* minister—first among equals.

Yet in practice, relationships between the person heading the government and other cabinet colleagues is loose and undisciplined. A provision in the 1984 NUG coalition agreement did confer on the premier the right to relieve a minister of his position. Yet to do so, in practical coalition terms, a head of government would have to think twice, for such an action might automatically trigger a cabinet crisis and a fall from power. Either the minister in question resigns, or the prime minister does; or else both must manage to get along somehow, reconciling their political or personality differences.

Then, too, there is Menachem Begin's rueful admission that of course he was always informed of actions by Defense Minister

Sharon—sometimes beforehand, sometimes only after the fact! That this could even be possible is reinforced by independent inquiries into the Pollard affair in 1987 that concluded that two successive heads of government, Shamir and Peres, had not known of a top secret intelligence operation being run in the United States. It was only after considerable damage had been done following Pollard's arrest by the American authorities that then Premier Shimon Peres, backed in an hour of stress by his ministers of defense and foreign affairs, asserted collective responsibility in piloting U.S.-Israeli relations through a particularly unpleasant crisis of confidence.

Furthermore, there is bureaucratic decentralization. It stems from divided spheres of responsibility, competence, and authority, not to mention from sharp policy differences. Thus it was that in the mid-fifties a pattern began to develop. Having already collided with each other more than once, the foreign office people and the defense establishment simply pulled apart and away from each other. In effect, the Foreign Ministry backed down, abnegating some of the functions, like policy planning, to the Prime Minister's Office but especially to the Defense Ministry and the army's General Staff. Each bureaucracy closed in within itself, working separately and in isolation from each other. An early clue as to what price such institutional autonomy and disregard for coordination might have for Israeli national interests came in the 1954 Lavon affair cited earlier, UN condemnatory resolutions, and a critical world press. To this day, such government functions as foreign information services, promoting Jewish immigration, and policy planning are parceled out among different ministries and agencies instead of being centralized within one department. Intelligence-gathering is the best example, especially those operations conducted abroad or involving foreign governments.

As shown by the accompanying flow chart (see Figure 1), intelligence activities fall in the domain of at least four different government institutions. This automatically poses the problems of (a) authorization and (b) supervision in addition to the theme of this chapter, (c) coordination. The Pollard case, again, exposed the defects of the arrangement in existence at the time. Nothing since then suggests any fundamental change for the better.

There are few established facts about the Pollard affair. What is known is that the secret operation began in the first half of 1984 and ended abruptly in November 1985, when Jonathan Pollard and his wife were arrested by the American authorities, charged with spying for Israel, and subsequently given long prison sentences. A Pentagon intelligence analyst with a high security clearance, Pollard had passed

Figure 1. Structure of the Israeli Security and Intelligence Community

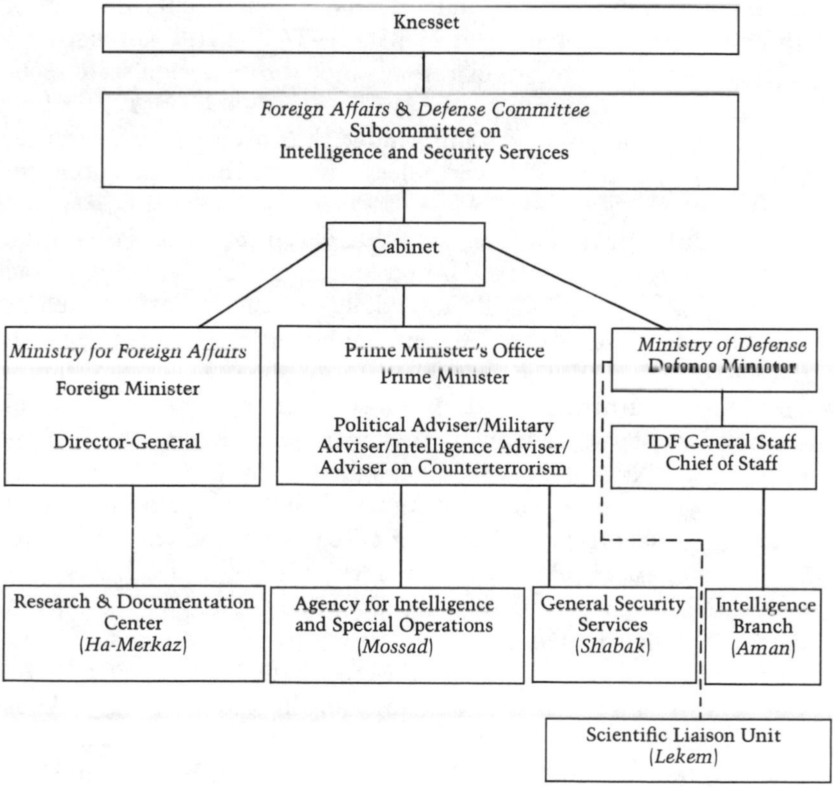

entire files of classified documents to his Israeli contact. Investigations in Israel unearthed that Pollard had been recruited and run by the head of a Scientific Liaison Unit (SLU, or *Lekem*) deep within the Defense Ministry whose very existence came as a surprise to many high government officials in Jerusalem. Caught totally unaware, the political leadership sought desperately to avert a crisis in U.S.-Israel relations and to provide outraged Reagan administration officials with a detailed account.

Two separate investigations were conducted into the circumstances and background of the affair: the Rotenstreich commission appointed by Prime Minister Shamir and the Eban parliamentary committee using the power of the Knesset to discuss the state's foreign policy, armed forces, and security. The summary findings of both bodies were published on 28 May 1987 (the full Rotenstreich commission report remains classified since it touches on state security); both focus primarily on the government's response *after* Pollard's arrest rather than detailing how the intelligence operation began and was managed. Nevertheless, some of the conclusions are remarkable.

Both investigations found conclusively that using Pollard, an American Jew, to spy on the United States, a friendly country, had been undertaken without the knowledge of the country's highest political leadership. The two Rotenstreich commissioners were convinced that neither of the two defense ministers, Arens and Rabin, "knew of the recruitment and running of Pollard, nor of the place of his employment and, obviously, they were not asked to approve his recruitment." At fault was the oversight system of the Ministry of Defense over *Lekem* that did not monitor its activities closely, so that something as seemingly basic as periodic checks and reassessments of *Lekem*'s operational policy were not carried out.

The Eban report puts the case differently. The head of *Lekem,* Rafi Eitan, failed to report Pollard's recruitment to his superiors. Defense Ministry Director-General Menachem Meron, centrally responsible for supervising *Lekem,* did so only superficially. Abba Eban's personal opinion was that the defense ministers, too, had been lax and should have created both the proper machinery and the atmosphere that would enable them to know whether there were any operations being sponsored within their ministry that might compromise the nation's security or international relations. Another committee member concluded there were only two possible explanations for the Pollard contretemps, neither of them satisfactory: either there had been no political supervision of the intelligence service, or there had been insufficient supervision.

Here was the exposure of poor coordination at still a third level: between the operational echelon and its civilian superiors, as well as within a single agency and between two or more rival agencies. Israel's claim that Pollard had been a "rogue operation" perhaps helped to appease American sensitivities. Yet the other side of the coin is that no prosecutor could rival the defense brief in delivering so stinging an indictment of past Israeli bureaucratic practices, exposing such an appalling lack of vigilance and coordination.

The existing system fosters both competitiveness and improvisation in an atmosphere of secrecy. Such competitiveness is encouraged by divided responsibilities and departmentalized chores. The ad hoc improvising style, in turn, stems from the need for quick responses to fast-breaking events, while restricted access is due to the sensitivity of most material pertaining to national security. All three features are very well illustrated in the first stages of Israel's role in Irangate. Prime Minister Peres elected to entrust the delicate negotiation, logistical arrangements, shipment, and payment schedules to three individuals only: Al Schwimmer, Yaakov Nimrodi, and David Kimche. Only Kimche was a government employee; the other two, businessmen experienced in secret operations and having Peres's complete personal trust. Peres preferred this to going through accepted bureaucratic channels.

THREE BUREAUCRATIC CONTENDERS

The competitive interplay of bureaucratic forces has become an accepted way of life in Israeli government service. In the area of external affairs this competitiveness is institutionalized in the bureaucratic struggles waged among three organizational actors: the Prime Minister's Office, the Ministry for Foreign Affairs, and the Ministry of Defense. Their rivalry is not exactly an equal one, however, because the sides are not evenly balanced. Serious differences in structures, spheres of competence, and status have left the Ministry for Foreign Affairs the biggest bureaucratic loser.

Prime Minister's Office

One serious contender is the Prime Minister's Office, whose growing prominence in the three overlapping spheres of intelligence, security, and statecraft is reflected by the increased number of government personnel employed by, and directly responsible to, the prime minister. Perhaps the strongest moving force behind this trend has been the personal operating style of three recent holders of the office: Begin, Peres, and Shamir. Each sought to put the direction and management of foreign policy under his control, which is merely another indication of how critical foreign affairs are perceived of by the country's leaders.

The range of activities within the Prime Minister's Office is extensive. One section, the government secretariat, provides clerical assistance to some forty cabinet committees, prepares the weekly cabinet agenda, records minutes, and circulates decisions requiring implementation. No less important, the secretariat is charged with coordinating interministerial efforts, maintaining contact between the cabinet and the Knesset, and in general keeping the prime minister informed of government activity. The Prime Minister's Office is also in charge of the Government Press Office, which provides information and services to the inordinate number of foreign journalists usually covering Israel and who, in turn, present developments in the country and its policies to the outside world.

A substantial portion of the office's activities, however, are covert. It is from here that clandestine intelligence and antiterror efforts are directed, as well as secret diplomatic contacts initiated. The director of the Mossad, Israel's intelligence agency, thus reports directly to the prime minister who also pursues sensitive diplomatic exchanges by working through a battery of close, personal confidants, including his political and military advisers. Teddy Kollek played such a role for Ben-Gurion; the late Dr. Yaakov Herzog, director-general of the Prime Minister's Office, did likewise for Levi Eshkol and Golda Meir, being instrumental in opening a discreet dialogue with the Vatican and also being the first Israeli to meet with Jordan's King Hussein, secretly in September 1963.

Recent practice finds the government (cabinet) secretary undertaking diplomatic assignments well beyond any purely technical or administrative role: Dan Meridor in Shamir's first premiership, Dr. Yossi Beilin for Peres, and Dr. Elyakim Rubenstein in the second half of the first national unity government. The latter, for example, was entrusted by Shamir with matters of great delicacy and urgency, such as smoothing ties with the United States over the Pollard debacle, Irangate, and the Shultz proposals.

Shimon Peres, during his two years in office, contributed significantly to building up the status and competence of the Prime Minister's Office and its personnel. To his credit, Peres emphasized staff work and discussion centering on position papers drafted by his aides. He surrounded himself with an inner circle of advisers and experts that, on security and foreign affairs, included Cabinet Secre-

1. Dr. Theodor Herzl, first practitioner of Zionist diplomacy, being granted an impromptu audience with Germany's Kaiser Wilhelm. Palestine, 1898. (Courtesy Central Zionist Archives)

2. Dr. Chaim Weizmann, Herzl's successor, dons a *kaffiya* in meeting the Amir Feisal as part of an early bid at allying Zionism with the Arab nationalist movement. Akaba, 1918. (Courtesy Central Zionist Archives)

3. The Jewish delegation to the St. James's conference on the future of Palestine. London, 1939. (Courtesy Central Zionist Archives)

4. Delegates to the Twenty-first Zionist Congress learn of the Nazi-Soviet pact dooming Europe to war and sealing the fate of European Jewry. Front row, left to right, Israel's future leaders: Moshe Sharett (first foreign minister), David Ben-Gurion (first prime minister), Chaim Weizmann (first president of the state), and Eliezer Kaplan (first finance minister). Geneva, August 1939 (Courtesy Central Zionist Archives)

5. Members of the Jewish community celebrating UN endorsement for the partition plan and Jewish statehood. Palestine, 29 November 1947. (Courtesy Central Zionist Archives)

6. David Ben-Gurion announcing the establishment of an independent state of Israel. Tel Aviv, 14 May 1948. (Courtesy Central Zionist Archives)

7. Flag-raising ceremony marking Israel's admission to the UN, one year after declaring independence. To the left of the flagpole, representing Israel, are David Hacohen, Abba Eban, Foreign Minister Moshe Sharett. Right, Gideon Rafael, future ambassador and director-general of the Ministry for Foreign Affairs. New York, 12 May 1949. (Courtesy Central Zionist Archives)

8. First fruits of nonalignment. President Chaim Weizmann on Independence Day, 1949. Left, U.S. Ambassador James G. McDonald. Right, Soviet envoy Pavel Yershov. (Courtesy Israel State Archives)

9. Golda Meir, Israel's first ambassador to the Soviet Union, attending High Holy Day services at Moscow's Great Synagogue, is overwhelmed by Russian Jews. 1948., (Courtesy the Ministry of Foreign Affairs, Jerusalem)

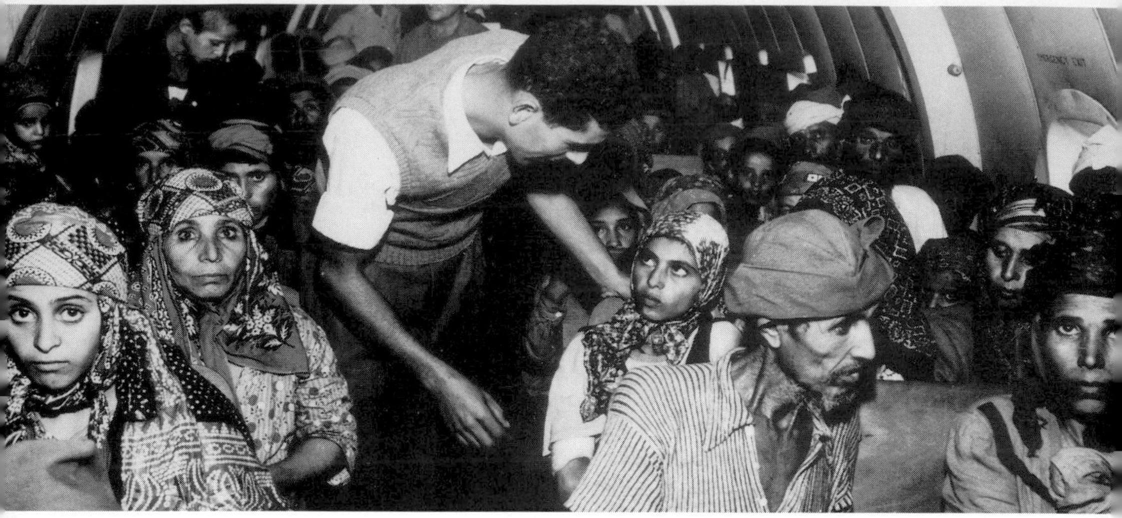

10. Yemenite Jews on their way to the Promised Land as part of Operation Magic Carpet, in keeping with the diplomatic goal of ingathering the exiles. 1949. (Courtesy Government Press Office, Jerusalem)

11. Foreign Minister Moshe Sharett just before his final split with Ben-Gurion. 1956. (Courtesy Government Press Office, Jerusalem)

12. Ben-Gurion meets French President Charles de Gaulle at the Palais de l'Elysée. Paris, 1960. (Courtesy Government Press Office, Jerusalem)

13. Reaching out. President Yitzchak Ben-Zvi dressed in Liberian tribal attire during a state visit to Africa aimed at cultivating ties with emerging Third World nations. August 1962. (Courtesy Government Press Office, Jerusalem)

14. The Israeli delegation, headed by Foreign Minister Eban (center), in attendance at the UN General Assembly special session to debate the Soviet proposal on the Middle East situation. Ambassador Gideon Refael (to Eban's right) and Golda Meir are also pictured. New York, 19 June 1967. (Courtesy United Nations)

15. The two great political antagonists. David Ben-Gurion and Menachem Begin, in a rare conversation, brokered by Gen. Ezer Weizman. King David Hotel, 11 December 1967. (Courtesy Government Press Office, Jerusalem)

16. Personal diplomacy. Following the Six-Day War victory, Premier Levi Eshkol confers with President Lyndon Johnson at his Texas ranch. January 1968. (Courtesy Government Press Office, Jerusalem)

17. Golda Meir, representing the Jewish state, received by Pope Paul VI.

18. Ambassador Chaim Herzog addresses the UN General Assembly after tearing up a resolution that condemned Zionism as "a form of racism and racial discrimination." New York, 10 November 1975. (Courtesy United Nations/M. Tzovaras)

19. Following the signing of the Camp David accords, Sadat and Begin clasp hands with President Jimmy Carter on the White House lawn. 26 March 1979. (Courtesy Government Press Office, Jerusalem)

20. Foreign Minister Abba Eban heads a delegation of Israeli diplomats paying respects to the memory of the 6 million Jewish victims of the Holocaust. Auschwitz, 1966. (Courtesy Israel State Archives)

21. The policy-making process. The Israeli delegation meets for informal consultation with Premier Menachem Begin. Camp David, September 1978. (Courtesy Government Press Office, Jerusalem)

22. Prime Minister Shamir greets Foreign Minister Eduard Shevardnaze at UN Headquarters. New York, 9 June 1988. (Courtesy Embassy of Israel, Washington, D.C.)

tary Beilin, political counselor Dr. Nimrod Novik, Avraham ("Abrasha") Tamir, the experienced head of the Prime Minister's Office and person in charge of strategic planning, Minister-without-Portfolio Ezer Weizman, and adviser for Diaspora affairs Avraham Burg. With their assistance Peres undertook initiatives on a broad diplomatic front aimed at improving Israel's international image and position while enhancing the ability of the Prime Minister's Office to compete more effectively in the bureaucratic struggle. Ironically enough, most of these team members accompanied Peres in late 1986 when he switched over to the Foreign Ministry and then proceeded to employ precisely these same techniques *against* the Prime Minister's Office!

Ministry for Foreign Affairs

Students of comparative foreign relations maintain that the higher the status of a country's foreign office the less policy will involve the use of force, and the more its policy will be reactive rather than active. The Israeli experience confirms the first hypothesis but refutes the second. Israeli diplomacy from the beginning has used coercive force alongside subtler forms of influence and persuasion in large part because the Foreign Ministry does not enjoy a high status and never did. But as for the second hypothesis, the opposite holds for Israel. Even though the ministry has a low status and does not exert a dominant influence over the policy-making process, foreign policy has some strong reactive tendencies, especially on the Arab and peace fronts.

The secondary status of the Ministry for Foreign Affairs is not at all evident to the outside observer. Indeed, on the surface it would appear to possess every requisite for securing a position of foreign policy preeminence. Taken together, the head office and staff in Jerusalem along with the diplomatic missions abroad can claim departmental seniority, expertise, and competence in addition to a wealth of collective experience in the field of world affairs. Moreover, the Foreign Ministry has projected a fairly coherent worldview and departmental approach rooted in basic precepts and sensitivities toward the core diplomatic issues facing Israel.

The Foreign Ministry arguably has it all and yet consistently has lost out to its bureaucratic rivals, most particularly the Defense Ministry, on specific foreign policy decisions and in the larger contest for authority and powers. There are various reasons for this marked loss of influence, prestige, and responsibility by the Foreign Ministry, beginning with the country's objective security situation and the inhospitable climate Israel confronts on its borders, which argue for tangible power over diplomatic subtlety. Another, bureaucratic explanation indicates that the rival agency, the Defense Ministry, is simply better equipped, or armed, and better positioned to fight the interdepartmental battles than the Foreign Ministry. These arguments are valid. Still, I would suggest another reason, which is that the interests and personnel of the Ministry for Foreign Affairs in most instances have just not enjoyed the leadership necessary to play a more assertive role.

On the one hand, the ministry in its first forty years had known greater ministerial stability than either of its rivals in the sense of fewer foreign ministers: seven (Sharett, Meir, Eban, Allon, Dayan, Shamir, Peres) as opposed to eight prime ministers and ten defense ministers (Ben-Gurion, Lavon, Eskhol, Dayan, Peres, Weizman, Begin, Sharon, Arens, Rabin). On the other hand, however, and upon closer analysis, Israeli foreign ministers have been of three kinds: inexperienced; eminently qualified but weak politically; politically strong and perhaps even qualified but independent. Examples of the first type were Mrs. Meir and Yigal Allon, neither of whom was selected for professional diplomatic training or experience but on grounds of loyalty or coalition-balancing. Two individuals with impressive qualifications were Sharett and Eban; although having a deep grasp of the issues, neither of them possessed the political muscle to fight aggressively for the ministry's positions and therefore enjoyed little political influence with their cabinet colleagues or in cabinet debate.

A third category has been strong, assertive foreign ministers. Dayan and Peres are the best, and probably only, examples. Both men enjoyed a reputation for political acumen: they had accumulated a wealth of personal foreign contacts as well as years of practical experience in matters of security; each was adept at bureaucratic politics and also knew how to gain government backing for their policy proposals. Consequently, each seemed the ideal candidate for bringing the Ministry for Foreign Affairs to a position of policy centrality. Instead, Dayan and Peres alike earned the reputation for preferring to act independently, reminiscent of Kissinger's diplomatic style in the American context. Like him, they chose to pursue overseas political initiatives by working outside of the bureaucratic-institutional framework and relying on a handful of trusted personal aides.

Bypassing of Foreign Ministry personnel by their own ministers is thus an additional source of demoralization. This became particularly apparent during the two years (1986–88) Shimon Peres served as minister for foreign affairs. He succeeded in enhancing the ministry's prestige to the extent that at times it appeared almost to be an independent center for policy making, conducting probes with Jordan and campaigning for an international peace conference. Also, the ministry was instrumental in prompting a cabinet review of policy toward the Republic of South Africa.

This, however, was not the same thing as building the competence and status of the ministry as a whole, so that resentment continued to build up among senior ministry officials. In January 1987, for example, several of them spoke out against signs of renewed politicization of the ministry evidenced through political appointments to overseas posts. References were made at the time to feelings of alienation and to a sense of professional ineffectiveness attributed to "the Olympian remoteness and inaccessibility" of the foreign minister and to the clique of his "boys" who "surround and insulate him from the professional staff and who often treat the staff with condescension." The perception, in short, was of yet another foreign minister deciding to run policy alone, without the ministry.

In fairness, though, whatever effect Peres's style of conducting foreign policy might have had on the ministry itself, it was less the cause of the despondency than the symptom of a much longer process of institutional decline. This situation could be arrested and possibly even reversed. But it would require a rare type of foreign secretary. Someone who understood the substance of foreign relations, its nuances, and dynamics. Someone who appreciated the advantage of working within an institutional framework and of drawing upon the expertise of its members. A political leader who, in addition, would know how to fight for the Foreign Ministry on behalf of its policy recommendations but, more important, on behalf of its claim (as is accepted in so many other countries like the United States and Britain) to be the government agency with primary responsibility for both the conduct and close coordination of Israel's extensive overseas efforts.

But for the present the Ministry for Foreign Affairs continues to be subordinate. It is subordinate to such influences as personal intuition and improvisation. It is understaffed and underutilized, being viewed by successive governments more as an auxiliary instrument for policy implementation, with restricted operational and functional responsibilities, than as the ministry that ought to have the heaviest input for policy recommendation and planning. And it is still subordinate to the rival Defense Ministry, the organization having the greatest influence on the foreign policy process.

Ministry for Defense

Military definitions of Israeli national defense doctrine have prevailed over the diplomatic approach to security ever since 1948. Ben-Gurion, as both prime minister and defense minister, held to a set of firm convictions passed on to future leaders:

1. Power takes precedence over persuasion;
2. Deterrence outweighs dialogue in effectiveness and in tangible results;
3. A tough stance will prove more effective with Arab leaders than accommodation or concessions;
4. Deeds are more important than words in world politics even if the deeds angered or possibly alienated outside actors; and
5. International guarantees are no substitute for physical ones centering on the right—and capability—of individual, national self-defense.

In much the same way, the Ministry for Defense from the beginning has tended to prevail over the Ministry for Foreign Affairs in their competition for policy influence and policy control. Almost systematically, over time the Foreign Ministry has been outmaneuvered, outvoted, and shut out of certain policy functions by its defense counterparts.

This trend, so critical for understanding Israel foreign policy making and behavior, was set in motion as early as 1949. For example, the question arose at the time as to which ministry should be responsible for representing Israel and for managing the armistice regime with the neighboring Arab countries. Foreign Minister Sharett and his people argued that the Mixed Armistice Commissions under UN auspices were Israel's sole channel for direct contacts with the Arab governments and therefore were essentially diplomatic rather than military. Ben-Gurion, for his part, saw the armistice agreements as an extension of the ongoing quest for Israeli security, making them the prerogative of the Israel Defense Forces and of its civilian authorities. Despite objections by Sharett, control over armistice affairs was vested in the Defense Ministry.

As mentioned earlier, in the 1950s and 1960s the Foreign Ministry did not participate directly in decisions on military reprisals across Israel's borders. Similarly, arms sales to West Germany and Latin American countries were negotiated and contracted for by Defense Ministry representatives without Foreign Ministry approval. Again, it has been shown that the Foreign Ministry was excluded in the 1970 decision to escalate the Suez Canal war of attrition through deep-penetration bombing against Egypt backed by the Soviet Union. Following the Sadat initiative, when Dayan on behalf of the Foreign Ministry insisted on heading the Israeli delegation to the autonomy talks with the United States and Egypt and met Defense Ministry opposition, a compromise of the jurisdictional dispute was worked out by Premier Begin. The delegation would be chaired by Israel's minister of the interior!

Military power and diplomacy, the army corps and the diplomatic corps: by right these ought to be equal, complementary tools in the service of national interests. Instead, in the Israeli case the relationship in institutional bureaucratic terms between the two components is patently one-sided (see Table 14). It is asymmetrical because the Ministry of Defense enjoys advantages over the Ministry for Foreign Affairs in every single determinant of bureaucratic politics. First, it has become one of the largest government agencies. Second, its budget is far greater, especially after the 1973 war when defense absorbed as much as half or two-thirds of the state budget and over 20 percent of the gross national product (GNP). Third, the Defense Ministry represents a far more extensive domestic constituency, given its control over a vast defense establishment comprising the IDF, the defense industries, and the ministry's own civilian personnel. Fourth, the Defense Ministry and its work are understood, appreciated, and supported by the Israeli public. This sense of attachment and grasp of what defense means for the country are reinforced for tens of thousands of Israeli men and women through direct contact in their early military service and subsequent annual reserve duty. Diplomacy is seen by a majority of Israelis as either distant from them or as marginal for the country's real security, being largely a matter of striped trousers, cocktail parties, and empty phrase-making.

For these and other reasons, the Foreign Ministry's struggle is an unequal one, especially in the face of its own leadership and morale problems. This has had two important results. The first is that a great many Israelis, along with most political leaders and Knesset members, are inclined to dismiss the Foreign Ministry and statecraft as little more than an extension of the larger, more crucial military effort. Consequently, the diplomatic outlook on intelligence operations, for example, or on weapons transfers, may not always be voiced in government policy decisions, and if heard, perhaps not loudly or forcefully enough.

The second result encouraged by the weaknesses of the Foreign Ministry is that we find the Israeli military exercising preponderant influence in specific policy areas that have major ramifications for

Table 14. The Bureaucratic Contestants

	Ministry for Foreign Affairs (FA)	Ministry for Defense (D)	Prime Minister's Office & Cabinet Secretariat (PM)	Ministry of Finance (F)	Ministry of Interior (I)	Ministry of Education & Culture (EC)
STAFF Personnel	818	2,205	584	5,724	650	2,169
Percent of Total Government Personnel[1]	1.25	3.38	0.89	8.78	0.99	3.32
BUDGET Ministry Budget (million IS)	185.05	8,905.86	17.415	254.96	36.43	2,472.98
Percent of Total Government Budget[2]	0.57	27.44	0.05	0.78	0.11	7.62

[1] Total government employees (1988): 65,149
[2] Total government budget (1988): 32,446 million shekalim

Sources: Ministry of Finance, "Government Budget Proposal for Fiscal Year 1988," presented to the eleventh Knesset (Jerusalem, 1988).

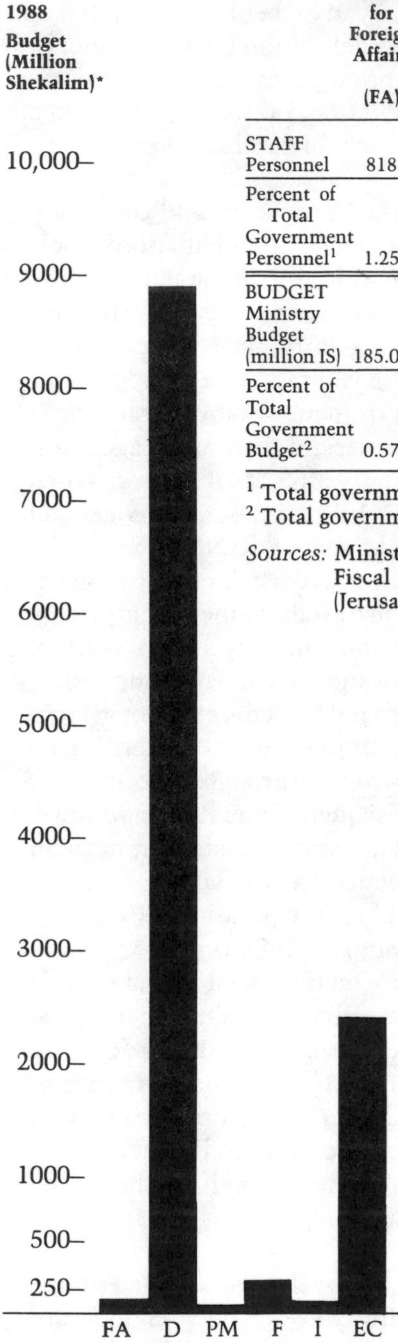

* 1 1988 IS = U.S. $.64

Israel's international position and that arguably ought to be entrusted to the Ministry for Foreign Affairs or at least require a greater involvement by it in forming policy guidelines.

Encroachment by the Ministry for Defense into foreign policy-related areas includes

- policy planning, strategic global assessments, and detailed position papers on a broad range of regional, bilateral (U.S.-Israeli ties), and international issues;
- negotiation with U.S. administration officials on all aspects of military cooperation but that cross into economic and trade policy and that affect the strategic, political relationship;
- coordinating Israel's ambitious and far-flung programs of foreign military assistance, including negotiation with other governments—a program with direct foreign policy consequences, both good and bad, for Israel; and
- administering the West Bank and Gaza territories, including the handling of the foreign media, in an area of considerable world interest affecting Israel's international standing and relations with many foreign governments.

By the rules of the game of bureaucratic politics any ascendant organization, such as the Defense Ministry, can be expected to exploit its advantages in resources, status, and competence in further extending its power and its influence over the policy-making establishment.

In one of the only instances where this serious trend was publicly aired, in October 1986 the departing director general of the Foreign Ministry, David Kimche, openly criticized the mounting institutional imbalance of power. He argued that the defense establishment had far too great a say in policy making and on political issues and the Foreign Ministry far too little. By way of example, Kimche revealed that no one at his ministry had known beforehand of the 1981 decision to bomb the Iraqi nuclear reactor nor of the decision in 1982 to invade Lebanon. Assailing "the atmosphere of arrogance in the defense establishment *vis-à-vis* the foreign service," he noted the long history of the problem, but he insisted that in the future Israel's struggle would focus on peace, not war. Hence, it is the Foreign Ministry that ought to be the leading policy-making body and not anyone else.

Nevertheless, Kimche's remained a voice in the wilderness. The present system that has evolved over forty years through trial and error seems impervious to change. Therefore, policy making on foreign affairs continues to be governed by an unequal interdepartmental contest, by decentralized accountability, and by poor overall coordination. Numerous references have been made about wasteful duplication, spitefulness, and other decision-making defects. Public, government, and parliamentary commissions—from the 1974 Agranat Commission inquiry into the Yom Kippur intelligence failure, through the Kahan Commission's investigation of the 1982 Lebanon intervention, and the state controller's report on the Lavi, to the two probes into the Pollard affair—have filled the public record with documentary evidence of structural as well as procedural shortcomings.

Academics and scholarly think tanks have presented recommendations for restructuring the decision-making system in Israel to give greater coherence and compatibility to the process. This includes the formation of a central body designed along the lines of a national security council whose function it would be to sort out options while estimating their risks, likely benefits, and probabilities of success. Certainly there is no shortage of creative ideas, almost any of which might help correct what too often constitutes a messy process—what Israelis refer to as a complete *balagan,* or disarray—that translates as well into a messy articulation of policy. Few specific proposals for reform have been adopted, however, even in principle. Fewer still have actually been put into effect.

As a direct result, foreign policy making in Israel is seldom both logical or tidy. It continues to suffer more than is necessary from the interplay of parochial interests and pressures instead of being what it ought to be, i.e., the product of an overarching strategy that is purposive and agreed upon.

Under the existing "system," it is easier to understand how as a state actor Israel has been caught by surprise. This is as true of the diplomatic arena as it is of the military-intelligence sphere. Looking back, Israel had the 1967 crisis sprung upon it and paid dearly for the unforeseen 1973 Yom Kippur contingency. Less remembered is how Israel was thrown off guard by the 1977 Soviet-American joint communiqué, taken unawares by the 1982 Reagan initiative, stunned by the Pollard and Irangate exposés, and completely unprepared for either the tenacity of the *intifada* or the 31 July 1988 surprise policy shift by Jordan's King Hussein removing himself as spokesman for the Palestinians.

Also instructive was Israel's belated policy reassessment toward South Africa. Only when overseas protests, especially in the United States, began to mount in 1987 against the military supply relationship with Pretoria, did the government machinery begin to operate.

At the personal insistence of Foreign Ministry Director-General Yossi Beilin, an interdepartmental committee drafted a set of ten recommendations for imposing sanctions against South Africa that were then adopted by the inner cabinet in September 1987 to follow-up the decision in March to ban all new defense contracts.

Entirely consistent with this tendency to be caught unprepared for likely eventualities was the American *volte face* on the issue of negotiating with the PLO in the last days of the Reagan administration in December 1988. In this instance, experts had been predicting it was only a question of time; the day would come when the United States would change its 1975 stand against dealing directly with the PLO and against Yasir Arafat as sole legitimate representative of the Palestinian people. Yet official Jerusalem had no contingency plan ready, did not respond promptly or effectively, and was painfully slow in pursuing any alternative initiatives of its own.

Major restructuring of the foreign policy-making apparatus is not politically likely soon. Consequently, in turning from policy coordination to policy implementation, we must conclude that in all likelihood Israeli foreign policy will continue to be conducted in the worst of both possible worlds. Juxtaposed are many of the inefficiencies and symptoms of waste inherent in complex organizations, along with some of the most flagrant abuses known to occur whenever power and authority are concentrated (not by design but through bureaucratic infighting) in the hands (no matter how competent) of a single, dominant, organizational actor such as the Defense Ministry.

This awareness at least should help explain the Israeli form of "muddling through" (*eichshehu, l'histader*): somehow we'll get by. Certainly, if nothing else, the discussion must caution the non-Israeli reader against assuming security and foreign affairs decision making is completely rational. Without a doubt, professional life is difficult for Israeli diplomats who invariably are hard pressed to explain and to implement whatever should happen to emerge from the political and organizational struggles being waged continuously back in Jerusalem.

CHAPTER 7

POLICY IMPLEMENTATION

Middle East diplomacy is very open. There is nothing secret.

—Yuri Dubinin, 1989
Soviet Ambassador to Washington

Foreign policies are unlike prophecies. They cannot be self-fulfilling. Only policies that are declaratory (an ultimatum, a public warning, a policy clarification) have an immediate effect through the announcement itself. And even these usually must be backed up by some act or show of resolve. Otherwise, unless executed, policies, like decisions, remain mere statements of purpose or intent. Successful execution, in turn, depends on two things: (a) that a range of cultural, political, economic, or coercive means be available from which the state and its authoritative representatives can choose; (b) that they select and follow through with strategies, tactics, and techniques that are most appropriate to the occasion, i.e., likely to bring the greatest payoff at minimum cost or risk. This is why implementing policy can be a more onerous and demanding exercise in international politics than its formulation.

THE ENDS-MEANS DILEMMA

For Israel, in particular, because of its limited means and national power, the implementation phase of the foreign policy process often becomes the most important and the most challenging. First, it is clear from our previous discussion that neither the carrying out of government directives nor their success can be taken for granted as something that follows automatically from decision making, however rational. As Israeli leaders by now have learned, simply issuing orders is not sufficient to overcome the interagency push and pull in

Jerusalem. Bureaucrats, operating from their own individual fiefdoms, have a different agenda along with ways for altering or reinterpreting their instructions. But then again, secondly, not to give orders must also be regarded as inadequate and inappropriate, since this allows others (whether they are one's own civil servants and subordinates or one's foreign opponents) to seize the initiative, as Egypt's Sadat did in the 1973 military surprise. Moreover, there is yet a third paradox, for in foreign policy few certitudes exist. Even wise and appropriate policy moves occasionally produce entirely unplanned and unanticipated results. Such was the case in American Middle East policy, for example, in the 1977 call by the United States for a return to the Geneva conference and a multilateral framework. Instead, this prompted Sadat to open a bilateral dialogue with Israel without consulting, or confiding in, the United States.

Unintended diplomatic consequences happen because the way decisions are implemented at home affects the conduct of Israeli foreign relations with other countries. Herein lies a key distinction between policy making and policy coordination, on the one hand, and policy execution, on the other. All three are phases of, and parts of, a single policy process. Implementation, in fact, is the culmination of this long and complicated process of framing foreign policy. Still, they do not share the same emphases. Phases one and two center on the actors: leaders, institutions, and agencies; phase three, on policy instruments. The first two determine policy output—decisions; the third phase determines the policy outcome. The Jerusalem merry-go-round—exactly how Israel goes about processing policy—is an entirely internal, domestic matter. It seems to have made peace with its special blend of centralized policy making and decentralized policy coordination. But how it then chooses to give meaning and effect to those decisions concerns outside parties and has a direct bearing on Middle East and international affairs.

Approached from a slightly different angle, the weighing of alternative implementation strategies by Israel raises a fascinating yet unaddressed question. Acknowledging that it faces a restrictive, often hostile external environment, how has Israel sought to break out of those confines? What tools and assets does it have to choose from? Which of these instruments does it favor? And with what degree of success?

Israel's range of policy instruments in following through on policy choices is at once both standard and exceptional. Standard in the sense of having the general categories of influence and power available to all sovereign states: cultural diplomacy, prestige, military force, political ties and alignments, and economic power. Where

Israel begins to be distinctive, however, lies in its having fewer of these options than most other countries; for example, it is one of only a handful of countries not affiliated with any formal treaty alliance. In addition, even in the categories of influence and power it possesses, Israel has smaller amounts—particularly in relation to its ambitious security agenda and foreign policy goals. As a small country deficient in natural resources, it is less attractive as an economic trading partner. As a country sometimes listed as an outcast or pariah state, its value as a diplomatic ally is diminished. As its dependency on the United States grows, its political leverage and independence of political action becomes subject to question. So, too, is its military capability dwarfed by the geographic depth and collective resources of the Arab world.

Assuming there is a strong correlation between a country's means and its pursuit of foreign policy objectives, logically Israel should not be expected to have quite so many diplomatic achievements and international links as its record shows. The central argument in this chapter is that while the range and quantity of its options for putting policies into practice are indeed limited, and despite internal policy-making deficiencies that are avoidable and of Israel's own making, Israeli foreign policy has been extremely resourceful overall in using the few nonmilitary bargaining chips it does possess to promote core national interests internationally. Four instruments in particular have been used in making a little go a long way. These Israeli "specialities" are (1) economic statecraft; (2) arms diplomacy; (3) backstage diplomacy; and (4) the Jewish connection.

THE MILITARY INSTRUMENT

Any discussion of implementation strategies by Israel must begin, however, with the basic distinction between force and diplomacy. Effective foreign policy execution requires two things: first, knowing how to choose between the two—when to apply coercion and when to persuade; and, second, knowing how to integrate power with diplomacy to achieve a balanced mix. In the past, Israel has been inclined to rely more on power than on diplomacy. It has attempted to apply a military solution not only to military problems but to political problems as well. Intervention in Lebanon in 1982, from this perspective, is only a more recent and most extreme illustration of this exaggerated confidence in some Israel military and even political circles in the efficacy of physical force.

Our task is not to justify but rather to explain this favoring of power. To a considerable extent we are thrust back once again to the existential security dilemma and its logical response. The perception of a serious, permanent threat to the country's physical existence necessitates having—and at times employing—a strong military capability. Then again, this overreliance on force projection may represent an attempt by Israeli leaders to overcome, psychologically and politically, the sin of weakness in the other nonmilitary, economic, and diplomatic categories of national power. Those who would have Israel rely on an overt nuclear capability, unintentionally perhaps, are catering to, and encouraging, this kind of simplistic approach. The answer to Israel's problems does not lie exclusively, or even primarily, in the nuclear option or deterrent. Having a "bomb in the basement" would not absolve the national leadership from either political movement or creative diplomacy.

Like most features about Israeli foreign policy, this attitude and the behavior pattern it encourages can be traced to the formative years of statehood, years that saw a combination of military success coupled with a growing distaste for diplomacy stemming from disillusionment.

- Superpower diplomacy? Israel had little to offer either the United States or the USSR initially. Furthermore, it was already apparent by 1952–53 that the country could not keep to its declared original course of strict nonidentification.
- Multilateral diplomacy? The United Nations rather quickly turned into an unfriendly forum, with Israel the object of criticism and one-sided resolutions. Instead of focusing its diplomatic efforts on international bodies, Jerusalem looked elsewhere for support, concentrating on fostering friendly bilateral relations with individual countries.
- Alliance diplomacy? Israel remained outside all the formal regional, economic, and security frameworks. Membership in an alliance might have proven the value of the diplomatic art while enhancing the security of the country. Still, the option never arose.
- Economic and cultural diplomacy? Not even the right to participate in peaceful, apolitical activities could be taken for granted. Competing in sporting events, signing cultural exchanges, sending delegates to various development panels—each and every small gain had to be contested and fought for. Meanwhile, the Arab economic boycott and Arab pressure on governments willing to deal with the Jewish state severely handicapped trade prospects.

- Middle East diplomacy? After 1949–50 there was a complete absence of any meaningful peace process through which a resolution of the dispute with the Arab states might have been pursued. So here also Israeli advocates of the diplomatic approach to security had little opportunity to prove its usefulness and little to show for their efforts.

During the first ten years Israel more or less accepted the fact that it had little ability to pursue diplomatic initiatives. In addition, when it came to ensuring minimum security, the IDF proved a far superior instrument than, say, the UN Security Council. The result was disillusionment with the very nature of the diplomatic process itself.

After the mid-1950s Israelis perceived themselves forced back upon the sole remaining option: a superior defense. Forty years later, a younger generation, although still without any proven better alternative, has come to realize that even—or especially—military superiority has definite political, social, and economic limitations. Fortunately, some Israeli leaders reached this conclusion even without the lessons provided by the 1973 and 1982 wars and explored other, more subtle, and more constructive means of persuasion by which the country could project its influence (however small) and its interests (however great) abroad.

ECONOMIC STATECRAFT

Some of Israel's finest diplomatic successes have been in the area of trade negotiation and economic relations, beginning with the West German reparations pact and continuing through the 1985 agreement with the United States establishing a free-trade area between the two countries. The importance for Israel of these international commercial ties cannot be overstated. In contrast, they have been terribly understated, perhaps because writers on Israeli foreign policy are not economists, perhaps because this kind of diplomacy has not brought Israel anything like economic independence. It then bears emphasizing that economic statecraft today is an essential part of the diplomatic art, and success is a matter of degree.

The central objective behind Israeli economic diplomacy is to improve the country's overall economic and trade position by compensating, through overseas links, for serious problems in the domestic economy and for the adverse effects of Arab economic warfare. From this general goal derive more specific aims. First, Israel constantly has lived beyond its means. Industrial expansion as well as the quality of life, or the standard of living, depend upon capital investment. Yet government development budgets and the gross domestic product, saddled with a huge defense burden, have never been able, by themselves, to generate such growth. Hence the encouragement of foreign capital and investment, including, in particular, direct aid, loans, and credits. Since 1953 the Bonn government, for example, has paid out more than $30 billion in reparations and restitution to Holocaust survivors, mainly in Israel. An even greater role is played most recently by U.S. economic aid, which stabilized toward the close of the eighties at $1.2 billion annually in outright grants, besides the $1.8 billion in military assistance. Two important additional sources of private capital are foreign tourism and the contributions by fellow Jews made through Israel Bonds and the United Jewish Appeal (UJA).

A second aim is providing assured sources of import and supply. Israel is lacking in just about every category of raw materials and strategic resources vital for industrialization and yet wishes to maintain a Western standard of living as well as economic growth. Hence the importance of guaranteeing three kinds of importation: (1) defense goods, now met primarily through the United States as primary source of supply; (2) energy supplies and raw materials, such as uncut diamonds, oil, coal, and steel, met through multiple sources of supply from Third World countries; (3) consumer products ranging from foodstuffs to electrical appliances and automobiles. Overseas success in this area has, of course, aggravated the country's twofold balance of payment and balance of trade problem, featuring, on the one hand, a consistently large foreign debt and, on the other, an excess of some 20 to 30 percent of imports over exports.

Seeking overseas markets for Israeli products thus becomes a third aim of economic statecraft. Although planners fully appreciate the need for Israel to export, fulfilling this assignment is left to economic affairs counselors in Israeli embassies abroad. Their task is not an easy one since success is both a function of Israel's competitiveness and the willingness of other countries to buy from Israel. Nevertheless, exports have been rising steadily (see Table 15). They increased, for example, from $5.5 billion in 1980 to $8.4 billion in 1987, jumping to $9.7 billion in 1988.

The leading export offerings currently include agricultural products, particularly citrus and flowers; polished diamonds; textiles and designer clothing; plus machinery, electronics, and transport, a large part (60 percent or more) of which are defense items. In terms of Israel's trading partners, Western Europe is the largest (see Figure 2).

Table 15. Total Exports by Region, 1987–88

Region	Export ($ million) 1987	1988
North America	2,848.5	3,091.3
Central America	43.8	29.6
South America	157.0	199.7
Europe	3,191.1	3,742.8
Asia	1,043.9	1,470.1
Africa	160.7	164.0
Oceania	89.2	118.8
Unclassified Countries	941.2	923.0
TOTAL	8,475.4	9,739.3

Source: Central Bureau of Statistics, *Foreign Trade Statistics Quarterly* 39, no. 3 (July–September 1988): 32–33, Table 10 and *Foreign Trade Statistics Quarterly* 39, 3 (October–December 1988): 32–33, Table 10.

Members of the European Economic Community accounted for 32 percent ($2.7 billion) of total exports in 1987. In second place and rising is the United States, to whom Israel sells over 25 percent of its products. Exports, particularly industrial exports, have been growing slowly but steadily. Such statistics in themselves suggest that economic diplomacy has made definite inroads.

Nevertheless, even in dealing with the developed and more favorably disposed countries of North America and Western Europe, Israeli commercial representatives continue to encounter formidable political as well as economic barriers: the Arab boycott and threatened sanctions against governments or corporations conducting business transactions with Israel, along with protectionist policies and high tariffs. Countering both types of restrictions and liberalizing trade therefore stand as a fourth pillar of economic statecraft. This bilateral negotiating process involves such agenda items as improving the terms of trade, lifting discriminatory protectionist measures by both sides, enforcing the principle of reciprocity, and stiffening resistance to Arab pressures.

All such commercial efforts through diplomatic means are informed by a common twofold strategy on the question of linkage between economics and politics. Israel sees an opening for promoting its trade offensive by gaining others' consent to a formula of separating the economic and political spheres. It suggests that both sides cooperate in the nonpolitical areas of commerce and culture while agreeing to discuss and possibly disagree on politically sensitive

Figure 2. Exports by Region (Percentage), 1987

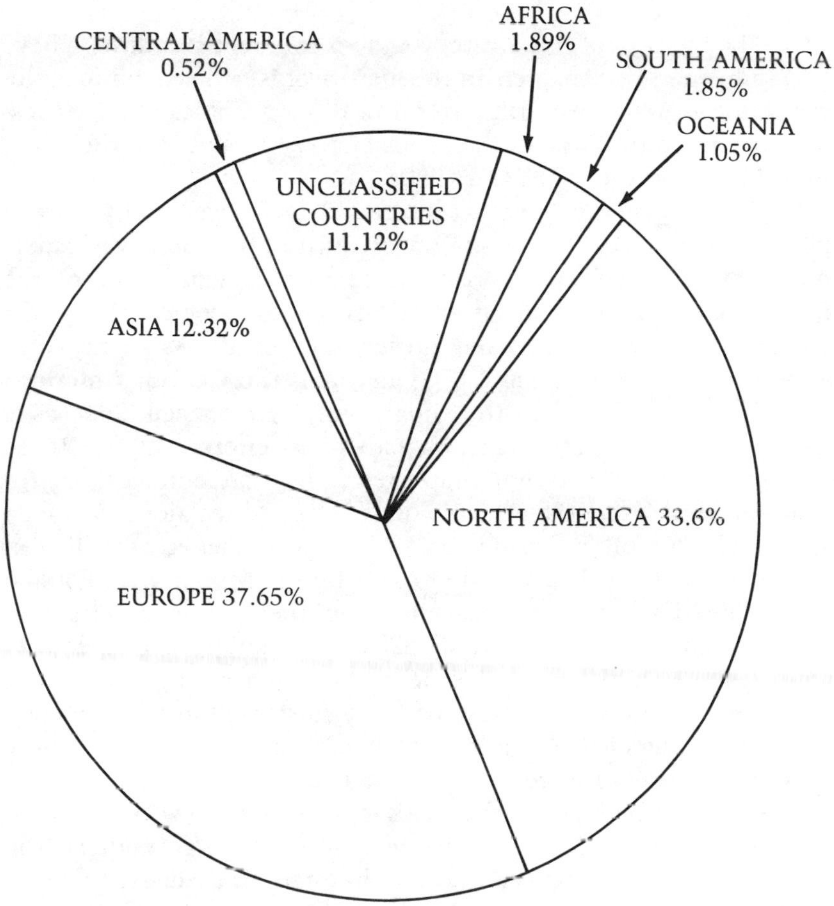

Source: Central Bureau of Statistics, *Foreign Trade Statistics Quarterly* 39, no. 3 (July–September 1988): 9–10.

issues. Yet at the same time, Israel cannot help but look one step beyond the purely trade considerations, hoping that establishing commercial relations will serve as a lever for advancing political interests as well.

The wisdom of this strategy and its inherent limitations have been proven in two chapters in the history of Israeli economic diplomacy and in relations with two quite different blocs of countries: toward the Third World in the 1950s and 1960s, and with the Common Market in the 1970s and 1980s.

Challenging the prevalent image of Israel as perenially slow in picking up on global trends and opportunities, the country's leaders made an early, correct assessment as to the significance of the independence movement among Afro-Asian peoples. They developed an early and extensive presence in Africa, Asia, and Latin America starting with Burma, Ghana, and the Central American republics. In 1957, after the Sinai campaign opened Eilat as a gateway to the east, Israel upgraded its efforts toward these emergent nations. Full diplomatic relations were entered into, for example, with more than thirty countries in Africa alone; between 1962 and 1968 official trade agreements were signed with fifteen sub-Saharan states. Israeli experts sent by the Ministry for Foreign Affairs provided technical assistance on the spot in hundreds of projects centering on housing construction, public works, tourist facilities, agricultural development, health services, and water resources planning. Over the years it hosted more than 90,000 technicians, medical personnel, teachers, and students from the developing areas for specialized seminars.

Progress in cementing these ties was arrested, however, after the 1967 war but especially in 1973 when no less than twenty-nine of the African countries befriended and aided by Israel proceeded to break off relations and to side with the Arab sponsors of anti-Israel UN resolutions.

Interestingly, despite this diplomatic setback, economic cooperation continued tacitly—an acknowledgment of the value of Israeli assistance. Moreover, in the 1980s Israel was in the process of returning to the Third World, but with a revised, more realistic objective. Retained is the desire to prove Israel a model for nation-building and economic modernization. Gone, however, are any pretenses of acquiring long-term influence or political benefits. The current rationale justifies such efforts strictly on the grounds of tangible economic rewards. The same applied at the close of the decade to efforts at building up trade contacts in Eastern Europe.

Certainly the potential for commercial gains is great and still largely untapped. Today Africa represents fifty-one states with 500 million people, a significant proportion of the world's natural resources, and a need for economic assistance unattached to political strings. At the same time, Israeli-African trade relations represents only about 2 percent of Israel's total trade balance.

Greater attention is also being shown in Jerusalem to the Far East, in particular to Japan and China, and to the prosperous, industrializing countries in the Association of Southeast Asian Nations bloc. As Avraham Tamir, director-general of the Foreign Ministry, presented the case in 1988: "The Far East has two-thirds of the world's population and its emerging economic superpowers . . . if we don't change our perception, we will lose the future." At the end of the eighties, China in particular has been moving, albeit slowly, into greater open commercial relationships with Israel. One confirmed indicator of such prospects was the visit by the Foreign Ministry's deputy director-general for economic affairs, Yitzchak Minervi, to Beijing, which was disclosed in October 1988. The Chinese reportedly expressed a willingness to supply Israel with coal and oil, while the Israeli representative was said to have come with a list of some twenty proposals for helping China in such fields as farming, technology, medicine, industry, fishing, and energy, well beyond restricted defense aid.

Another part of Israel's economic future centers on Western Europe and the EEC, with its geographic proximity and 320 million sophisticated consumers. That Israel has any prospects for beneficial trade relations owes to diplomatic astuteness and perseverance going back at least thirty years. Israel was one of the first countries to grasp the full potential of the 1957 Treaty of Rome and its call for a common market. It was the third country (after the United States and Greece) to appoint an ambassador to the EEC and already in 1960 began to explore prospects for association.

The negotiations with the EEC have been long, tedious, and marked by slow progress in the face of institutional, economic, and political resistance on the part of the Common Market or its individual members. A few of the milestones include

1965: an agreement granting customs reductions to a few Israeli products far short of the preferential status requested by Israel.
1970: signing of a revised five-year pact extending preferential treatment to a list of Israeli industrial commodities; and
1975: associate status conferred on Israel and supplemented in

> 1977, providing for the lowering of all tariff barriers on Israeli manufacture imported into the EEC and similar phased reductions on Common Market imports into Israel through 1985.

Owing to this persistence, by the end of the 1980s the EEC played a major role in Israel's foreign trade.

The accomplishment is all the more impressive considering the political complications intruding at each stage of the Israel-EEC dialogue. One powerful disincentive since 1973 is heightened concern by the Western Europeans to guarantee the uninterrupted flow of oil from the Arab petroleum-producing countries. Objection to Israeli policies in the administered territories and on the Palestinian question are a further, related constraint. The Community's members did not even give the Camp David accords or the peace treaty with Egypt a warm reception, and in June 1980 the European Council issued the Venice Declaration calling for Palestinian self-determination, which the Israeli government promptly rejected.

That the close relationship with a uniting Europe still faced future strains was made apparent by another crisis in late 1987–early 1988. A new economic agreement had been negotiated and signed in 1986 but not ratified. Final approval of the three agricultural, trade, and financial protocols giving Israel greater access to the market was deferred by the European Parliament. As EEC representatives admitted, the delay was part of a political campaign to pressure Jerusalem to change its position on the future of the West Bank and Gaza; specifically, allowing Arab farmers to express their separateness by exporting farm produce independently rather than through the Israeli marketing boards. Israel, for its part, criticized this as unfair interference for political reasons rather than being a decision about the new accord on its commercial merits alone. Once Israel agreed to grant export permits expeditiously, the European Parliament ratified the trade protocols long sought by Israel on 12 October 1988 by a vote of 314 in favor, 25 against, and 19 abstentions. This at least opened the way for Israeli agriculture, industry, and tourism to prepare for the 1992 date set by the European Community to become one huge competitive market.

Economic statecraft, in short, is a double-edged policy instrument. It has worked exceedingly well in the "open bridges" policy with Jordan; far less well in normalizing relations with Egypt. Still, on balance, in its quest for four specific economic objectives—investment, import, export, and ease of access and commercial opportunity—this kind of diplomacy has proven one of the most advisable, constructive, and effective foreign policy tools in Israel's possession.

ARMS DIPLOMACY

If Israel clings to its tenuous political and military independence, part of this success can be traced to an intense, sustained program of foreign military assistance. For a people previously the object of ridicule and a symbol for powerlessness, the status of the Jewish state in the realm of international defense, security affairs, and the conventional arms trade is of far more than passing importance in the total picture of Israel among the nations.

In its isolation and defensiveness for the past two decades, Israel's sale of weapons technologies on a global scale is another of the few successful foreign policy techniques at the disposal of policy makers in Jerusalem. This leads us to the interesting proposition that through its ability to market defense products abroad at an annual rate of over $1 billion, Israel's political, commercial, and strategic influence exceeds its formal diplomatic influence and standing. Indeed, owing to the discretion and confidentiality governing all such supply relationships, Israel has, but is prevented from publicizing, ties with more states than have normal diplomatic relations with it.

The motives of necessity and opportunity prompting Israel to be so involved in security assistance are too complex to be analyzed in detail within this broader foreign policy study; elsewhere the author has reviewed the significance of arms exports for the country's defense and economy. Suffice to state here that the reasoning behind this policy is often misrepresented by outside critics and many Israeli outsiders because of their own ideological biases and for propaganda purposes. Arms diplomacy is hardly confined to Israel; over forty countries currently are reported to be engaged to varying degrees in weapons transfers. Nor is this diplomacy imprudent or a matter of caprice where Israel is concerned. Military aid has given Israel a modest yet sometimes critical influence with Third World countries and in entire regions where other standard instruments of foreign policy do not work so well. In a word, helping others meet their defense needs has proved to be a multipurpose technique for pursuing vital national interests.

The military-security argument is the centerpiece of Israeli arms export policy, serving at least four defense functions:

1. to strengthen the Israeli army's immediate as well as longer-range preparedness by extending local defense production

and reducing the unit cost of local items while reducing dependence on outside procurement or the threat of a supply cut-off;

2. to enhance Israeli deterrent capability in Arab eyes by projecting an image of strength and worldwide defense links;
3. to fit Israel into a broader Western strategic perspective; and
4. to demonstrate support for countries befriending Israel.

The latter two goals introduce the diplomatic argument into the economic-security calculus.

At this point any of seven or eight different foreign policy considerations are involved in Israel's search for international defense relationships. Briefly, these include the following. First, the acquisition of influence. Although the connection between weapons and influence is unclear even to superpowers and may only be transient, nevertheless the belief shared by Israeli policy makers is that weapons aid gives them a presence, such as in offering the opportunity to present Israel's position on various issues, including the Middle East conflict. Such a presence—"a foot in the door"—may actually be more important, and more attainable, than any pretenses at controlling other countries' politics. As a matter of fact, Israel's patent inability to dictate or to punish—recall the wave of unilateral decisions by Third World nations to sever diplomatic ties in 1973–74—becomes something of an advantage for arms customers suspicious of interference or dominance by the great power suppliers (see Table 16). A second consideration, reinforcing the first, is the use of arms not necessarily to gain influence for Israel so much as, at a minimum, to deny influence to Arab adversaries in those same client countries. This represents a form of preemptive diplomacy for Israel.

As noted, however, the Israeli arms export strategy goes beyond preemption. It seeks to establish a presence that can promote the third goal of military and commercial contacts. Attention is thus given to specific target groups in the recipient countries. These elites include government leaders, officials in charge of arms procurement contracts, professional military officers who in many of these countries already are, or are likely to be, in positions of power, and last but not least, the local business community. Concentration on the latter group reflects the hope that credibility in the initial role of military supplier might eventually lead to additional avenues for political and economic cooperation. Such would seem to be the case with the People's Republic of China in the 1980s and would be fully consistent with the pattern of relationships among Israel, Iran, and South Africa built up during the previous decade. Probably the earliest

Table 16. A Partial List of Military Aid Recipients (1970–90)

North America
- Canada
- United States

Central America
- Costa Rica
- Dominican Republic
- El Salvador
- Guatemala
- Haiti
- Honduras
- Mexico
- Nicaragua
- Panama

South America
- Argentina
- Bolivia
- Brazil
- Chile
- Colombia
- Ecuador
- Paraguay
- Peru
- Venezuela

Europe
- Belgium
- Denmark
- Federal Republic of Germany
- Finland
- Greece
- Ireland
- Italy
- Portugal
- Spain
- Switzerland

Africa
- Cameroon
- Ciskei
- Ethiopia
- Ghana
- Kenya
- Liberia
- Morocco
- Nigeria
- South Africa
- Swaziland
- Tanzania
- Uganda
- Zaire
- Zimbabwe

Asia
- Australia
- Fiji
- Indonesia
- Malaysia
- New Zealand
- Papua–New Guinea
- People's Republic of China
- Philippines
- Singapore
- Sri Lanka
- Taiwan
- Thailand

Middle East
- Iran

Source: Aaron S. Klieman, *Israel's Global Reach: Arms Sales as Diplomacy* (McLean, VA: Pergamon-Brassey's, 1985), pp. 135, 137, 140, 142; International news service reports and military trade journals.

example of the flag and trade following, instead of preceding, arms is that of West Germany. In 1959 it was disclosed that the Federal Republic had for some time been buying Uzi submachine guns as well as other light weapons made in Israel. Formal relations between the two countries were established only in 1965.

A fourth function of arms exports is bringing about closer alignment with the West in general and with the United States in particular. Weapons support for pro-Western Third World regimes is part of what Israeli and American representatives diplomatically allude to when portraying Israel as a strategic asset—a fact better known to officials in the West from classified documents than to their publics at large, or, for that matter, to the average Israeli. Preventing small and vulnerable countries from falling prey to destabilization is a constant concern; any Israeli success in enhancing the ability of those governments to cope with internal or external threats must be regarded as promoting this larger community of interests. Israel's own foreign military aid program thus falls within the broader context of an effective security framework for the free world, under American leadership, and answers Washington's call for greater contributions from allied and friendly countries able to render various forms of assistance.

Israel's own special agenda on military aid contains a unique Jewish factor. A survey of its arms sales practices over the years discloses a fairly strong correspondence between those countries with a Jewish presence, mostly in the non-Western world, and their status as recipients of defense equipment or advice from Israel. A partial list includes such diverse countries as Argentina, Brazil, Chile, Ethiopia, Guatemala, Iran, Mexico, South Africa, and even Morocco. Here the purpose is to maintain free and continuous contact with every one of these Jewish communities, to facilitate their movement to Israel, and to guarantee their religious and cultural rights as Jews. Friendly military support, although imperfect and morally problematic, most certainly represents one such vital opening.

Next in the pro-arms calculus is the prestige value of defense exports. Even though being associated with the international traffic in arms has its uncomfortable moments, drawing exaggerated prominence and subjecting Israeli policies to moral criticism, policy makers nevertheless insist there are symbolic as well as material benefits. For a small state like Israel, power is often a function of reputation, of how others perceive it. In today's world the marketability of Israel's armaments is the equivalent of showing the flag. In this sense, defense assistance is a signal to enemies and to friendly countries alike of Israeli strength and resolve, suggesting Israel has more than moral support to offer those on good terms with it. Paradoxically, judging from the current interest in Israeli arms for sale and its defense assistance worldwide, Israel may be encircled in the Middle East and still capable of demonstrating a global reach.

A seventh and final utility derived from arms diplomacy is that it offers Jerusalem a greater degree of latitude politically. Not complete independence (which country is genuinely sovereign in a world of interdependence?), but an essential margin for diplomatic maneuver. Staking out a course of its own serves to counter the negative side of close association with the United States, where Israel is susceptible to overreliance. For Israel, with its options so limited to begin with, pragmatism argues for exploiting any opportunity to pursue independence in foreign affairs. And if Israel clings doggedly to the status of an independent-minded, security-conscious state, some of the credit must be attributed to the defense export drive—perhaps the best response Israel has yet given to those who would have it completely isolated in world affairs.

BACKSTAGE DIPLOMACY

Arms sales have been a technique used by Israel for opening doors. Secret diplomatic contacts have gotten Israel into still other countries via the back door. So much so that it has become one of the world's foremost practitioners of quiet diplomacy. This statecraft in the dark, in turn, is really the bright side of Israel's anti-exclusionist foreign relations.

What makes Israel of all countries so intimately involved in such unconventional diplomacy in a century dedicated to the ideal of "open covenants, openly arrived at"? The foundations for diplomatic secrecy where Israel is concerned owe to the following:

- walls of Arab rejectionism that pose an abnormal situation for Israel;
- vital national interests that must be safeguarded, with physical security acting as the prism through which all other policies and issues, domestic or foreign, are filtered; and
- closure to Israel of regular diplomatic channels usually open to sovereign states, thereby inhibiting the free exercise of statecraft.

These obstacles have been compensated for, however, by evidence that otherwise indisposed or even openly hostile world leaders and governments (some of them Arab and Muslim) might still be prepared to engage Israel in a businesslike manner, on a quid pro quo basis, on condition that the relationship be maintained with absolute discretion on both sides. Only by seizing this opportunity and acceding to these stipulations has the Jewish state avoided the fate of "a nation that dwelleth alone."

The formula for secret diplomacy has worked exceptionally well for Israel over the years, an outstanding instance being the covert Israeli-French connection initiated in 1953. Gradually deepening by 1956 into a secret military pact, the Paris–Tel Aviv axis fulfilled two of Israel's most pressing needs: it met immediate defense requirements, and it prevented Israel's political isolation. This harmony of interests did not endure beyond the 1967 crisis. Still, in Israel's diplomatic perspective fourteen years are not an insignificant block of time.

Schematically, behind-the-scenes efforts have proven invaluable when it comes to administering foreign policy on four of Israel's most sensitive national concerns. In fact it would be hard to imagine where the security of the state would be, as well as its trade position, political contacts, and links to world Jewry, were it not for back-channeling. Quiet diplomacy plays a role in each of the following: military procurement (less so in recent years when America has sought openly to meet Israel's military requirements); fulfilling overseas defense contracts and arms transfers; intelligence operations; importation of strategic minerals and energy supplies; and commercial transactions premised on anonymity for the contracting party. There have been innumerable political contacts—with Arab representatives, with non-Arab states, and with countries further afield in both the Soviet bloc and the Afro-Asian nonaligned bloc—that came about only because conditions of strictest confidentiality were respected by Israel. Lastly, secrecy has made possible Israel's upholding its special Jewish agenda: facilitating immigration, intervening to protect Jewish hostage communities like that of the Soviet Union, and most characteristically, negotiating hostage releases involving Jews and prisoner-of-war exchanges to gain the release of captured Israeli military personnel held by Arabs.

The tacit relationship maintained for many years with prerevolutionary Iran in the era of the shah is the best single illustration of the fruits of quiet diplomacy. This example happens to have involved all four concerns: security, trade, political contacts, and keeping a line open to Persian Jewry. Teheran shared Jerusalem's preoccupation with militant Arab unity, supplied Israel with oil, coordinated efforts in secret meetings with Israeli leaders at the highest levels, and pursued an enlightened policy toward the Jews of Iran. That as strategic and important a relationship as that between Iran and Israel functioned almost exclusively via back channels for so long, from the 1960s until the end of the seventies, tells a great deal about the central role of quiet diplomacy.

This strategic secret bilateral relationship with Iran facilitated, in turn, the so-called "periphery policy" of the late fifties in which Israel successfully interwove a network of discreet ties with Ankara and Addis Ababa as well, which derived from shared regional concerns. In another example, in the 1960s Spain's refusal to recognize Israel did not prevent high officials in the Franco regime from cooperating with the Mossad in secretly transferring 76,000 North African Jews to Israel by way of Spain.

The workings of back-channel diplomacy, and its results for Israel's struggle, are a story in themselves. Merely to provide the readers an inkling of the importance attached by Israeli leaders to keeping open as many lines and doors and options as possible, we can recall what was probably the most intense month of secret statecraft in Israeli history: from mid-August to mid-September 1977. In memoirs published shortly before his death, the late Foreign Minister Moshe Dayan relates how during those hectic yet heady weeks of activity he carried out no less than four secret missions: to New Delhi to press (unsuccessfully) for upgrading relations; to Teheran for consultations with the shah; to London for a meeting with King Hussein of Jordan; and to Morocco where King Hassan was instrumental in setting up the Dayan-Tuhami (deputy Egyptian premier) meeting of 16 September that would set in motion the historic journey by President Sadat to Jerusalem.

Nor has the pace or the diversity of Israeli quiet diplomacy abated in more recent years, judging from press reports and unauthorized leaks. Some of the confirmed items:

- the secret airlift of some 15,000 "Beta Israel" Jews of Ethiopia to Israel with the complicity of officials in Sudan and Ethiopia—neither having relations with Israel!—until prematurely disclosed in January 1985 while the operation was in progress;
- confirmation by Jerusalem in 1986 that Israeli personnel had been helping Cameroon rebuild its security forces since 1984, two years prior to renewal of diplomatic ties;
- behind-the-scenes efforts by Israel were rewarded in January 1986 when Spain announced full diplomatic recognition;
- mounting evidence in the late 1980s of a tacit relationship between Israel and the People's Republic of China (PRC) in

such fields as countertrade, technical, and military assistance and agricultural programs;

- comments by the Austrian foreign minister in late 1987 to the effect that more than five thousand Iranian Jews had passed through Austria from Pakistan on route to Israel or the United States with the consent of the Khomeini regime—this after the Irangate probe had highlighted Israel's retaining important private contacts in Iran even after the shah's fall from power;
- secret preparations leading to a formal visit, revealed at the last minute, by Foreign Minister Peres to Budapest in May 1988 as part of delicate moves toward improving relations with Eastern Europe;
- a secret meeting, all but confirmed, between Peres and King Hussein in London on 11 April 1987 at which principles were worked out for the convening of an international peace conference and, no less interesting, the admission by a Jordanian Foreign Ministry official in February 1988 that a Shamir-Hussein meeting had been canceled at the last moment due to a press leak; and
- disclosure in June 1988 of authorization by Premier Shamir for an Israeli Arab, Dr. Ahmad Tibi, to meet privately with PLO officials in Tunis on the sensitive humanitarian quest for three Israeli soldiers missing in action since 1982—this despite a long-standing official ban against either contacts or negotiation with representatives of the Palestine Liberation Organization.

These examples may suffice in conveying the real flavor of Israel's public and also not-so-public diplomatic history over four decades.

Backstage diplomacy, involving many unsung heroes, has been instrumental in preventing setbacks, breaking up hostile coalitions, and deterring diplomatic as well as military threats. It has been no less crucial for furthering the four positive goals dealt with here. Yet quiet statecraft and its emphasis in this chapter as a principal diplomatic instrument take on a larger function in the debate over the success or failure of Israeli foreign policy. Standard critiques all rest on the public record and at that level seem both cogent and persuasive. Let it be noted, however, that in the case of Israel, open, formal diplomatic ties are little more than the tip of the iceberg. Were critics to have the complete files at their disposal, there is no question Israel's foreign affairs would appear in an entirely different light. Then Israeli diplomacy would reflect a good deal more subtlety, initiative, and imaginativeness than it is usually given credit for. Only by reference to the less conventional and the less conspicuous tools for administering foreign policy goals set by Jerusalem do students and scholars stand any chance of compiling a more complete picture of Israel in the international community.

THE JEWISH CONNECTION

As discreet and undocumented as back-channeling may be, the Jewish element is perhaps the most elusive aspect of Israel's entire external relations. It is impossible to define in exact terms the special bond existing between the people of Israel and the rest of world Jewry in this century of the Holocaust and Zion's rebirth. Nevertheless, the Diaspora represents both a commitment *by* Israel and a resource—a strategic reserve—*for* Israel and therefore merits inclusion in the discussion of the instruments used in implementing foreign policy (see Table 17).

For one thing, the relationship of Jews to Israel may not be so firm. Yet in international politics perception often becomes as important as reality, if not more so. What matters in the end in practical terms is that many foreign governments are absolutely convinced Israel commands the support of the Jewish world, therefore making it prudent for them to be on good terms with the Jewish state. In the eyes of Third World leaders, from Morocco's King Hassan to Zaire's President Mobutu, for example, Israel is seen as a key to improving their own standing in the United States with the media, Congress, and the White House. The assumption, which diplomats in Jerusalem have no reason to refute, is that by appearing sympathetic toward Israel these countries will have better prospects for gaining an appreciative audience in Washington through the "Jewish lobby" for their own aid requests. Thus, during a visit to the States in September 1988, then Foreign Minister Peres met with a group of American Jewish businessmen and asked them to promote Hungary's trade links with the United States. The meeting was at the Hungarians' request, took place with the knowledge of the State Department, and came as part of attempts by Budapest to upgrade ties with Israel. These assumptions regarding Israel's relationship with the world's Jews underscore the reciprocal, two-way nature of the Israel-Diaspora support system. Zionism pledged to use Israeli sovereignty on behalf of Jews in distress—the post-Holocaust vow of "Never again!" The Jewish state has held itself responsible for the fate of helpless Jewish communities. Witness its intervention and quiet diplomacy on behalf of the captive Jews in Syria, Persian Jewry, the "Beta Israel" villages

Table 17. The Jewish Diaspora (Estimated Jewish Population Distribution, 1986)

Country	Jewish Population	Country	Jewish Population
NORTH AMERICA		EUROPE (continued)	
Canada	310,000	Spain	12,000
United States	5,700,000	Sweden	15,000
		Switzerland	19,000
CENTRAL AMERICA		Turkey	20,000
Bahamas	300	U.S.S.R.	1,515,000
Costa Rica	2,000	Yugoslavia	4,800
Cuba	700		
Dominican Republic	100	ASIA	
Guatemala	800	Hong Kong	1,000
Jamaica	300	India	4,200
Mexico	35,000	Iran	22,000
Netherlands Antilles	400	Iraq	200
Panama	3,800	Japan	1,000
Puerto Rico	1,500	Lebanon	100
Virgin Islands	300	Philippines	100
Other	300	Singapore	300
		Syria	4,000
SOUTH AMERICA		Thailand	300
Argentina	224,000	Yemen	1,000
Bolivia	600	Other	300
Brazil	100,000		
Chile	17,000	AFRICA	
Colombia	6,500	Egypt	200
Ecuador	1,000	Ethiopia	12,000
Paraguay	900	Kenya	100
Peru	4,000	Morocco	12,000
Suriname	200	South Africa	115,000
Uruguay	25,000	Tunisia	3,000
Venezuela	20,000	Zaire	400
		Zambia	300
EUROPE		Zimbabwe	1,200
Austria	6,400	Other	1,000
Belgium	32,000		
Bulgaria	3,200	OCEANIA	
Czechoslovakia	8,200	Australia	77,000
Denmark	6,600	New Zealand	4,000
Finland	1,200	Other	100
France	530,000		
Germany, East	500	DIASPORA	9,401,400
Germany, West	32,700	ISRAEL	3,562,500
Gibraltar	600		
Great Britain	326,000		
Greece	5,000	GRAND TOTAL	12,963,900
Hungary	60,000		
Ireland	2,000		
Italy	31,800		
Luxembourg	700		
Netherlands	26,000		
Norway	1,000		
Poland	4,400		
Portugal	300		
Romania	21,500		

Source: The American Jewish Year Book, 1988 (New York: The American Jewish Committee, 1988) pp. 420, 422, 424, 425.

in Ethiopia, Jews behind the iron curtain. In return, Israeli leaders felt they had every right to expect the loyalty and unflinching support of Jews in the Diaspora in making Israel strong, secure, and economically sound. Ben-Gurion argued this thesis in typically forceful style when he stated: "The State was created, as I understand it, for and by the whole Jewish people. But henceforth, the future of the Jewish people depends on the existence, growth, and consolidation of the State."

This Israel-centric perspective has endured for more than three decades, resulting in, on the whole, a mutually beneficial partnership that, at the start of this decade, finds both Israel and at least the major concentrations of Jews in the West strengthened and more confident in facing the future. Nevertheless, certain tensions centering on respective duties and obligations remain unresolved. Ben-Gurion's original formulation of the relationship would not gain a ringing endorsement of late from world Jewish leaders because it implies an almost one-sided adherence to the Jewish agenda set forth by Israeli leaders.

The Israel-Diaspora dialogue now takes place in a changing environment. Some Jewish observers have gone even further than deriding Israeli leaders for insensitivity to the needs of the Jewish world or charging them with paying mere lip service to their Jewish commitment. Here and there a few voices have been heard against Israeli arrogance to the point of meddling, gross interference, and manipulation in Diaspora communal affairs. Less extreme and closer to the truth is the view suggesting that while the lot of Jewish communities outside Israel is not the number one determinant in Israel's foreign policy calculus, neither does it mean Israel is free to formulate its policy like other countries strictly on the basis of its own *raison d'état*. Professor Shlomo Avineri, a former director-general of the Foreign Ministry in the mid-seventies, feels

> that Israel cannot remain alien to the concerns of Jewish minorities the world over . . . has entangled Israel in many complex relationships; and since Jews suffer, by definition, not in open and liberal societies, but in totalitarian and authoritarian ones, it follows that Israel sometimes feels itself a hostage of some of the nastiest regimes that happen to populate the globe.

Some of which he then goes on to name: the Soviet Union, South Africa, the Argentinian military junta, Iran, and Ethiopia.

Admittedly there have been situations where sensitivity for the welfare of local Jews constrained Jerusalem. This lesson was brought home perhaps most forcefully in 1961, when Israel took an unequivocal and principled stand in voting on behalf of a UN resolution condemning apartheid in South Africa, to which Pretoria promptly responded by revoking Israeli exemption from commodity and transfer restrictions—an avenue used by the Jews of South Africa to liquidate business assets and transfer money out of the country. Five years of quiet diplomacy were needed before the preferential status was reinstated and political fences mended.

On the other hand, the Jewish world often has been an asset for Israel, supporting it out of a strong identification with the state and its people. This backing can take any of several forms. First, in times of previous crisis and war, Jewish individuals and entire communities rallied around Israel. This solidarity stretched all the way from increased fund-raising to political demonstrations, tourism, and volunteering personal services, as Jewish musicians, doctors, and nurses did in 1967 and again in 1973. Just after the Six-Day War, Prime Minister Eshkol convened an economic conference for world Jewry. In March 1989 the government sponsored a "Conference on Jewish Solidarity with Israel," scheduled for the eve of Premier Shamir's visit to Washington to meet with President Bush and members of the new administration. Invitations sent to over one thousand participants from sixty communities and organizations explained that, in view of recent developments in the Middle East, "there is an urgent need to strengthen the relationship of solidarity between Israel and all Jews around the world." The intent was more explicit yet: "The government of Israel expects the entire Jewish people to stand at Israel's side in its quest for peace, security, and prosperity."

Second, on an ongoing basis the Jewish Agency for Israel provides an institutional umbrella, facilitating communication and contact. Taken solely for the purposes of illustrating the network of possible Israel-Diaspora links, consider the schedule maintained by the agency's chairman, Simcha Dinitz, during 1988, his first year in office. The itinerary of the former ambassador to Washington included

January • New York, to participate in a Jewish Agency conference and World Zionist Congress meeting

March • Zurich, for the Keren Hayesod conference
• England, for a Zionist Federation meeting

April • Poland, a "march for life" demonstration at Holocaust sites

- South America, visiting Jewish communities in Brazil, Uruguay, and Venezuela

July
- Bucharest, to represent world Jewry at local synagogue events and for meetings with Romanian government officials
- Hungary, where he met with the Hungarian foreign minister
- New York, for a series of working meetings on agency business

August
- New York, for discussions on the Soviet Jewish question and further consultation with U.S. Jewish leaders
- Yugoslavia, to a rally and conference of Jewish student bodies in Europe, also expanded to permit talks with government officials

September
- Zurich and Basel as a follow-up to the earlier Keren Hayesod conference

October
- again, New York, to attend the World Jewish Congress (WJC)
- Mexico, on behalf of Keren Hayesod and to address a conference of the Zionist Federations of Latin America

November
- Moscow, accompanying two leaders of the WJC on the first official visit to the USSR for meetings with Soviet officials as well as with Jews awaiting permission to leave for Israel
- once more New York, this visit prompted by a UJA conference, followed by the annual conference of Jewish Federations held in New Orleans
- Zurich, to speak before a gathering of the European Zionist conference
- Helsinki, for the Israel-Finland Friendship League and to visit the local Jewish community

December
- the United States, to carry out an extended cross-country lecture tour before local Jewish federations in the major cities, during which he also

> managed to attend the conference of American Zionist Federations.

All told, the Jewish Agency chairman undertook some seventeen trips around the globe as an unofficial ambassador to the Diaspora, strengthening cooperation among diverse Jewish organizations, providing a means of communication between far-flung Jewish communities, and bringing the message of Israel.

Under the Jewish Agency, Israelis and non-Israelis, committed Zionists and non-Zionists, religious and secular Jews, have worked together on such consensual issues as immigration absorption, agricultural and settlement policy, strengthening Jewish youth education in Israel and abroad, and financing urban renewal as well as economic enterprises. This is a major expression of the support system mentioned earlier; world Jewry constitutes Israel's hinterland and security-in-depth, so to speak.

Third, and meriting separate mention, is the U.S. Jewish community, which has been singularly committed and active on behalf of Israel and Israeli causes. Showing exceptional understanding for how the U.S. political system works, Jewish leaders and major organizations in the United States on more than one occasion have proven their political acumen and organizational skill in mobilizing the Jewish rank-and-file; in arousing American public opinion by an effective media effort; in building a wider base of political support by going beyond the Jewish community itself; in gaining an appreciative ear among U.S. congressmen through professional lobbying; and in carrying Israel's case to successive presidents and administrations. The danger in this success is not so much the danger of a backlash, although the possibility exists, but in that Israeli statesmen find it convenient sometimes to leave what Professor Steven Spiegel (University of California-Los Angeles) has called the "other" Arab-Israeli conflict—the struggle to shape America's Middle East policy—to American Jewish experts and lobbyists instead of accepting direct responsibility for promoting U.S.-Israeli relations. At the forefront of this effort in Washington is the American-Israel Public Affairs Committee (AIPAC), with a membership of over 50,000, a staff of some 80 professionals, a budget of more than $8 million, and contacts in every congressional district.

Notice that the above approaches share efforts at demonstrating the extent of mass Jewish support for Israel by mobilizing large numbers of Jews and perhaps entire communities. The Conference of Major American Jewish Organizations is but one expression of this effort by Jerusalem to work at the communal level and through Jewish establishment leaders. Israeli emissaries strive to maintain close contact and an ongoing dialogue with myriad and diverse groups representing American and world Jewry, some of the best known and active of which are the United Jewish Appeal (UJA) Federation, the American Jewish Committee, the American Jewish Congress, the Council of Jewish Federations, Hadassah, the Anti-Defamation League, B'nai Brith, the Synagogue Council of America, and the America-Israel Cultural Foundation. In addition, the worldwide Israel Bonds organization, headed in 1989 by former Israeli ambassador to the United States Dr. Meir Rosenne, had since 1951 raised $9 billion for economic projects through the sale of investment bonds.

The list of such voluntary educational and philanthropic agencies is long and impressive, representing millions of concerned and committed Jews. Israeli speakers appear at annual conferences held by such bodies, while a stream of study groups and special missions are sponsored to visit Israel firsthand and to be exposed to Israeli viewpoints in meetings with Israeli political figures and academics. This two-way stream has been outstandingly successful in forging a bond between the two vibrant communities in the United States and in Israel.

Seeking the assistance of Diaspora Jewry can also work no less effectively at a completely different level when individuals volunteer their personal services on behalf of Israel and Jewish-related causes. In doing so they bring to bear their expertise and political or professional contacts with both home governments and foreign countries. Witness the close involvement of the U.S. industrialist Armand Hammer in gaining the release of Ida Nudel from the Soviet authorities and bringing her to Israel.

Cooperation at this level may involve nothing more than providing important local contacts that ease the way for Israeli businesspeople or official representatives arriving into an otherwise unfamiliar cultural setting. A still more invaluable service finds Jewish leaders and public figures acting as special emissaries. One person who comes to mind is the late president of the World Jewish Congress, Dr. Nahum Goldmann. Despite his well-known differences with Ben-Gurion and other Israeli leaders, they were able to enlist his help in the 1950s and 1960s. Goldmann was involved in a number of delicate missions to which official Israeli government sanction could not be given. Three of the most notable were conducting initial reparations talks with West German officials, a dialogue with Tunisia's moderate President Bourguiba, and unfruitful attempts at arranging a meeting with the Egyptian strongman leader,

President Nasser, as one way of starting an Arab-Israeli negotiating process.

This pattern of discreet parallel initiatives on behalf of convergent Israel-Diaspora Jewish interests and concerns has been honored by Dr. Goldmann's successors as well as other world Jewish dignitaries. To cite merely one example, WJC President Edgar Bronfman has used his international contacts and travels to raise the anomalous absence of formal diplomatic and commercial ties with Israel with government leaders from Eastern Europe to India and China. For instance, in July 1985 Bronfman paid a visit to the USSR, carrying with him a personal letter from Prime Minister Peres to General Secretary Gorbachev that recalled the historical debt of the Jewish people to the Soviet Union, expressed the desire for a better mutual understanding in the future, and welcomed "an opportunity for constructive dialogue with you." Here, too, the record of Jewish "good offices" is as fascinating and full of potential, and as relevant for Israeli foreign affairs, as it is inaccessible.

There is the ever-present and too real danger certainly that Jewish organizational leaders could pursue a separate, independent course due to divergent assessments over a particular issue or how it might best be pursued. This potential for divisiveness and friction in the Jewish connection already has been exposed on at least several occasions, with each side resentful at what it saw as being used by the other and as being taken for granted.

The entire Pollard affair, which was most unfortunate from every standpoint (Israeli decision-making procedures, U.S.-Israeli intergovernmental consultation), will have been viewed in the long run as a setback in American Jewish confidence in Israeli judgment. The dramatic change in American policy toward the standing of the PLO late in 1988 was another such instance. American Jewish representatives were inclined to accept administration assessments of PLO moderation and renewed their call for new peace proposals by Jerusalem in meeting the challenge. Binyamin Netanyahu, deputy foreign minister in the new NUG, complained to many of these representatives in a closed-door meeting and frank exchange in January 1989 about their weak and ineffective response. He expressed concern about the Jewish community's apparent confusion, embarrassment, and lack of self-confidence and called for rallying forces in support of Israel's positions.

These strains notwithstanding, the fundamental Jewish connection still held tight, providing those responsible for carrying out Israeli foreign policy goals and operative decisions with yet another unorthodox but invaluable policy implementation tool.

Economic statecraft, arms diplomacy, back-channel diplomacy, the Jewish connection: each demands patience and perseverance. Likewise, each is not usually thought of in conventional diplomatic terms. And yet each, separately and jointly, has contributed meaningfully to keeping Israel viable.

PART THREE

ISRAEL'S DIPLOMATIC MAP

What other European or Third World "second tier" country of comparable position or size comes readily to mind as Israel's peer in the intensity and also the diversity of its international relations? The question is not intended to be leading, or self-serving. Rather it is meant to make a sobering point about the compulsions motivating Israel and Israeli foreign policy. If in fact Israel is unrivaled, it is also because few countries are so dependent upon external forces or as compulsive, assigning such importance to having the greatest possible number of overseas affiliations.

Citizens of Israel still view Jewish sovereignty as precarious. Needing to be convinced of permanence, they are thus forever seeking fresh confirmation of the country's acceptability abroad. Each state visit to Israel by a foreign leader, every new scientific, cultural, or trade pact, any upgrading of diplomatic or commercial ties is eagerly seized upon and usually blown out of proportion as proof that Israel at forty is indeed a geopolitical reality, a going concern.

During the 1988 Seoul Olympics, for example,

the Israeli media had no Israeli medalists to dote on. A substitute was found in the person of Foreign Minister Peres. In lavishing attention on his activities at the opening session of the UN General Assembly, readers were provided with a daily tally sheet of official, semi-official, and unofficial meetings held with other heads of delegation. What made it a virtuoso performance were Peres's talks with representatives from countries like China, Czechoslovakia, and Ethiopia that were still estranged from Israel and without formal links to Jerusalem.

In this atmosphere of combined anxiety and expectancy, each and every one of Israel's bilateral relationships is not only important but interesting and distinctive as well. From Argentina to Zaire, each set of ties has its own special history and problems, just as each probably offers some insight into the larger style and conduct of Israeli statecraft. A country-by-country survey, however, would run counter to a central theme of this section, which is the highly selective nature of Israeli foreign policy and how concentrated is Israel's diplomatic map.

The plain fact is that not all of the relationships entered into by Israel are of equivalent weight. The country lacks the budget, the bureaucratic slots, and the depth of expertise to pursue every set of ties with the same priority and urgency. Clearly, some determination has had to be made by Jerusalem concerning which states are more crucial than others and must be given greater attention.

Countries on the scale of Costa Rica, Fiji, or Malawi cannot hold the key to Israel's fulfillment of its maximum national interests. That they do nevertheless receive close attention merely reconfirms the point made earlier about Israel's desire not to lose friendly nations however small. Still, with all due respect, such countries are unlikely to determine whether the Jewish state continues to be an active, participating member of the world community and at what level. Only a handful of countries truly has this capacity whether, like France and Iran in earlier years or West Germany and Egypt at present, because of their contribution to Israeli development and security or, like China and Japan, for their potential.

The following section takes this reductionist view a step further. It argues that Israel's diplomatic preoccupation is narrower still. From the dozen or even handful of genuinely pivotal countries, the list in recent years comes down to really two vital relationships: the United States in terms of the global and superpower arena and, in the context of Middle East and Palestinian affairs, the Hashemite Kingdom of Jordan.

As we have stressed throughout, peace and—of necessity—immediate security are the overriding criteria underscoring all government policy. This line of reasoning extends also to targeting countries important to Israel politically, militarily, and diplomatically. Again, in the most immediate sense, security becomes the prism through which the world is addressed, international developments filtered, and individual country assessments formed. The average Israeli clings pretty much to a bifurcated image of the external environment, divided into the adjacent Arab region and the rest of the world. So, too, official Jerusalem professes to see Israel's security as a function of the two great political contests of our time: the Soviet-American worldwide rivalry and the inter-Arab power struggle dominating the Middle East and Islamic subsystems.

To stay afloat in this sea of local and international change, Israeli policy has tilted perceptibly in each of these distinct yet interrelated political struggles. It is fair to say the nation and its leaders have long since chosen sides. Globally, Israel is firmly positioned in the Western camp, whereas, regionally, it prefers conservative, moderate Arab regimes against Muslim fundamentalists, Arab radicals, and Palestinian irridentists.

More specific still: in the eyes of Israeli political and military strategists it is really the United States and Jordan that have stood at the epicenter of the respective power alignments. Both countries have also been held to be indispensable, whether directly or indirectly, for vouchsafing Israel's own national security. "How goes Washington and Amman, so goes Jerusalem" may be as good a shorthand definition as any of Israel's constricted map of the world. The rest, in keeping with the Talmudic saying, is merely commentary.

Improved relations with the United States of America exemplify the one-great-power doctrine that is a carryover from the Zionist era. Jordan is the Middle Eastern equivalent: a one-Arab-power doctrine. Each has provided Israel with a "minimum winning coalition," especially after 1967, in its global and regional policies.

Were the American commitment toward Israel to be withdrawn for any reason, or should Jordan River stability in force since 1970–71 suddenly be undermined along Israel's long and vulnerable eastern frontier, the implications would be negative and serious in the extreme. Either scenario would rock Israeli foreign policy to its very foundations. It would challenge deep-seated beliefs about American friendship and Jordanian peaceful coexistence while upsetting traditional policy premises in Jerusalem and, in particular, the tendency to take for granted steadfast opposition by both the United States and Jordan to an independent Palestinian state. Moreover, instead of this concern being purely theoretical, in Israel's forty-second year of statehood there were indications that policies in Amman as well as in post-Reagan Washington could be undergoing slow yet meaningful change prejudicial to Israel.

It is only appropriate therefore that the following two chapters be devoted to a closer look at, first, the Israeli-American relationship and, then, at the less appreciated Israeli-Jordanian relationship. In the author's opinion, these are the only two sets of ties that qualify as "strategic" and "special." For this same reason they are the ones where Israel is also most vulnerable. Neither the United States nor Jordan can be taken for granted as a permanent, unshakable ally.

CHAPTER 8

ISRAEL AND THE SUPERPOWERS

Please tell the Israeli government and the people of Israel that there is a lot of goodwill and friendship in the Soviet Union toward Israel.

–Mikhail Gorbachev, 1988

. . . as close a friendship as can exist between two sovereign nations.

–former U.S. ambassador to Israel, Thomas Pickering, 1988

That the dominant Soviet-American contest impinges on Jerusalem, denying it complete freedom, hardly qualifies Israel as exceptional. Large or small, all nations were forced to operate since 1946 within this cold war environment. Where Israel does stand out, though, is in the profound impact the superpowers have had on its foreign policy.

The global rivalry between Moscow and Washington can be argued to have worked to Israel's advantage by elevating an otherwise peripheral eastern Mediterranean country into a strategic asset for the United States and the West. But with this possible exception the U.S.-USSR confrontation for the most part has been a source for apprehension among Israeli policy makers, acting as a diplomatic restraining wall. The superpowers have armed the Arabs, for example, and thus prolonged the Middle East conflict. Another source of consternation is the way bipolarity in the past has frustrated Israeli hopes for normalizing relations with both East and West.

BETWEEN MOSCOW AND WASHINGTON

Other Third World nations have been good at cold war neutralism, which consists of knowing how to play off one side against the other in order to survive and, if particularly astute or lucky, perhaps even to enhance one's own bargaining position and leverage with both camps. India comes immediately to mind as an excellent case in point. Israel, by way of contrast, has fared rather poorly in this strategy of nonalignment. But not for lack of trying, especially at the very beginning. Ben-Gurion's pragmatism, as we have seen, led Israel at first to steer the middle course between Moscow and Washington. His efforts were stillborn, however. Indeed, when we recall the fierce tug of war at the height of the cold war that saw the United States and the Soviet Union competing against each other for the most marginal ally, it is sobering how poorly Israel fared. For the first two decades Israeli statecraft failed to win the friendship of *either* superpower.

More important in the long run is that once nonidentification proved untenable, Israel eventually managed to make a virtue of necessity. Successive governments in Jerusalem labored long and hard to solidify the country's moral and political allegiance to the West. Most specifically, over the years Israeli policy has succeeded in moving closer to the United States or perhaps in drawing the United States closer to Israel, so much so that by the nation's fortieth anniversary Israeli global relations showed a profound diplomatic imbalance. At the heart of this disequilibrium was the one-sided pro-American orientation that, for all its logic and many tangible benefits, nevertheless posed two serious concerns. The first was excessive reliance on a single patron, the United States; the other, alienation from the Soviet Union.

ISRAEL'S MEANING FOR THE SUPERPOWERS

Gross distortion at either end of Israel's superpower equation leads us to suggest the influence—both past and present—of three considerations that seem to determine how American and Soviet leaders view the Jewish state. In comparing U.S. and Soviet positions at any given moment, Israel's fortunes rise or fall on the basis of ideology, domestic politics, and geopolitics. With the Kremlin, every one of the three conspires against Israel, while the intermix of American political philosophy and social values with consensus politics at home, together with larger American foreign policy objectives, have facilitated close Israeli–U.S. ties.

The contrasting patterns can be represented graphically in Table 18. Nowhere are the two perspectives more sharply drawn than in the realm of social tenets and political philosophies as espoused by American and Soviet elites. This ideological variable is purposely cited first for an additional reason. As students of world affairs most of us are

Table 18. Israel's Relationship with the Superpowers

United States	Intervening Variable	USSR
+	ideology	–
+	domestic politics	–
+/–	geopolitics	–

schooled in twentieth-century political realism and therefore are prone to attributing state behavior to national interests and power motives while downplaying the role, if any, of ideology. Yet shared values form the bedrock of Israeli-American relations. Even more so are traditional Russian attitudes toward Jews and Communist ideological blinkers a serious obstacle in terms of Israel and the Soviet Union.

In approaching the Kremlin, Israel begins immediately with one major limitation. The Zionist idea itself arouses Soviet sensitivities to an extent that outside observers may find impossible to comprehend. Yet, on doctrinal grounds, Zionism and Marxism have always been antithetical, with Bolshevik ideologues realizing the appeal of Zionism for the Jewish proletariat on the basis of ethnic, religious, and national consciousness rather than Communist internationalism. Following the 1917 revolution, therefore, suppression of Zionism became official policy within the Soviet Union, reaching its peak in the Stalinist era.

If identification with Israel is untenable for Soviet leaders on ideological grounds, then the internal policy setting inside the Kremlin and its foreign policy priorities represent two additional calculations that work to Israel's disfavor.

There is to this day no known representative arguing for a pro-Israel policy in the Soviet Union, for example. Befriending Israel remains, as it has always been, unpopular with the Soviet public as much as within the state and party bureaucratic apparatus. Nor does it help matters that Jerusalem is hardly perceived of as the key instrument for advancing Soviet interests in the Middle East or anywhere else, except possibly in opening the United States to more favorable trade relations with the USSR. Without a compelling political or strategic argument, or a vigorous advocate to promote close ties with the Jewish state, there has been little incentive for a major policy revision by the Kremlin even in the era of *glasnost* under Gorbachev.

But if friendship toward Israel has been neither necessary nor expedient ideologically, politically, or geopolitically in the case of the Soviet Union, the opposite is true of the United States. Here we find an entirely different intermix of the basic determinants, with overseas considerations and American politics, like the American value system, having a positive and supportive role in Israel-U.S. relations.

Ideologically, Israel is often held up as a mirror image by Americans. Many see in the Jewish state a reminder of their own early pioneering ethic and experiences with overcoming adversity. Many Americans, because of the Holocaust, express their support for Israel as a moral commitment; others may relate to it in religious terms as a spiritual center and holy land or in terms of democracy as a progressive society pledged to safeguarding individual freedoms. Still others identify Israelis as a people determined to defend their homeland and independence.

Politically, these perceptions of Israel have stood the country in good stead when inserted into the calculus of American foreign policy. To take only one example, Israel's democratic performance in contrast to authoritarian rule prevalent among the Arab states and in many industrializing countries offers no small measure of ideological satisfaction and renewed confidence to the United States as leader of the free world democracies.* Nor is Israel's proven military capability lost on Pentagon strategists for whom it appeals as an anchor and major point man for the United States in the Mideast. The one reservation, and the cause for an ambiguous plus/minus symbol in the previous diagram under "geopolitics," is concern that defense cooperation with Israel prejudice America's military and economic ties with the Arab world. Otherwise, American defense circles acknowledge that a strong Israel contributes to Western deterrence and collective security as well as to regional and global equilibrium under America's leadership.

Shared ideals and global threat assessments find their expression, thirdly, in American politics and policy making. They account for the largely sympathetic hearing Israel receives inside the United States. Understanding and political support derive from a broad domestic coalition. This national consensus may benefit from a vocal American Jewish community, although it ripples outward to include major segments of the non-Jewish public, the media, both national parties, both houses of Congress, the military, and the executive branch of government.

In sum, despite moments of friction, standing by Israel has been

* When national elections were held in November 1988 in both countries, 79 percent of eligible Israelis voted, compared with just under 50 percent of the voters in the United States. The Israeli figure is actually higher considering the substantial number of Israelis residing abroad and that Israel makes no provision for absentee voting.

regarded, especially since the late sixties and in complete contrast with the USSR, as correct policy on all three counts: ethical consistency, good politics, and sound strategy.

ISRAEL AND THE KREMLIN

Addressing the General Assembly of the United Nations on Israeli policies, Foreign Minister Peres found it necessary to avow, "The Soviet Union is not our enemy." This was on 29 September 1987, just two months shy of the fortieth anniversary of General Assembly Resolution 181, when on 29 November 1947 the Soviet representative unhesitatingly raised his hand in support of statehood for the Jewish people in a partitioned Palestine. By their very incongruity these two scenes are helpful in reviewing what has been an uneasy, strained Israel-Soviet relationship.

After all these years, questions persist. If, as just postulated, the triad of Communist doctrine, politics, and statecraft pose constant, immutable disincentives to friendly ties, what prompted the original Soviet support for the Israeli state? Why should the Kremlin have been at the forefront of the Zionist struggle, assuring adoption of the historic 1947 resolution by delivering the five decisive Communist votes of Byelorussia, Czechoslovakia, Poland, Ukraine, and the USSR (Yugoslavia abstained) and then in May 1948 becoming the second country (after the United States) to recognize the infant state? Why, after such an auspicious start, would relations deteriorate so badly that a high Israeli official found it necessary openly to disclaim enmity toward the Soviet superpower? What caused the deep rift between the two countries? And, in particular, was the reversal Israel's fault, as widely assumed by scholars who cite Israel's voting with the United States and the United Nations in 1950 to condemn Communist aggression in Korea?

The latter argument assumes that had it not been for Israel unnecessarily alienating the Kremlin the relationship with Moscow might have continued and flourished. The assumption is false. When understood in their historical and political context, the years 1947 to 1952 are a departure from the dominant theme of Soviet estrangement not only since then, but also from the prestate period. Those early years of positive contacts throws into sharp contrast the otherwise consistently negative influence of ideas, politics, and world power balances on Kremlin policy toward Israel.

In the fall of 1947, weakening the West guided Soviet foreign policy. Chaos in Palestine therefore presented an unexpected windfall. Here was an opportunity to outmaneuver both England and the United States, at long last, to penetrate the eastern Mediterranean, to displace Western influence in the Near East regions adjacent to the Soviet Union, and to substitute for it a direct Soviet presence—all this at almost no risk or even material commitment. This larger geopolitical and foreign policy perspective strongly argued for increasing UN and world pressure on the British to carry out their announced termination of the Palestine mandate.

At that critical juncture, for the first and probably only time in the history of Soviet-Zionist relations, Marxist-Leninist ideology actually worked in Israel's favor. To the undisguised amazement of Zionist onlookers the USSR's representative showed not a trace of embarrassment in contradicting the traditional anti-Zionist line during an early UN debate held on 14 May 1947 dealing with the situation in Palestine. A special point was made in warning of the injustice were the right of all peoples to realize their national aspirations to be denied the Jewish people. Self-determination provided the rationale for this quite profound ideological adjustment by Communist party leaders. It may also have been thought possible from the standpoint of internal politics to keep domestic and foreign policy separate. Suppressing Jewish nationalists inside the USSR was one thing; expressing verbal and diplomatic support for a separate group of Jews already in Palestine was another thing entirely.

It is also possible Red Army intelligence assessments might have been more sanguine than American estimates in 1947–48 about the fighting capability of the Jewish community in Palestine and its resolve. One scenario argued that the threatened Arab attack might fail to materialize altogether. A second scenario reasoned that even if launched, an invasion by the ill-prepared and disorganized Arab armies could be repulsed by a united Jewish *yishuv* (community), its back to the sea and stiffened by Communist bloc arms supplies. The latter scenario proved correct.

On the whole, however, this Soviet ideological-geopolitical calculation painted too roseate a picture of *yishuv* politics. It was believed, for instance, that Israeli founders would adopt policy positions conforming to those of other fraternal socialist countries out of gratitude for the timely Soviet military and political backing. Orthodox Marxists similarly were led into thinking of support for Israel as ideologically consistent, for who were the political elites of the *yishuv* if not Russian Jews, committed socialists and sworn opponents of Western capitalist imperialism? Lenin's theory of the vanguard also encouraged overestimating the influence of the Israeli

Communist party, formed in the early 1920s, of the Moscow-oriented Mapam party, and of its Hashomer Hatzair youth movement.

Translated into political action the new Kremlin policy directive supporting the Zionist cause resulted in a string of specific decisions:

- endorsement of partition for Palestine, both in principle (May 1947) and as a concrete plan (November 1947);
- strong oppostion to a last-minute American proposal of trusteeship for Palestine (April 1948) that would have suspended partition and Jewish statehood;
- prompt recognition of Israel (May 1948), followed by the opening of a Soviet legation in Tel Aviv (August 1948);
- condemnation of the Arab armed attack on Israel as unlawful invasion (May 1948), while justifying Israel's response as legitimate self-defense;
- authorization for the shipment to Israel of urgently needed small arms, mortars, and artillery via Czechoslovakia (spring and summer 1948); and
- objection to the Bernadotte plan (July 1948) calling on Israel to yield territories and to the idea that the Negev be taken from Jewish possession.

Soviet support also continued once the War for Independence ended. This was expressed in

- support for the first attempt by Israel (December 1948) at gaining unconditional admission to the UN and, again, in the vote granting membership (May 1949);
- calling for direct peace negotiations (October 1948) and adopting a moderate stand on issues relating to the Arab-Israeli conflict, including the refugee problem; and
- withdrawing support for internationalization of Jerusalem (April 1950), consistent with Israel's own position.

Even as late as September 1951, the Soviet Union joined in the Security Council resolution calling upon Egypt to permit Israel use of the international Suez Canal waterway.*

* The date is instructive, for the Suez Canal resolution asked for by Israel took place more than a year after the Korean decision aligning Israel with the West and angering the Soviets. However, when a similar appeal to Egypt came up for UN vote in 1954 the Soviets vetoed it, reflecting the deterioration in relations during the intervening few years.

Israel may have been the primary beneficiary of this Soviet policy. But so, too, did working with and through the Zionist state bring the Soviets early and also not insignificant political returns.

The outcome of the Palestine struggle was an embarrassment for Britain, its Arab allies, and the West. Israel's undisguised eagerness for close ties with the Communist countries reflected appreciation for Soviet help in the birth and defense of the state. Tel Aviv provided a useful listening post for monitoring Middle East developments in and around Israel. Furthermore, due to its support for Israel, the USSR was assured of a voice in future UN efforts relating to the Palestine problem in all its aspects—a bonus in terms of Soviet international prestige.

Nevertheless, Kremlin leaders must have realized almost immediately the problems with this approach, as evidenced by the "Golda tremor" in the fall of 1948 when attendance at High Holy Day synagogue services by Israel's first ambassador to Moscow, Golda Meir, brought a spontaneous outpouring of latent Soviet Jewish consciousness and affection for the Jewish state. The embassy and flag of Israel threatened to become a rallying point for Jewish nationalist and religious sentiment. In the deeper ideological and political sense, the scene at Moscow's Great Synagogue implied that Soviet policy toward the Zionist question could not be compartmentalized for long: repressing it at home while endorsing Israel.

Just how well-founded these Soviet suspicions were about the challenge of Zionism for communism is confirmed by the "prisoners of Zion" phenomenon at the end of the sixties when Soviet citizens, most of them brought up exclusively on the teachings of Marx and Lenin, asked to exchange the socialist model for the right to immigrate to the Jewish homeland. More than just defying the authoritarian state and reinforcing the wider dissident movement, the reawakening of Soviet Jewry fundamentally questioned the validity of Communist theory.

Accordingly, already in 1949 harsh steps were taken against Jews in Moscow and in the Ukraine. Accredited Israeli diplomats suddenly found their movements inside the Soviet Union heavily restricted. The Soviet Foreign Ministry refused to discuss the issue of Soviet Jewry, calling it unwarranted and an arrogant interference in internal affairs.

The final prop for the short-lived policy of identification with Israel to buckle and then collapse was the strategic argument. First, the Ben-Gurion government clung to its balanced approach of cordiality toward East and West alike rather than tie Israel firmly to the socialist camp. Second, and far more determinant: Arab world openings and opportunities during the fifties presented an alternative to Israel and what seemed from the Soviet standpoint like a more sound option.

Israel per se offered the USSR little it did not already have: a bare foothold. Israel's conflict with the Arabs, however, presented fertile ground for Soviet access to, and activity in, the Middle East, opening out to oil fields, military bases, strategic naval chokepoints, and potential converts to socialist revolution in the southern tier of emerging Afro-Asian nations.

Israeli historians in particular insist on holding Israel responsible for alienating the Soviets by opting to line up with the West during the Korean crisis. This interpretation cries out for reconsideration. Michael Brecher, for one, stresses Israel's "early disenchantment" with the Soviets, whereas it was probably the exact opposite. Our thesis, in other words, is that it remained only a matter of time until Kremlin policy makers confronted their own early overblown expectations of what Israel might, or could possibly, offer the Soviet Union. Korea 1950 at most provided the catalyst and pretext for revising the policy adopted in 1947.

Israel's position at the start of the Korean War was hardly partisan or unequivocal. Even its verbal support for a 27 June 1950 Security Council resolution calling on all members to help end the breach of peace in Asia came only after Israel was directly canvassed by the UN secretary-general in July. Material support from Israel fell considerably short of the arms and troop contingents asked for by Washington of all UN members; on 22 August Israel offered the Republic of Korea medical supplies estimated at worth $63,000. Both decisions, condemning the violence and sending aid, were minimal given the circumstances of a flagrant violation of the UN Charter and of heavy pressure from the United States to do more. And as declassified Israeli state papers now confirm, even these decisions were reached only following agonizing cabinet debate, which suggests the deep reluctance of cautious Israeli leaders to give offense to the Soviet Union.

Israel's stand in comparison with other countries was also unexceptional. When, for example, the General Assembly on 1 February 1951 found Communist China responsible for aggression, Israel was only one of forty-two members besides the United States voting in favor. Yet none of the others incurred Soviet wrath or suffered serious political retaliation by Moscow. Blaming Israeli decisions from July 1950–February 1951 on the single Korean episode is unconvincing and surely not enough to account for the change in Soviet thinking. Soviet leaders could have lived with the Israeli position on Korea. In fact they did, since Moscow broke off diplomatic relations with Tel Aviv in February 1953 as the war in Asia was winding down. Renewed in July of that year, bilateral ties were maintained in a strained atmosphere until a final rupture at the Six-Day War in 1967, again at the insistence of the Soviets.

When the break came the real causes were, first, a return to anti-Jewish repression inside the Soviet Union; second, intensification of the cold war; third, a revised reading by the Kremlin of Middle East trends. In all three instances, Israel had become a liability. During the fifties the collective Soviet leadership and centralized bureaucracy shifted gear to support the new generation of Arab revolutionary leaders like Egypt's Nasser, committed to Arab independence, modernization, and unity; to ousting Western imperialism; and to a "second round" aimed at Israel's destruction. Only the last posed any difficulty for the Kremlin. To its credit, neither then nor at any time since has Soviet estrangement from Israel gone so far as to call for disqualification of its rightful existence, sovereignty, or security needs in encouraging closer relations with the Arab world. Rather, under Khrushchev the Soviet policy for dominating the Middle East sought to win over the Arabs through indirect means: arms deliveries, economic assistance, and support in the United Nations, including on issues related to Israel. This formula came to light in the 1955–56 transitional phase. The famous Czech arms deal opened Egypt to Soviet penetration. Moscow backed Nasser's sponsorship of the Bandung founding conference on nonaligned countries. And it roundly condemned Israel during the Suez crisis, impressing the Arabs and opening opportunities for further penetration into Syria, Iraq, southern Arabia, and even the Horn of Africa.

It was this fundamental readjustment in Soviet foreign policy ends and means that made Israel expendable by the close of the first decade. If we have stressed this early change in Soviet attitude, it is more for its contemporary rather than historical insight. A grasp of how Communist teachings, Russian domestic sensitivities, and Soviet global pretensions conspired against Israel in the 1950s enables tracing the disappointing record of the 1980s. The basic pieces of the Israel-USSR relationship were all essentially in place no later than 1956. Nor was there much in Israel's power to improve its position or prospects with Moscow given this structured situation. In retrospect, Soviet alienation began considerably before 1967 and had nothing to do with the captured territories from which the Soviet Union demanded a full Israeli withdrawal as the precondition for restoring diplomatic relations in following years.

And because relations were broken off, there is little of substance in the record after 1967. From Khrushchev through Brezhnev and into the Gorbachev era, the Kremlin persisted in turning a cold shoulder toward Israel while emphasizing warm ties with the Arabs. This hard-line policy produced some unpleasant exchanges. Four serious confrontations were

June 1970—As the Soviets escalated their military commitment to Egypt during the war of attrition, a number of close aerial encounters took place in the Suez Canal sector. It was revealed later that on one occasion five Soviet planes had been downed by Israeli pilots in a single dogfight.

October 1973—The Soviets threatened direct military action unless Israel halted its advance and relaxed its siege of the Egyptian Third Army even though Sadat a year earlier had removed the keystone of Soviet Middle East policy by ordering an end to the heavy Soviet presence in his country.

July 1982—The government of the Soviet Union delivered a strong protest through Finland at what it saw as the deliberate shelling of the Soviet Embassy complex in Beirut by Israel, warning very firmly that Israel "will have to assume all responsibility for its actions."

May 1986—After Jerusalem accepted the U.S. invitation to participate in the Strategic Defense Initiative (SDI, or "Star Wars"), Moscow cautioned against Israeli involvement and in following months expressed serious concerns at Israel's development of the Jericho intermediate-range rocket with a capability of reaching targets in the Soviet Union.

Despite these sharp encounters, and perhaps because of them, Israel was not cut off completely.

Communication between Jerusalem and Moscow was maintained through a variety of channels, direct as well as indirect. First, through lower-level officials or outside intermediaries. Thus, for example, representatives of the Russian Patriarchate were sent periodically to Israel, ostensibly to look after the interests of the church and its property in Jerusalem; the Embassy of Finland represented Israel's interests in the Soviet Union. Second, through backdoor diplomacy, as took place in September 1977 when two envoys flew from Moscow to hold secret meetings with Premier Begin or whenever Israeli and Soviet ambassadors were authorized to conduct private meetings in Vienna or other European capitals.

A final channel were some nine confirmed public talks at the ministerial level, almost all of them in New York at UN General Assembly opening sessions and between the foreign ministers of the two respective countries: Eban-Gromyko (December 1973 during the Geneva Conference); Allon-Gromyko (September 1975); Shamir-Gromyko (September 1981 and September 1985); Peres-Shevardnadze (September 1986 and September 1987); Shamir-Shevardnadze (June 1988); and Arens-Shevardnadze (December 1988 in Paris at a special conference on banning chemical warfare; again, at Cairo, in February 1989). It is hard to detect a pattern for these sporadic exchanges. Two logical motivations, however, were (a) the interest of both parties in preventing actual hostilities and (b) the growing awareness in the USSR that Israel was not easily intimidated and, increasingly in recent years, that Israel had to be acknowledged as a central factor and could not simply be written off. Such awareness usually occurred whenever the Soviets felt themselves being squeezed out of the Middle East and out of the Arab-Israeli peace process by U.S. hegemonial policies.

When these occasions for dialogue presented themselves, Israel had every reason to encourage them. It was the Soviets who showed greater reluctance, proving that superpowers have as difficult a time as smaller states in admitting error (in cutting ties in 1967 and then refusing for so long to renew them; in depending on the Arabs, and the most extreme and undependable among them; in assuming Israel could either be ignored or coerced) and in overcoming inhibitions (letting Soviet Jewry go; alienating Arab allies). Consequently, the pace of normalization depended primarily on the Kremlin restructuring its basic approach: deemphasizing the ideological component; domestically and politically by tolerating proponents who do not hold a view of Israel as inherently unfriendly; in replacing foreign policy adventurism with a more discriminating and evenhanded Middle East policy consistent with the rules for U.S.-Soviet global détente.

Israel's role called for patience as well as for creating opportunities to dispel Soviet hesitancy. Wisely, economic trade relations with the countries of Eastern Europe were expanded in the late 1980s whenever such an opening presented itself (see Table 19). Two opportunities that Israel did not create but was quick to seize upon came unexpectedly in December 1988. When a hijacked Soviet airliner landed in Israel the government immediately complied with an official request for the return of the plane, its crew, and hijackers. The action earned Moscow's gratitude for handling the affair in a "noble

Table 19. Trade with Eastern Europe, 1987 ($ million)

Country	Export	Import
Bulgaria	1.150	2.708
Czechoslovakia	2.541	.191
East Germany	2.040	.109
Hungary	8.040	9.572
Poland	4.258	.053
Romania	6.770	30.593
USSR	—	—
Yugoslavia	24.138	15.295
TOTAL	48.956	58.628

Source: Ha'aretz, 7 October 1988.

and humanitarian way." This cooperation was then followed by prompt rescue help in the Armenian earthquake. There remains a long way to go, however, and many issue differences are yet to be resolved. Improving relations with the USSR remains one of the top priorities in Israeli foreign policy for the 1990s.

For more than half of its history Israel has been cut off from one of the world's two superpowers. This has certainly made Israel's diplomatic life much more difficult. Nevertheless, the disappointment on the Jerusalem-Moscow axis has been more than compensated for by success at the other end of the superpower scale: the Jerusalem-Washington relationship.

ISRAEL AND THE WHITE HOUSE

Both Moscow and Washington figured prominently in Israel's creation. Between May 1947–May 1948 these two cold war superpower rivals uncharacteristically stood on the same side of the political fence in supporting the Zionist claim to Jewish statehood. From then on, however, Israeli-Soviet and Israeli-American relations took a divergent rather than parallel course: the former became a source of frustration and regret, the latter provided comfort and reassurance.

The majority of Israelis unhesitatingly subscribe to the belief that ties with the United States far surpass the independence struggle itself and also the 1979 Egyptian peace as the single most outstanding achievement in forty years of Israeli foreign affairs. And judging from the state of relations at the start of the fifth decade they certainly deserve to be viewed in Jerusalem with satisfaction. But not smugness. Precisely because of the supreme importance attached to developing the American connection in the right direction, Israeli leaders and public alike have to guard against being taken in by the conventional literature and rhetoric of the relationship. All too often these yield high traces of exaggeration and hyperbole in dealing with the present, compounded by selective memory toward the past and wishful thinking about the future. Realism, in short, dictates U.S.-Israel relations be demythologized.

That the capacity for self-delusion exists on both sides of the Atlantic-Mediterranean axis is best seen from frequent popular references to the "special relationship." Yet, freed of such embroidery, Israel's relations are proving more conventional than special. Similarly, the political closeness between the two countries is more recent than traditional or "historic." Although described as a two-way street the relationship is unequal rather than balanced. For these same reasons, lastly, the relationship remains susceptible to political hazards instead of offering a picture of perfect health.

The "Special" Relationship

Israeli enthusiasts should begin by disabusing themselves of the notion that U.S.-Israel ties are "special" in the accepted dictionary sense of being extraordinary, "one of a kind," *sui generis*. As the world's leading great power, the United States points with pride to any number of special allies and friendships: historically, France; culturally, Britain; geographically, Canada and Mexico; strategically, the USSR and China; commercially, Japan. Some of them would make a case for being more vital than Israel to the United States. In the Middle East context, the United States has worked long and hard at cultivating what are seen as being pivotal actors. Its sensitivity extends both to the pro-Western regimes in Egypt, Jordan, and oil-rich Saudi Arabia as well as to countries like Iran, Iraq, and Syria yet to be won over.

Consequently, Israel will always face stiff competition in vying for America's attention and support. Nor is the word "special" particularly helpful in this struggle because of its other, less flattering interpretation. Critics, in opposing the close relationship with Israel, are quick to single Israel out as the largest recipient of American foreign aid and to deny any fair compensation by Israel in return; they employ "special" as meaning a liability instead of an asset. Who would predict with any confidence, therefore, how American foreign policy might react to a direct conflict-of-interest situation, one necessitating an either-or choice between any one of the other sensitive bilateral links pursued by Washington and its commitment to Israel?

An iron rule of world politics is that all political friendships are liable to change. As Lord Palmerston once confessed about England's foreign policy: it embraced neither eternal allies nor perpetual enemies—only interests that remained "eternal and perpetual." Modern diplomatic history in fact teaches that self-interest and expediency dominate alliance politics, as demonstrated by the recent experience of Taiwan and South Vietnam. The warm affinity shown toward Israel by the government and people of the United States is fully documented. Yet this note of caution is necessary, for it argues against painting the relationship between the two countries as anything more than what it is, or can be: a normal set of ties based on mutual interests. It merely follows from this that the U.S.-Israeli connection is subject to the same historical and political forces that operate on other nations and alliances.

The Israeli-American alliance arouses further concern because it has never been formalized. Assigning undue weight to the relationship is discouraged when we realize that no binding treaty exists between the two countries. It rests on mutual trust alone.

Israel before 1967 would have prized an explicit defense undertaking from Washington but was turned down repeatedly. Since 1967 it is Israel that indicates greater hesitancy, suspecting that an American commitment, possibly as part of international guarantees, might be used in baiting it to relinquish possession of the disputed territories short of a genuine Arab peace. Nor for that matter have American officials been overly eager to pledge themselves in advance to undertaking specific actions on Israel's behalf. In fact, both sides have deep reservations, each for its own reasons, about an explicit security guarantee, viewing it as a form of entanglement. Opposition to the idea of a security treaty is couched in arguments like (a) even legal pledges can and have been broken; (b) they are subject to conflicting interpretation (i.e., defining an act of aggression against Israel) or reinterpretation (the 1988 abrogation of the 1975 pledge not to recognize or negotiate with the PLO); (c) the unwritten commitment reflects a deeper moral bond and a far stronger assurance of Israel's security, survival, and well-being than any legal instrument could possibly give. During the last decade, in lieu of a formal treaty the relationship has been regulated by a combination of implicit understandings, institutionalized consultation, and formal memorandums of agreement (MOAs) that include recognition by the United States of Israel as a major "non-NATO ally" and a bilateral free-trade agreement.

The "Traditional" Relationship

As with the USSR, Israel's historical record, and especially the early formative period 1947–53, promotes a greater sense of realism by pointing out certain objective limitations to the relationship. Those years correspond to the Truman presidency, which is remembered for having set relations on a positive course from the outset and for having provided policy guidelines to later administrations on constructing a closer partnership with Israel. In particular, Truman's recognition of the Jewish state on 14 May 1948 has been given great symbolic importance.

The positive attitude toward Israel under Truman compares most favorably, for example, with the Eisenhower-Dulles era, which was marked by a coolness toward Israel that is brushed aside as a temporary departure. Typical of this viewpoint is Steven Spiegel's description of Eisenhower as "the one president after Israel's establishment" who confronted Jerusalem and demanded changes in Israeli policy; Nadav Safran refers to 1953–57 as the four lean years of Israeli-American relations. The diplomatic annals indicate otherwise, however; subsequent White House occupants also found it necessary to pressure Israel. Not only is it unfair toward Eisenhower by presenting him as the negative example and exception, but, above all, it is overly indulgent toward the Truman record.

The Truman administration did establish the pattern for future relations with Israel; only it was a pattern with disquieting features. Among them: divided counsel over policies toward Israel; a certain unease or ambivalence in fundamental perceptions reflected in the periodic debate over whether Israel constitutes an asset or a liability for the United States; support for what Spiegel terms the "press-Israel strategy"; and attempts at keeping Israel at a safe distance ("evenhandedness"). Each of these found early expression under President Truman.

For instance, the act of recognizing Israel was indeed courageous and statesmanlike. However, it was not the "grand opening" for cordial or even normal ties. If anything, it stands as the high point of the Truman commitment when we recall that he then went on to serve a full four-year term during which American policy on Israel was guarded and at best half-hearted. Usually overlooked are less complimentary acts of either omission or commission as a follow-up to recognition. Even ignoring the furtiveness by which the decision and its announcement were made—so fierce was opposition within the executive branch to the direction Truman was taking—the form of recognition itself was qualified and only de facto instead of de jure.

Later files add to this reassessment. Truman and his administration

- imposed an arms embargo and turned down appeals for arms by Israel in defending itself from the Arab invasion;
- supported the 1948 Bernadotte proposals that called for territorial concessions on Israel's part;
- were slow in extending economic assistance, with a loan promised in May 1948 for construction and settling displaced persons finally approved only at the end of January 1949;
- joined Britain and France in the 1950 Tripartite Declaration against military aid to the Middle East that clearly discriminated against Israel since its Arab adversaries (Egypt, Iraq, and Jordan) continued to be supplied under bilateral treaties with the U.K.; and
- pressed Israel not to pursue ties with Red China and to align itself with the United States on Korea.

Rather than breaking with Truman's legacy, what Eisenhower and Dulles did in effect was to take already existing reservations about Israel several steps further in keeping it at arm's length and by continuing to view it as a mixed blessing if not a political embarrassment.

From 1946 to 1972 the United States distributed $55 billion in military grants worldwide; none of this went to Israel. Even the direct purchase of arms by Israel from the United States involved a long and difficult struggle by Israeli diplomats in overcoming resistance in Washington—to the idea and to the association (see Table 20). Only in 1961 did President Kennedy part with established policy in authorizing the direct sale of Hawk defensive missiles. The arms pipeline opened wider with approval by the Johnson administration for the supply of offensive Skyhawk A-4 aircraft and then F-4 Phantom fighters.

Beginning with Truman himself, each president and adminis-

Table 20. U.S. Government Foreign Grants and Credits to Israel ($ million)

Years	Grants and Credits
1948–55	390
1956–65	483
1966–75	3,760
1976–85	25,416

Source: Statistical Abstracts of the United States, 1988, p. 764.

tration added a new page to the evolving relationship, a page chronicling both misunderstandings and achievements. Aside from Truman and Eisenhower, Kennedy's short tenure may have featured improved ties with Israel but also overtures to Egypt, Israel's chief adversary. President Johnson stood behind Israel following the 1967 conflict but had disappointed Jerusalem at the height of the June crisis. Nixon likewise expressed appreciation for Israel's timely cooperation in the 1970 Jordan alert and yet sponsored the Rogers plan and permitted delays in the Yom Kippur military airlift. While Gerald Ford maintained support for Israel, he also supervised the painful 1975 reassessment. Carter may have staked his personal credibility in reviving and brokering the Israel-Egypt peace negotiations in 1978–79, but he will be remembered for blocking Israeli sales of Kfir planes with American components to Latin America, for pressing a return to the 1973 Geneva conference format, and for advocating a homeland for the Palestinians. The record of the Reagan era is similarly mixed: mounting recognition of Israel as a strategic asset contrasts with arms cutoffs, the Iran-contra affair, and the surprise 1982 Reagan plan.

For these reasons, and whatever else its strong points, the U.S.-Israel bond cannot really qualify as either long-standing or traditional. If friendship is taken as meaning close, intimate political collaboration and an identity of interests, then this quality is a comparatively recent phenomenon. Nor has the friendship been consistent. It traces not through a steady linear progression, but in a spiral of ups and downs. Bilateral relations have moved forward incrementally, by fits and starts. Certainly the path has not been a smooth one. But what matters from an Israeli standpoint is that these relations were moving in the right direction. Consequently, there is little that can be gained from papering over the differences or in doctoring the history of the mixed relationship.

The "Equal" Partnership

Nor is much to be accomplished by denying that the relationship is not one of equals. Now it is probably true that Israeli services to the United States and contribution to the cause of global stability are greater than meets the eye or that can be gleaned by historians from the public record, particularly in the field of intelligence and security. The concept of Israel as an anchor for America in the Middle East should not be dismissed as empty rhetoric. Yet, by the same token, the fundamentally asymmetrical nature of the relationship cannot be hidden, notwithstanding frequent references to *mutual* admiration, *shared* values and *common* interests, complete *reciprocity*, and "strategic consensus."

Critics, of course, are the first to note and to accent the disparities, starting with objective inequalities. A superpower having worldwide interests and global capabilities is matched with a small, defensive, introverted country. Israel's "world" lies on its immediate borders, while America's frame of reference girdles the entire international system. Where Washington has broad concerns and commitments, Jerusalem has extremely narrow ones. And if America's security dilemma is nuclear, Soviet oriented, and hypothetical, Israel's is conventional, Arab directed, and palpable.

Moreover, how equal can any alliance or partnership be when it contains intrinsic role disparities? For most Americans the Jewish state ranks as an important friendly country; whether it qualifies as a vital ally is debatable. For Israel, on the other hand, the United States in recent years has become increasingly indispensable and is likely to remain so in the future.

American policy toward Israel over the last decade or so seems to vindicate the notion in Israeli diplomacy of enlisting the support of at least one major world actor. Because, whether referred to as the "critical mass," the "margin of difference," or the "force multiplier," American support at present supplies the missing components in Israel's ends-means equation, thereby extending and enhancing the nation's staying power. The economy is sustained by subsidies and investment capital from the United States. Since 1949 the United States has provided over $43 billion in assistance (see Table 21). Aid for Israel in 1989 consisted of $1.8 billion in Foreign Military Sales Financing (FMSF) grants and $1.2 billion in Economic Support Funds (ESF), all provided on a grant basis. Israel's major weapons also come from the United States (see Table 22). Within the $1.8 billion total for military assistance, $400 million was authorized in 1989 for offshore procurement expenditure in Israel, providing an added injection into the Israeli economy in the form of jobs, technology, and increased production. Another $100 million was in the form of direct offsets, mandated purchases of Israeli defense articles by the United States. These offsets, plus another sum of more than $250 million in U.S. Defense Department procurements of Israeli military items through a defense industrial cooperation program, were over and above the $1.8 billion figure. Under the 1988 Fair Pricing Initiative Act, Israel would save $90 million in costs associated with the purchase of F-16 aircraft. The United States agreed to provide Israel $100 million for joint research under the Arrow antiballistic missile research project as part of the SDI program.

Table 21. U.S. Military and Economic Aid to Israel (1977–88) ($ million)

	Economic Aid			Military Aid			Total Economic & Military Aid		
Year	loans	grants	total	loans	grants	total	loans	grants	grand total
1977	245	490	735	500	500	1,000	745	990	1,735
1978	260	525	785	500	500	1,000	760	1,025	1,785
1979	260	525	785	2,700	600	3,300	2,960	1,125	4,085
1980		525	525	500	500	1,000	760	1,025	1,785
1981		764	764	900	500	1,400	900	1,264	2,164
1982		806	806	850	550	1,400	850	1,356	2,206
1983		785	785	950	750	1,700	950	1,535	2,485
1984		910	910	850	850	1,700	850	1,760	2,610
1985		1,200	1,200		1,400	1,400		2,600	2,600
1986		1,200	1,200		1,800	1,800		3,000	3,000
1987		1,200	1,200		1,800	1,800		3,000	3,000
1988		1,200	1,200		1,800	1,800		3,000	3,000
TOTAL		10,130	11,155	7,750	10,650	19,300	8,775	21,680	30,455

Source: U.S. government official figures.

In effect the United States figures prominently in every issue-area that makes up Israel's foreign policy agenda. Identification with Israel upholds its legitimacy. Military aid helps confer a sense of security in holding out against the Arab threat while sustaining hopes for an eventual peace. Expanding trade links are a stimulant to industrial and technological growth as well as an antidote to Arab-induced economic discrimination. So are America's support in international forums and use of its veto power in the UN Security Council a counter to efforts at excluding and isolating Israel. In the period 1972 to 1989 the United States cast no less than eighteen vetoes to prevent passage of resolutions deemed by the White House or the State Department to be blatantly one-sided against Israel and unconstructive in terms of the peace process. Lastly, friendship with the United States provides ease of access to the largest and most influential community within the international Jewish Diaspora.

What more could any small state like Israel ask for than to have its diplomatic efforts crowned by affiliation with a superpower, particularly the United States? A clue to a problem with the relationship is its capacity for summoning up a recessive Jewish trait among Israelis: "If everything is going so well, then why am I so worried?" For no matter how we look at the present state of bilateral affairs or

Table 22. Major American-Supplied Weapons

1. Fighter or Attack Planes	5. Tanks
A-4 Skyhawk	M-60
F-4E Phantom	
F-16 Fighting Falcon	6. Missiles
F-15 Eagle	Harpoon surface-to-surface
	Hawk ground-to-air
2. Transport Planes	Lance surface-to-surface
C-130 Hercules	Maverick air-to-ground
	Redeye ground-to-air
3. Surveillance Aircraft	Shrike air-to-ground
E-2C Hawkeye	Sidewinder air-to-air
	Sparrow air-to-air
4. Helicopters	Walleye air-to-ground
CH-53 Sea Stallion	
Bell 206	7. Engines
Bell 212	aircraft
UH-1 Cobra	naval vessels
Hughes 500-MD	

what the deeper causes for it might be, the partnership reflects a distinct imbalance. It casts the United States in the dominant role of superpower patron in direct contrast to Israel as subordinate: as client, as recipient. This dependency invites attention to a final component of the complex yet fascinating connection: its psychological undercurrents and possible repercussions.

How "Healthy" Is the Relationship?

On the surface, relations seem stable, healthy, and vibrant. Institutional and commercial links include the Joint Political Military Group, concerned with strategic cooperation; the Joint Security Assistance Planning Group, coordinating U.S. military assistance; the Joint Economic Development Group, focusing on economic issues; and the 1985 Free Trade Agreement. As further tangible evidence one could cite the growing number of formal bilateral accords starting with the 1975 Memorandum of Agreement (see Table 23).

Still, it is as true of interstate as of interpersonal relations that any superior-inferior status will produce unhealthy side effects. After four decades of close association and occasional discord, undertones of resentment have been becoming audible in the Israeli-U.S. dialogue—and from both sides.

Table 23. U.S.-Israeli Memorandums of Agreement/Understanding

1. 1 September 1975 MOA
   A corollary to the Israel-Egypt interim agreement ("Sinai II"), it committed the United States to be "fully responsive" to Israel's defense, energy, and economic needs; to consult with Israel in the event of a "world power" interfering militarily in the Middle East; to accept the Israeli view that further negotiations with Egypt, or possibly Jordan, be within the framework of an overall peace settlement; to coordinate diplomatic initiatives; and not to recognize or negotiate with the PLO so long as it denied Israel's right to exist and refused to accept UN Resolutions 242 and 338.
2. 26 March 1979 MOA
   Pledges assistance in the additional economic, military, and security burden imposed by complete withdrawal from the Sinai and implementing the treaty of peace signed that day between Israel and Egypt.
3. 26 March 1979 MOA
   Also relating to the peace treaty and providing oil supply arrangements for a period of 15 years but dating back retroactively to 1975.
4. 30 November 1981 MOU
   Sets out general areas for strategic cooperation between the two countries.
5. 29 November 1983. National Security Decision Directive 111
   A further bilateral strategic cooperation agreement within the framework of the Joint Political Military Group (JPMG) commissioned to coordinate military planning, joint maneuvers, and the stockpiling of equipment in Israel.
6. 7 March 1985.
   Congressional approval for establishment of a free-trade zone in Israel.
7. 17 February 1987. National Defense Authorization Act
   Section 1105 of the act declares Israel a major non-NATO ally for purposes of cooperation in aspects of military research and development.
8. 21 April 1988. MOA
   Signed to mark Israel's fortieth anniversary, it formally institutionalizes U.S.-Israeli coordination on strategic, economic, military, and diplomatic matters; to remain in force for five years.

Symptomatic were the responses to the Pollard spy episode. American officials felt offended, protesting that friends should not spy on each other. Embarrassed Israelis, for their part, insisted the operation would not have been called for had Washington been more forthcoming in sharing intelligence data anxiously requested by Jerusalem.

Even before Pollard, however, one could find American newspaper editorialists, Arab propagandists, and foreign policy establishment members beginning to raise pointed questions as to just why Israel merited being the beneficiary of U.S. largesse and whether there was any real return on the expenditure. People like Seth Tillman called for getting tough with Israel, while George Ball railed against the "excessively ingrown and convoluted relations," accused Israel of "dependence without responsibility," and criticized it for repeatedly disregarding America's advice, protests, and own interests. In short, from an American perspective such a situation in world politics encourages in the patron a tendency to make demands, to extract a price for services rendered, and to expect that the client state defer to the dominant partner.

At the receiving end, Israelis more and more have begun to look beyond the benefits to the cost side. The essence of the problem can easily be stated. It is this: at the same time that the United States serves as benefactor and protector, it also imposes indirectly on Israel's sovereignty, on its freedom of decision and freedom of action. There is no dimension of Israeli national life—from culture to statecraft—in which America's influence and presence have not made themselves felt.

Such intimacy is known even in international politics to result in an ambivalent love-hate relationship that breeds a kind of schizophrenia leading to unpredictable reactions. It is one thing to admit dependency but altogether different in having it put to you in as blunt terms as *Time* magazine did in its April 1988 feature story on Israel at forty: that without the $3 billion in U.S. annual aid "the very existence of Israel might fall into question." Sensitive Israelis found the partnership comforting for being so close . . . but also becoming too close for comfort.

From the standpoint of Israeli pride there is something demeaning in the very act of soliciting and accepting massive outside assistance. One unhealthy reaction would be resentment. But no less disturbing as an insight into Israeli self-respect would be for the leadership and the country's people to become hooked on American support, acknowledging the debt of gratitude without remorse while coming to assume unquestioning support.

Developments in the late eighties called attention, inter alia, to this important psychological or attitudinal aspect of the relationship. Respective views on the *intifada* and over Israeli handling of the West Bank–Gaza uprising revealed a certain impatience by both the United States and Israel; contradictory positions toward the PLO and its peaceful intentions led to a trace of disappointment with each other.

Whatever else, events cautioned against taking each other entirely for granted.

Cementing the Relationship

What we have done here is look at Israel's association with the United States from four different perspectives:

- Conceptual—Is it special?
- Historical—Is it time-honored?
- Political—Is it founded on reciprocity and shared interests?
- Psychological—Is it on a sound, healthy, solid footing?

This done, the reader can better grasp the immensity of the challenge now before Israel in how it goes about cementing this paramount relationship.

The problems and pitfalls, as experience teaches, are considerable. Indeed, they are about as formidable as the bilateral agenda is long, touching on issues from aid levels to regional and global trends but with the Arab-Israeli conflict and peace process as the centerpiece. Nevertheless, the obstacles, although real, are by no means insurmountable. Surely one major source for encouragement has got to be the essentially solid foundations that have girded and sustained relations to the present, above and beyond any single discordant note.

At the beginning of this chapter a hypothesis was made that the contours of Israeli superpower relations are defined by three key influences: each superpower's principles, politics, and foreign policy designs. When applied to the United States, all three continue into the fifth decade by interacting in a positive manner. But if any given issue retains the potential and the capacity for jeopardizing what has been built up, it is the unresolved dispute among Israelis, Palestinians, and Jordanians.

CHAPTER 9

ISRAEL AND THE ARAB WORLD

I would like to address the Palestinian people. The time for recrimination is past. . . . Now is the time to turn from violence to dialogue and travel to a different destiny.

–Shimon Peres, September 1987

External affairs end essentially where they begin: in the bitter conflict still raging on Israel's immediate frontiers. Despite having been reserved for last in our survey, nevertheless, by far the most challenging, important, and least satisfying foreign relationship that Israel has is with the Arabs of the Middle East. It is they who deny the Jewish state the goals it covets of recognition, safety, and a normal existence. And it is through them alone that such vital national interests can ever be truly realized in the long term. As the oldest diplomatic handbook in existence, the Bible, advises, "Neither is it beyond the sea, that you should say: who will cross the ocean and fetch it for us" (Deuteronomy 20:13). Israel's quarrel is not with the international community, just as its future assurance lies not in the UN in international guarantees, or in a distant superpower. It is with the neighboring Arab people, in whole or in large part, that Israel must make peace.

MIDDLE EAST PEACEMAKING AND ISRAELI PREFERENCES

Any blueprint for resolving the Arab-Israeli dispute must address not one but all five of what veteran peace brokers insist on seeing as the modalities or parameters for successful conflict termination. Briefly, these are

Agenda Setting

Defining exactly what the dispute is about is problematic in itself. What are the outstanding differences at issue and the major interests at stake? If it is a dispute of the classic kind, involving a fight over land and resources, then a straightforward territorial solution would seem to be called for. Far less tractable, however, are disputes involving deeper values or felt needs on the order of national legitimacy and self-determination, religious vindication or historical revenge, prestige and status, the quest for perceived or possibly even absolute security.

Climate Control

How might Arabs and Israelis better relate to each other? It is clear that if a settlement is to be negotiated rather than imposed, those psychological barriers once described by the late President Sadat as two-thirds of the problem must first be removed. In the language of game theorists the conflict has got to shift from the category of zero sum (one winner and one loser; winner take all) to non-zero sum (compromise). In effect, nothing less than the entire political and psychological environment needs to be improved as part of this attempt to reshape basic images and reciprocal attitudes from negative to positive. Here any number of specific confidence-building measures, such as a suspension of violence, are extremely helpful but difficult to gain consent for. Yet concessions and serious bargaining are unlikely without an atmosphere conducive to a real dialogue.

The Negotiating Format

How might a negotiating process best begin and gain momentum? Highly technical and very specific questions concerning style, technique, and approach have always arisen when determining how to initiate and then conduct meaningful Middle East negotiations, consuming unbelievable amounts of energy and goodwill. This one facet of peacemaking deals essentially with matters of (a) format and venue (where talks are to be held), (b) representation, (c) agenda, and (d) procedure. Not surprisingly, over the years it has yielded a large repertoire of ideas and disagreement: direct vs. indirect negotiation, bilateral vs. multilateral, with or without third-party intermediaries, an international conference or not, and "step-by-step" diplomacy that tries to negotiate each contentious issue separately as opposed to nothing less than a full, comprehensive solution.

The Peace Strategy

Since a solution to the Arab-Israeli conflict is everyone's agreed objective, all sides wish to know in advance what the final peace arrangement is going to look like. Rather than talking in abstracts, the key issue becomes, where should the peace process end and the peace map and final borders be drawn? Unlike the imaginativeness shown on matters of procedure, the repertoire is embarrassingly impoverished on this touchy and all-important substantive question. For one thing, the struggle has gone on far too long for any ideal or original solution to present itself. For another, every idea and formula without exception is flawed because of objective conditions already prevailing, in particular the demographic distribution and close intermix of Arabs and Jews. As a result, of the countless schemes that have been tabled and discarded as unsound or unworkable, only three frameworks have survived this process of elimination and are based on the alternative principles of partition, autonomy, and federalism.

Party Identification

Who besides Israel are the concerned parties? In fact, how many principal protagonists to the conflict are there? Systematic thinking requires distinguishing among the various possible players in the dispute and hence to a reserved place for themselves in an eventual settlement. Using such criteria as immediate geographic proximity and one's degree of actual involvement, there is room for differentiating directly concerned parties from those who, strictly speaking, are really secondary and indirectly concerned parties. The questions for Israel are not only to whom it should talk and with whom must it make peace, but with whom must it live in peace in the future.

In reviewing the record of peace proposals, Israel's basic position toward the five peace "levers" listed above shows remarkable consistency over time, with very few revisions made in policy since the early 1950s. Its preferences concerning the agenda and nature of the dispute, the Arabs, proper procedure, the peace map, and the players were expressed authoritatively at an early stage.

It has always been the official government view that the conflict goes on because the Arabs cannot bring themselves to accept the existence of Israel in any part of former Palestine. Once recognition was extended to Israel, and its right to security provided for in any final settlement, then all other issues became negotiable, whether territorial questions, the refugee problem, economic cooperation, or regional and security arrangements. Similarly, on the second or psychological aspect, Israel professed no hatred or permanent animosity toward the Arabs, as proved by the warm reception given Sadat in 1977. Writing in 1952, Ben-Gurion insisted that cooperation between "the Jewish people in its Land and independent Arabia" was a "historical necessity" but was feasible "only on a basis of equality, mutual respect, and reciprocal aid." That Israel stretches out its hand in peace and looks forward to cooperation and friendship with the Arabs in a prosperous Middle East is the constant theme promoted in Israeli information campaigns.

Broad generalities are of little use, however, once the issue becomes peace*making*. On this third variable of diplomatic procedure Israel has had to be more explicit. Here it is categorical in calling for direct, face-to-face talks with the Arabs without preconditions. With the exception of the 1987 London agreement entered into by Foreign Minister Shimon Peres, Israeli leaders uniformly discouraged proposals for convening an international conference to negotiate a solution. This strong objection rested on the three arguments of (a) the multilateral format being too large and unwieldy, as seen from (b) previous experience (Britain's failure at the 1939 Round Table conference on Palestine in 1939, the abortive 1949–50 Lausanne negotiations regarded to have been a tragic farce, and the largely ceremonial 1973 Geneva conference); and also because (c) the dynamics in such a multilateral setting work to the advantage of the most extreme Arab delegate in attendance in opposing concessions, while placing Israel at a distinct disadvantage in the sense of being outnumbered and subject to combined Arab, international, and great power pressure. This reasoning lies behind the long-standing consensus in Israel that favors the direct, bilateral approach as the best-suited negotiating format.

Where the Israeli consensus is weakest is over the substantive solution and which fourth lever to press: territorial compromise or autonomy? In national politics bipartisanship ends here, at the water's edge of what peace framework serves Israeli interests and how the final peace map ought to look.

Since 1967 at least the Labour Alignment position has adopted the principle of partition, which implies a willingness to cede some or even most of the disputed West Bank and Gaza areas through a partial withdrawal and in the spirit of "territory for peace." The Likud strategy was and remains antipartitionist. Thus, when thrust into a position of power in 1977 and forced by Sadat's peace initiative to come up with a political and conceptual alternative, Menachem Begin presented his counterproposal of autonomy, a plan offering self-rule to the Arab residents. This reluctance to yield Israel's control, presence, or claim to the West Bank districts of Judea and

Samaria is reflected in the less forthcoming motto of "peace for peace."

This question of a central peace principle for crafting the final settlement is the great dividing line in Israeli society and politics from 1967 to the present. Even as the debate continued to polarize opinion, a minimal working consensus remained in effect, restored by wide agreement on three further aspects of the peace map and framework. The first two are expressly laid down in the second national unity government coalition program of 22 December 1988:

- "united Jerusalem, Israel's eternal capital, is one indivisible city under Israeli sovereignty"; and
- the NUG, like every government before it, "will oppose the establishment of an additional Palestinian state in the Gaza District and in the area between Israel and Jordan."

The other point of general agreement is that neither Labour nor Likud objects to the federalist principle per se, but only wants it as a later supplement to the peace settlement and within the framework of regional economic cooperation.

This leaves Israel with the fifth peacemaking dilemma: specifying whom it sees as the Arab party or parties that will help bring the conflict to an end.

BETWEEN HASHEMITES AND PALESTINIANS

Quite remarkably, the most elementary of the five peace questions has probably been the least explored by peace researchers and practitioners alike, at least until recently. This oversight, if such it was, is inexcusable on the part of those with the greatest interest at stake, Israelis themselves. Representatives for Jerusalem often have found it necessary to remind others that for its small size Israel nonetheless represents one-half of the Arab-Israeli conflict as well as of its solution. But who makes up the other, missing half?

The possibilities are not infinite and, indeed, most candidates can immediately be struck from the list. To begin with, the Arab world's twenty-two states are too fractious and diverse a grouping to comprise an opposing side, and individual members like Iraq, Lebanon, Morocco, and Saudi Arabia are either unable or unwilling to assume a diplomatic leadership role. Egypt, on the other hand, was long regarded in Israeli eyes as the voice of the Arabs and therefore the most likely candidate, except that Cairo by its own admission lacks the mandate to speak for the other Arab countries or to represent Palestinian interests, as made evident during the 1977–79 negotiations with Israel and since. Under the bilateral peace with Egypt, Israel's objective is more narrowly defined. As formulated in February 1989 by Foreign Minister Moshe Arens, it is to dissuade Egypt from returning to the "circle of war" by building a dam "so that this stream [of normal relations] cannot run backwards anymore." Similarly with Syria. Damascus may hold the key to Lebanon's future in the same way that it is pivotal for the Israeli-Arab strategic military balance. In the long run the possibility exists for an understanding between Damascus and Israel acknowledging Syrian preeminence in its immediate sphere under a broader Middle East peace regime. Still, in terms of the core Arab-Israeli political dispute—or, Who gets What in former mandate Palestine?—like Egypt, Syria must be regarded as a secondary rather than primary diplomatic actor.

Hence, in the final analysis for Israel, the choice in nominees is pretty much an either-or situation. Bargaining, and then coexisting, with either Jordan or the Palestinians. Many important Israeli figures have clung at different times to one form or another of a third option: a hyphenated solution in the sense of a joint Jordanian-Palestinian delegation to peace talks, for instance; or of a single Jordanian-Palestinian entity (one state, two people) to the east of Israel and preferably under Jordanian rule. Such unconstructive ambiguity is little more than a sophisticated means of avoiding a hard yet inevitable choice—and one better made by Israel than made for it by other actors or by circumstance. Moreover, this third, intermediate position simplistically presumes an essential compatibility of interests and aspirations between Jordan and the Palestinians that is contradicted by their history and politics.

Actually, official government thinking on this question of a direct peace partner has involved relatively little soul-searching, hesitancy, or deliberation. Here the preference was clear-cut and unambiguous, with the Hashemite Kingdom of Jordan the odds-on, overwhelming favorite. How Israeli policy arrived at this pro-Jordanian stance is fascinating as a case study in disjointed and incremental decision making, as well as in the formative influence of prestate Zionist diplomacy on the post-1948 period, which is where most scholars take up the study of Israeli foreign relations. Published state papers do not present the so-called Jordanian option as resulting from a specific, conscious policy decision reached only after thorough cabinet debate at the highest level. Rather, this preference emerged as the logical conclusion from a chain of assumptions. The sequence of premises underscores the following links:

- first, insistence by Israel that the dispute is restricted to states and that peace must be conducted exclusively at the level of governments on the basis of sovereignty and equality; and
- second, implicit in this stand was the a priori denial of any legal or political status to the Palestinians as a nonstate actor.

Both principles are already apparent in the first detailed blueprint for peace by Israel, presented to the General Assembly of the United Nations on 1 December 1952 by Ambassador Abba Eban. No less than twenty references to "the Arab states and Israel" appear in the text. In contrast, "the Palestinians" as such are not mentioned even once. There is a single reference to "the peoples of Palestine"—Arabs and Jews—in recalling the pre-1948 situation; otherwise the Palestinians are referred to solely as "Arab refugees."

This latter point served, in turn, as the third premise. Israel would take the view that the former Arab residents of Palestine were indistinct from the rest of the Arab nation. While they did pose a serious humanitarian refugee problem, this would best be resolved through their resettlement and absorption in the neighboring Arab countries. The fourth link is the two-state solution, in effect ever since 1948 but given its clearest formulation by Prime Minister Golda Meir in her statement to the Knesset on 12 April 1973: "Between the Mediterranean Sea and the eastern desert, there is room for two States only: a Jewish State and an Arab State—Israel and Jordan." Lest there be any lingering doubts, she added for emphasis, "We oppose the establishment of an additional Arab State in the region between Israel and Jordan." The consistent formula of two states reappears almost word for word in the more recent basic national unity government foreign policy guidelines of 22 December 1988, quoted above.

Of interest, however, is the policy statement delivered by Mrs. Meir's successor, Yitzchak Rabin, because it involved something more than yet another unexceptional rephrasing of the standard official position. Indeed, in addressing the Knesset on 3 June 1974, the prime minister was unprecedented for his candor in embracing Jordan. He began by declaring, "We are interested in conducting peace negotiations with Jordan," and he went on to repeat the other proviso: "We aim at a peace treaty with Jordan which will be founded on the existence of two independent states" but without explicitly mentioning Jordan. Instead, Rabin reflected perhaps the first traces of caution and hesitancy ("waffling," in the statesman's dictionary) when he professed that in "the neighboring *Jordanian-Palestinian* state, the *independent* identity of the Palestinian *and* Jordanian Arabs can find expression in peace and good-neighborliness with

Israel" (emphasis added). Regardless, however, Israel would reject the establishment of a "further separate" Arab state west of the Jordan.

What this possibly suggests is that by 1974 there had to have been a nagging suspicion, a creeping awareness within Jerusalem's intimate policy circle, of the complications in insisting on direct, bilateral, government-to-government negotiations—and only with Jordan. By the early seventies, in short, the reemergence of the Palestinians as a political factor was working slowly to convert the essence of the Arab-Israeli dispute from the classic two-party model held by Israel into a triangular conflict. From Israel's standpoint such a fundamental restructuring was extremely undesirable, posing the future dilemma of ultimately having to square the triangle by either clinging tenaciously to the Jordanian option or else breaking with traditional bedrock policy and adopting a Palestinian-based scenario.

The latter option suffered, as we shall see, from profound drawbacks. Not the least of them was that partnership with the Palestinian national movement flew directly in the face of entrenched official policy. Yet it would not be entirely accurate, popular impressions notwithstanding, to say that Zionist and Israeli leaders never had or never bothered to entertain such a notion. Closer to the truth, the prospect actually had been tested at times, only to be found unworkable, ill advised, or both. Peace with the Palestinians—directly, exclusively, definitively—was ruled out certainly no later than 1947–48. Yet the option was reconsidered on at least three known occasions between 1948 and the Rabin formulation of June 1974.

CLOSING THE PALESTINIAN OPTION

Long before 1974—and even before 1948—a series of documented conversations had been held with the Arabs of British-mandated Palestine by Chaim Weizmann, David Ben-Gurion, and others aware of how growing opposition from the resident Arabs in the 1920s and 1930s was beginning to threaten the entire Zionist enterprise. These various probes failed, in large part because no local Arab spokesman stepped forward and offered the two qualifications that might have made possible a meaningful dialogue and an eventual accord: realism and authority. Such a bargaining partner had to be someone prepared to acknowledge the Jewish presence, if only to avoid the descent into intercommunal strife. But someone who, in addition, as their authentic representative, could commit the Arabs of Palestine to a final understanding.

Israeli statecraft would be plagued for decades to come by the absence of such a Palestinian interlocutor as the Zionist experience repeated itself. Dominant leaders like Haj Amin al-Husayni in the mandate period, Ahmed Shukayri in the fifties, and Yasir Arafat adopted a position of hostility toward Zionism and Israel and were uncompromising. On the other hand, any Arab "notables" who dared so much as to enter negotiations were, like the Nashashibis in the 1930s, either impotent politically or else intimidated by extremists.

Frustrated at the local level, Zionist leaders widened their search for a bargaining partner. Hoping to gain acceptance by Arab nationalism, they went far beyond the confines of Palestine in meeting with Egyptian, Iraqi, Lebanese, Saudi, Syrian, and Transjordanian government officials.

These prestate negotiations are extremely important for understanding the evolution of Israel's later Arab policy. First, they were no more conclusive in averting the Palestine struggle than talks at the communal level. If anything, secondly, they encouraged regionalization of the struggle through the intervention of the Arab states in Palestine affairs, first politically and diplomatically, then militarily in 1948. Third, these probings and soundings provided a disincentive to redoubling efforts toward the Palestinians and helped frame the later insistence on interstate peacemaking only. Contacts with the wider Arab world outside Palestine deluded Zionist and Israeli strategists into believing that this was the better political alternative; that Palestinian nationalism might be neutralized and perhaps erased entirely with the help of non-Palestinian Arab leaders. Finally, it was at this stage prior to the 1948 showdown that the groundwork was laid in particular for a pro-Hashemite orientation as the substitute for the Palestinians and later redesignated the "Jordanian option."

If anything, dismissal of the Palestinians by Israeli foreign policy after 1948 has to be judged as regressive when compared to the prestate diplomacy. On two memorable occasions, 1937 and 1947, Zionists endorsed the principle of partitioning Palestine. Since both the British and the UN partition proposals called for a Jewish state living alongside a second sovereign unit that logically could only have been a Palestinian Arab state, this was tantamount to Zionist consent in sharing the country with the Palestinians. Had the latter exhibited realism and compromise at either of these critical junctures, it is likely they, and not the Hashemites, would have been co-partitionists with Israel. Instead, their categorical rejection of partition—the very concept as much as any specific plan—instead gave the founders of the Jewish state a free hand in looking further eastward, across the Jordan River to Amman, for the missing pragmatic bargaining partner.

The events of 1948 thus mark the decisive turning point in the choice of Israeli options. What had begun as a quarrel between two communities resident in Palestine now changed course profoundly. One community, the Jewish *yishuv,* emerged even more cohesive while the other virtually disintegrated. Moreover, as the Zionist national movement rose in status, gaining recognition as a full-fledged sovereign state, its rival, the Palestinian national movement, slipped back. Not only did the Palestinian movement fail to gain comparable international standing, but it became subordinate to other Arab regimes, disappearing as a Middle East political factor for fifteen years, until 1964 when revitalized as the Palestine Liberation Organization.

Interestingly, however, the Palestinian option did not entirely disappear. It resurfaced briefly in 1949 in connection with the Lausanne conference. Preliminary discussions in Tel Aviv revealed two schools of thought when Foreign Minister Sharett put forward his formulation of a Palestinian alternative to Ben-Gurion's "Hashemite option" and belief that "the key to peace with the *Arab world* is our agreement to cede the Arab part of western Palestine to Abdullah" (emphasis added). Sharett cautiously argued that an independent Palestinian state was less of a threat to Israel than a "greater Jordan." A year earlier, on 8 August 1948, he had written of "establishing self-rule in the Arab part of western Palestine." Now he was urging the wisdom of striving for renewed contact and mutual understanding with Palestinian representatives, aside from pointing out the Hashemite Kingdom's uncertain future.

Sharett's viewpoint failed to gain adoption, however. Ben-Gurion had the clear upper hand in mobilizing ministerial and bureaucratic support for his position. Nor once again was there the requisite Palestinian leader to provide assurances of cooperation, whereas discreet channels had already been reopened to the royal court in Amman. Indeed, there is some indication that part of Sharett's thinking was tactical: the very act of being seen as flirting with a Palestinian policy might induce the Hashemites to be more compromising. After 1951 even Sharett's Foreign Ministry personnel related to Jordan and the West Bank Palestinians as a single entity.

The next flirtation with a possible Palestinian-based option did not take place until after the 1967 war. In possession of the entire West Bank area that had been under Hashemite rule since 1948, the Eshkol government sought ways to utilize this revised strategic situation in pushing for an end to the 19-year-old conflict. As part of this reassessment of all policy options, top leaders, but Defense Minister Dayan in particular, held a series of secret discussions with prominent West Bank mayors and other political figures. At the center of these talks, extending from February to August 1968, was the possibility of agreement on the principle of local Arab autonomy as a first step toward a wider permanent arrangement. But nothing of substance emerged from these meetings as, once again, the Arab moderates-pragmatists came under intimidation. But this time the threats were not so much from Palestinian rejectionists as from the Hashemites who announced a death penalty for anyone daring to negotiate with Israel—and thus posing as an alternative to the Hashemites themselves.

The only other significant airing of a Palestinian alternative came in the early seventies in the context of the Jordan crisis when, for a moment in September 1970, it appeared the Hashemites might lose power under the combined pressure of civil war and military intervention from Syria. Destabilization in Jordan and overthrow of the regime confronted government and military leaders in Israel with the question of whether Israeli interests in peace and security might conceivably be better served by having Palestinian nationalism find at least partial satisfaction in an East Bank takeover, with Jordan becoming Palestine.

The scenario and its possible longer-term implications were not thoroughly considered in September 1970, however, for several reasons. For one thing, partiality toward Jordan as we shall see had by then become deeply entrenched in Israel's Middle East strategy. It represented institutionalized thinking in Jerusalem and Tel Aviv. Moreover, it drew much of its logic from lines of tacit cooperation across both sides of the Jordan River. Understandably, caution argued in favor of the known and against a leap in the dark. Switching allegiances suddenly to supporting the Palestinians would have meant nothing less than a fundamental revision of traditional premises and break with conventional wisdom. Such policy departures are rare in themselves and are least likely during an international crisis, especially not during one as acute as Jordan's. The crisis came unexpectedly, raged intensely, and then ended almost as quickly as it began, leaving insufficient time for careful policy review.

It is true that IDF General Ariel Sharon made a name for himself in championing replacement of Hashemites with Palestinians in Amman, but this was in 1974. By then the power struggle in Jordan had ended; during the interim King Hussein had firmly if brutally reconsolidated control over the East Bank, his confidence bolstered by Israel's overt show of deterrent support against Syria and by its tacit vote of confidence. Consequently, the Hashemite-Palestinian confrontation in 1970 and the role indirectly played by Israel to this day represent the strongest confirmation of Israeli steadfastness in favoring the Jordanian option in any of its variant forms to a Palestinian one.

Throughout the 1970s, therefore, Israeli policy and PLO strategy effectively converged on the central sticking point: definitions of the directly concerned parties. At the level of grand design both dismissed out of hand the notion of an Israeli-Palestinian axis. In refusing to recognize each other, both increased their dependence on Jordan as the indispensable ally and partner within the Palestine triangle.

For many years Israeli leaders had the weight of argument almost entirely on their side when negating prospects for a Palestinian solution (even in theory) to each other, before the public in endless debate at home, and in discussions with foreign governments. Bedrock premises insisted

- the Palestinians—as a *people*—did not exist culturally or historically apart from other Arabs and hence could not qualify as a distinct nation in any accepted legal or political sense;
- the PLO—as an *organization*—was but a terrorist body pledged to Israel's destruction;
- Yasir Arafat—as a *leader*—was self-appointed and unrepresentative;
- Palestine—as a *state*—would directly threaten both Israel and Jordan, thereby menacing regional stability and Western security; and
- Palestine—as an *economic unit*—would be nonviable.

Depending on the Israeli speaker and on the particular target audience this core argument could be reinforced by additional debating points.

One such theme was that recognition of a Palestinian claim would require Israel to yield substantial territories on the West Bank (Judea and Samaria) prized for reasons of history, religion, and security. Another consideration was the absence of a compelling reason, since the United States, too, had committed itself diplomatically to working toward peace through Jordan.

Furthermore, this convergence of Israeli and American approaches went deeper. The firm conviction prevailed in Washington as much as in Jerusalem that the breakthrough with Jordan was imminent. Peace became merely a matter of patience and perseverance; of styling the correct wording for an understanding, then waiting for the propitious moment when King Hussein could step forward and triumphantly present himself as Israel's ideal peace candidate. Waiting for Hussein, in effect, became the only game in town, sustained by well-timed signals or moderate statements from across the river whenever hopes flagged.

Finally, of course, the Palestinians themselves had a hand, for in the absence of mutual confidence-building Israelis saw no reason for risk taking. Whereas Hussein appeared eminently reasonable, the PLO, in sharp contrast, projected intransigence. In this way it made a major contribution to hardening Israel's anti-Palestinian policy and to discouraging any new line of reasoning. Repeatedly during the seventies and eighties, whenever it appeared as though the public mood in Israel might become more receptive to considering either the wisdom or the practicality of sitting down and talking directly with the Palestinians, some timely act of violence by Fatah or any of the other PLO factions silenced voices for change, poisoning the atmosphere for months and years to come.

Munich 1972 and the murder of eleven Israeli athletes by Black September during the Olympics . . . Ma'alot 1974 with twenty-two Israeli school children slain by Palestinian infiltrators . . . Tel Aviv 1978 and the death of thirty-seven Israeli bus passengers on the coastal road. The impact of this litany of atrocities was to drive open-minded Israelis once again back into their protective shell. Public opposition toward the PLO only further stiffened, precluding reconciliation with Palestinian nationalism. Under such circumstances the choice was stark and unmistakable: not to talk to Hussein would leave no choice but to deal with Arafat.

The Palestinians, by avowing that the only way to deal with Zionism was by force and power, may have done little to nudge Israel or Israelis in their direction. Jordan, for its part, did absolutely nothing. Which is not surprising since the Hashemites continued throughout to be the chief beneficiaries of this deep-seated and historical Israeli-Palestinian estrangement.

PURSUING THE JORDANIAN OPTION

In retrospect, the late seventies and early eighties mark Israel's rediscovery of the Palestinians in every sense but politically. Instead of providing the stimulus for redefining the direct parties, the encounter only encouraged Israel's greater dependence on Jordan.

The explanation traces to the domestic political setting. Because of its basic imprecision, the Jordanian option actually satisfied both streams of pessimistic and optimistic thought dividing public opinion, as well as policy makers, on the central issue of the unresolved Middle East conflict. Those of the political right who concentrated their energies on maintaining the territorial status quo were only asking King Hussein to continue to respect and to preserve the existing, satisfactory situation of quiet coexistence on the eastern frontier. Those to the left politically, who rejected the status quo as unrealistic and ultimately perilous for the future of Israel on the twin arguments of democracy and demography, hoped to engage Hussein's Hashemites in a straight, two-way territorial redivision. In sum, one school of thought treated Israel-Jordan as the minimal security regime; the other, equally dominant, went further and visualized Israel-Jordan as forming an optimal peace regime.

For this reason, in one of the most important speeches of his long reign since 1953, His Majesty King Hussein could insist, without fear of Israeli censure, on 31 July 1988 that "Jordan is a principal party to the Arab-Israeli conflict and to the peace process"—even though in the same breath he struck at the very heart of both conceptions (the security regime and the peace regime) by renouncing dynastic claims to the contested West Bank and Gaza areas in deference to the Palestinians. The vast majority still had no real problem in accepting the King's assertion, for he was merely restating what was in fact a major—and possibly the oldest—orientation in Israeli foreign policy.

Historically and politically, what had begun in the earlier mandate period with friendly informal contacts between members of the Jewish yishuv and Abdullah, the aspiring amir of a desert kingdom to the east of the Jordan, enlarged during the turbulent years 1947–52 into something more substantial—a geopolitical bond—and eventually into a central pillar of Israeli defense and Middle East foreign affairs. Thus, for instance, ever since the fifties the Israelis have regarded Jordan's destabilization, a Palestinian seizure of power, an attack on Jordan from another Arab state, or the stationing of foreign troops on Jordanian soil as *casus belli.* This declaratory policy, in turn, strengthens the Hashemite throne against domestic and external threats, as tested and confirmed in Jordan's worse crisis in 1970. In the course of a half-century, Jordan has progressed from a co-belligerent in 1948 to a co-partitionist (with Israel) of former Palestine, eventually emerging after 1967 into Israel's de facto associate in what has become a multifaceted relationship.

The relationship is fascinating and quite remarkable for existing at all. Discreet and therefore not well-known, it is not exactly Israel's best-kept secret, but it is downplayed and low-key. The Israel-Jordan relationship is both strategic (security in the course of exploring peace) and tactical, observed in small matters of everyday administration. It rests on interdependence in such fields as commerce and defense. Not least, these close-knit ties disprove the conventional notion that countries locked in a state of belligerency (as have Israel and Jordan since 1948) are precluded from more meaningful exchanges other than undiluted hostility.

Indeed, so meaningful and strategic is the Amman-Jerusalem axis that it ranks on the select list of Israel's foremost bilateral relationships—a relationship almost on a par with the United States and world Jewry. Both of the latter are relatively distant from Israel, whereas the Hashemite Kingdom is directly adjacent. Therefore, whatever happens in Jordan, its regime and stability vitally affect Israeli hopes now and in the future for a normal, peaceful, and secure existence. This highlights yet another quality about the association since, in much the same way as the American and the Jewish connections, it, too, is informal and uncodified. There is no binding instrument to commit the two parties, Israel and Jordan, to any agreed or defined set of privileges and mutual obligations. For Israelis this may be a source of assurance, seeing that the arrangement nevertheless has held for so long, but there is also an element of concern and risk involved.

So exceptional and so pivotal is Jordan's part that its main features merit brief discussion. For example, when did the Hashemite orientation originate? On what is it based? Where has it led?

The roots of the Jordanian option, as we suggested earlier, can be traced to the formative, prestate Zionist era when many of the foundations for later collaboration between Jerusalem and Amman were put in place. Then and now the logic rests on two core considerations: one geographic, the other political. What brings Israel and Jordan together is the physical proximity of shared borders: they constitute the western and eastern banks of the Jordan River—Cisjordania and Transjordania respectively. The only thing that might distance and detach them from each other is the insertion of a third geopolitical entity, a Palestinian state somewhere in between. Yet this is precisely what both parties politically have long sought to prevent. In their separate but parallel quest for security and viability, the Hashemites—like the Zionists—shared identical priorities: exclusion of a third contender, the Palestinian national movement; and, if not that, then at least its subordination. *Realpolitik* considerations of this sort explain attempts by Ben-Gurion and King Abdullah in 1946–47 to reach a secret "gentleman's agreement" designed to facilitate an orderly partition of the country when the British mandate terminated.

Their tacit understanding unraveled, however, in the subsequent military struggle for Palestine. Still, the end of the 1948 fighting saw the two parties, the new state of Israel and the enlarged Hashemite Kingdom of Jordan, emerge as the two sole successor states, with Abdullah possessing those West Bank lands earmarked for Palestinian self-determination by the original 1947 UN partition plan. Both parties understandably had every interest in proceeding as quickly as possible to stabilize and legalize this new status quo. Annexation of the West Bank by Abdullah and the Hashemites in 1950 offers insight into a symbiotic relationship then only beginning to take shape. From the entire international community Britain and Pakistan alone formally recognized Abdullah's unilateral move. What really mattered, though, for the stability of this territorial restructuring was Israel's studied silence, which amounted to tacit acquiescence, just as Israel and Jordan came to accept Jerusalem as a divided city.

On the whole, however, Israeli-Jordanian relations in the next phase, 1952 to 1967, were less than satisfactory. They suggested little more than a coincidence of convergence and were governed by a minimal armistice regime—and an imperfect, unstable one at that—rather than any kind of mutual security regime. Neither side placed real trust in the other, nor were there secure lines of direct communication as yet. Hence the two neighbors did not seek closer collaboration but merely tried to preserve a semblance of quiet all along their shared yet permeable borders . . . and with only limited success. The 1950s reveal independent actions by both sides. They were a time of tension, with a spiral of border violations, stern warnings, and Israeli reprisals against Jordanian targets, which on more than one occasion unintentionally caused challenges to the Hashemite regime by opponents from within Jordan. This unacceptable state of the relationship can be accurately summed up as a "deterrence dialogue." It is a term that Yair Evron applies to Syria and Israel, but which is most apt for the eastern front as well, since until 1967 the emphasis was on dissuading each other from any gross violation through a network of negative sanctions.

This deterrence dialogue broke down completely in June 1967, owing to King Hussein's defection in taking up arms against Israel. At first glance the outcome and Israel's lopsided victory seemed to end the need, or the possibility, for a continuing relationship. First, Hussein had shown bad faith. Second, Israel's gain in prestige and in territory meant Jordan's loss and humiliation. Third, the responsibility for containing Palestinian sentiment, which previously had been interstate and executed jointly in 1967, now essentially became Israel's alone.

Nevertheless, the Israel-Jordan crisis of confidence did not cause an irreparable breach. Instead, it had the opposite effect, reinforcing the basic foundations and deepening the tacit relationship in the coming years. Rationality and pragmatism by both sides helped greatly in putting the pieces of the relationship together again and in focusing on mutual interests: in particular, avoiding a repetition of hostilities, coping with renewed Palestinian activism, preventing an imposed superpower or international settlement, and administering the West Bank.

In this sense the original geopolitical equation had not been altered so profoundly by the 1967 war. Geographic proximity-contiguity remained in effect, save for the fact that the Jordan River had replaced the old 1949 armistice "green line" as the Israeli-Jordanian security border. Similarly, an enduring interdependence remained politically, because the only hope the Hashemites had of repossessing the West Bank short of risking war would be through Israeli consent to territorial concessions. To the same extent, if Israeli leaders were earnest in searching for an end to the conflict short of recognizing Palestinian claims to legitimacy and separate statehood, then Jordan still represented the only real peace partner. These, then, offered the makings for the Jordanian option, as it came to be known in the years following 1967—a diplomatic approach premised on compromise and on exchanging lengths of territory for degrees of peace.

Consequently, the decade of 1967–77 not only marked a significant turning point in the evolving relationship, but also probably its high-water crest. The dialogue intensified while tacit cooperation broadened appreciably, made possible by several procedural and substantive arrangements. King Hussein and Israeli leaders entered into a fairly regularized secret dialogue based upon face-to-face meetings at the highest level. Secondly, both parties came to appreciate that their adversarial partnership involved an *affinity* of interests rather than any *identity* of interests. Therefore, they agreed to disagree on the larger political questions. Such tolerance was necessary for covering any of three political eventualities:

- *When views coincided but without being coordinated.* Example: Israel and Jordan each encouraged America's active participation in the peace process—in the hope Washington might endorse its stand while faulting the other's.
- *When positions ran diametrically opposed.* Examples: Amman's initiatives at the United Nations in sponsoring resolutions censuring Israel and embarrassing to Jerusalem. Opposition by Israel to any U.S. and Western arms transfers giving the Jordanian army sophisticated weaponry and an

offensive capability. The fact that Israel and Jordan took different sides during the Iran-Iraq War.

- *When respective positions meshed.* Examples here include eyeing a militaristic and expansionist Syria with suspicion; seeing themselves potential victims of Islamic fundamentalism as well as of Arab political extremism in any form; and appreciating that each would stand to lose from another round of Israeli-Arab conflict.

More often than not, Israel and Jordan could be found on the same side in favoring the regional status quo. Nor did symmetrical interests end there, since both shared an interest in a strong American and Western presence in the area. Last, but certainly not least, the royal court in Amman and the Israeli government both gave the highest priority to containing PLO influence and political and terrorist activity.

Israel and Jordan continued to build on shared interests and concerns after 1967. They consciously sought to mute points of friction between them for the sake of more immediate, tangible—and mutual—gains. Together, they reached a core consensus and, better still, a working relationship premised, again, on overcoming political insecurities. The period 1970 to 1973 probably best confirmed what payoffs might be had from discreet collaboration, when King Hussein reciprocated Israel's commitment to East Bank stability during the 1970 Jordan crisis by not being party to the Syrian-Egyptian surprise Yom Kippur attack and by refusing to be drawn into any real fight with Israel. Experts agree that Jordan's direct involvement in opening an eastern front might have strained Israeli reserves in manpower and equipment to the breaking point. Both events highlight the concept as well as the political-military framework by which these two small, interlocked neighboring states could reinforce each other. By the terms of the unconventional security regime Israel and Jordan represented two complementary parts: the sword and the shield.

Given these reassurances, Israeli and Jordanian leaders proceeded cautiously to give additional meaning and substance to the relationship, taking their security regime considerably beyond the one salient issue of defense. They applied tacit cooperation to other functional areas that in the aggregate suggested nothing so much as a West Bank condominium.

The situation prevailing in the administered territories from 1968 until at least 1988 was tantamount to shared rule. This involved Israel directly and Jordan indirectly; a silent partner as it were who, nonetheless, was encouraged to maintain and even increase its financial and administrative involvement. This strong Hashemite presence was particularly apparent to the Arab residents in the towns and villages on the West Bank in their daily life and commerce. Consider just a few manifestations of this presence and of joint action.

Item. Texts published by the Ministry of Education in Amman and screened as inoffensive by Israeli officials were used in West Bank schools.

Item. The Jordanian dinar served as legal tender in Jerusalem, Gaza, and the West Bank for all business transactions, along with Israeli currency.

Item. The government of Jordan paid the salaries of thousands of West Bank civil servants.

Item. The Israeli military administration permitted Islamic religious institutions and local chambers of commerce to act as agents for King Hussein, representing Jordan's interests and preserving its influence on the West Bank by dispensing funds and through other forms of patronage.

Item. Amman's approval usually was sought before Israeli authorities made municipal and other appointments.

Item. Pro-Hashemite loyalists frequently were permitted, and at times even encouraged, to go to Amman to consult with officials in the royal court, often serving as messengers or go-betweens between Israel and Hussein.

In fact, crossing from Israel to Jordan and back became something of an everyday occurrence under what became known as the "open bridges" policy.

This "open bridges" policy, in effect since 1967, actually best symbolizes Israeli-Jordanian peaceful cooperation. It facilitates the trucking of West Bank agricultural produce and other local manufacture across the Jordan River for transshipment and sale to Arab markets. Israeli and Jordanian border police and customs officials daily process tourist groups, Christian pilgrims, busloads of West Bankers wishing to make the hajj to Mecca in Saudi Arabia, and individual Arabs going to and from the East Bank for family visits or reunification. As late as 1986–87 Jerusalem encouraged Hussein to consolidate his power base in the territories under the guise of "quality of life" projects geared to improving economic conditions by promoting trade, investment, and tourism. Toward this end, and in the spirit of de facto power-sharing, Israel appointed three Arab mayors acceptable to Jordan, agreed to reopening the Cairo-Amman Bank, and nodded assent to a five-year development plan for the West Bank announced by Jordan. It is this same spirit that has enabled Israeli and

Jordanian farmers in the fertile Jordan Valley for years to work their fields and orchards in peace, a spirit that also accounts for the development, side-by-side, of Aqaba and Eilat as major tourist and Red Sea recreation centers.

Underlying these and other practical understandings are several basic constants. For Jordan, the opportunity to assert its continued West Bank and Gaza influence in direct competition with the PLO. For Israel, the need for Jordan's assistance in easing the heavy burdens of a prolonged and difficult military administration. For Israel as well as Jordan, "open bridges" functionalism offered the sole alternative to clashing head-on. As secret talks with King Hussein confirmed, the two outstanding political issues were unbridgeable: the specific terms of a peace settlement and the final status of the disputed territories claimed by both countries.

Still, if you were an Israeli in the mid-1980s it would have been impossible not to notice or appreciate the fruits of condominium. Border tensions were almost nil, while many smaller and mundane problems had been resolved constructively. Less understood were the limitations in such a tacit and loose arrangement and the attendant risks for Israel in holding firmly to the Jordanian option or even in loosening it into a hyphenated Jordanian-Palestinian option to cover all bets.

The key here is the distinction between "peace" and "peaceful coexistence," which is not only useful but necessary. Applied in its Israel-Jordan context, the latter framework was instrumental, to be sure for ensuring conflict avoidance and de facto military disengagement and also in encouraging, as we have seen, functional cooperation and confidence-building between these two friendly antagonists. On the other hand, however, condominium had not been crowned by a just and lasting peace.

This repeated inability to consummate the long political courtship of Abdullah and Hussein did not particularly disturb Israeli intellectuals or politicians. Their rationalizations may have varied but remained within a basic national consensus. Most strategists urged the government to continue pursuing the elusive Jordanian option with renewed vigor by offering more attractive terms. Their thinking and influence are apparent at every step of the way: the Allon plan for territorial compromise with Hussein in the late sixties, the Jericho plan of the early seventies, Begin's autonomy plan at the end of the seventies, cresting in acceptance by Labour Foreign Minister Peres of the Jordanian position that an international conference be convened in the hope of drawing Jordan into open negotiations (the 1987 London agreement).

Basic building blocks for this pro-Jordan edifice featured an entire set of implicit and unquestioned premises. These articles of faith, briefly, included (and, for a good many Israelis, still include) that Hussein and the Hashemites are willing and politically able to commit themselves; are intent upon regaining the territories; will agree to an offer by Israel of less than total withdrawal, including Jerusalem; and, most important, on recrossing the Jordan will succeed in regaining an upper hand, taming Palestinian nationalism, whether by the carrot or the stick, assuring a viable, stable "dual monarchy" to Israel's east.

Parenthetically, many of these same people appreciated the unlikelihood that all the pieces of the Jordanian puzzle would fit nicely together. In private off-the-record discussions it was not uncommon to hear predictions, even from enthusiasts of the option, that in the long run of course East Bank/West Bank demographics combined with the dialectic of repressed Hashemite-Palestinian antagonism would conspire to bring about Palestinization of Jordan. Meanwhile, however, for Israel it would be best either to pull Hussein into a pact now or else to sit back and do nothing, letting events take their own natural course. Whichever, the effect was to preserve the interests of the Hashemite Kingdom, its central peace and security function, and its privileged status for the majority of Israelis as the other directly concerned party.

The language of the 1978 Camp David framework accords suggests how widespread this predisposition toward Jordan was since it is the formula endorsed by Likud hard-liners: at the time by Menachem Begin and in more recent years by Yitzchak Shamir and Moshe Arens. Jordan, in spite of its demonstrative refusal to endorse either the Sadat initiative or the Camp David formula, is mentioned in the document no less than fourteen times as a direct participant at every stage of the peace process: from instituting administrative self-rule in the territories to regulating and even policing the transitional arrangement until concluding negotiations over the final status of Gaza and the West Bank. Within this broad and even sympathetic consensus toward Jordan and King Hussein it is understandable why so little thought was given in political, military, or academic circles to Israel disqualifying the pro-Hashemite strategy. Or to the possibility that Hussein might take himself out of the picture by unilaterally denying to his subjects and to the world, including Israel, the existence of a Jordanian option.

Which is precisely what the king did on 31 July 1988 in a speech from the throne. Bowing to wishes of the Palestine Liberation Organization for separating the West Bank from the Hashemite Kingdom of Jordan, Hussein announced the dismantling of legal and administrative links between the two banks. As he explained the historic shift of position away from claiming the territories for Jordan, these moves were meant to encourage liberation of the occupied lands and to respect the rights of the Palestinians to establish their independent state.

Hussein's unilateral decision came as a complete shock to Israeli analysts. Not that such a defection had not been a distinct possibility. Ever since 1967 the palace in Amman had been of two minds about the longer-term wisdom of returning to a politicized West Bank. Hussein astutely understood that he could act with impunity from the standpoint of Israel since the latter had left itself no option other than relying on Jordan, whereas Hussein retained both a Palestinian option and an Israeli one. Also, by 1988 there was some basis for reciprocal distrust, arising from mutual disillusionment. Israel after 1967 had inherited a restless West Bank because in nineteen years the Hashemites had failed to deal effectively with the Palestinians. Now it was Hussein's turn to feel betrayed. Twenty years later, Israel's inability to put down the *intifada* uprising meant the conflagration might easily be exported across the "open bridges" onto the East Bank, presenting the Hashemite regime with yet another threat in its heartland. Neither Israel nor Jordan, independently or jointly, had succeeded in defusing the Palestinian problem.

Had they not been so locked into the Jordanian option in all its variants, the situation by 1987–88 ought to have reminded Israelis about the nature of alliance politics. All international coalitions present really only two choices: either to progress or to backslide. How much greater is this likelihood when dealing with a tacit defensive arrangement that encouraged the twin dangers of miscalculation and defection? In reality, the Israel-Jordan connection, for all its practical daily stabilizing effect, had begun in the 1980s to lose the momentum of earlier years. Conceivably what plagued it at heart was the gap—the cognitive dissonance—between inflated Israeli expectations of King Hussein "delivering the goods" and Hussein's greater caution and reserve. Israeli enthusiasts of the Jordanian option in Jerusalem thought in terms of peace, but Hussein was obligated to approach his relations with Israel in the narrowest terms of self-preservation. By this symbiosis, restraint by King Hussein—his penchant for fence-sitting—however understandable on his part, translated into Israeli indecision and paralysis on the most vital issue of bringing the Arab-Israeli conflict to an end diplomatically.

Reexamined in the larger context of Israeli foreign policy, the tacit relationship so carefully pursued with the neighboring Hashemites seems to have evolved into something it was never designed to be in taking on semi-permanence. It had also for some time become suspended: well beyond the pole of minimum security, yet far short of the pole of definitive peace. Nor did prospects for a strategic diplomatic breakthrough seem particularly inspiring in light of the double set of constraints: in Jerusalem, the bottom-line consensus insisting that even by the principle of "territory for peace" Israel at least had the right to expect a territorial *compromise*; while in the case of Amman, Hussein's checks at home (Jordanian ambivalence toward the territories as a mixed blessing, plus economic and political dependence upon other Arab states) as well as a complicated relationship with the Palestinians and Arafat's PLO dictated extreme prudence.

For Israel to continue endorsing the Jordanian option in so structured and restrictive a political setting served as a disincentive against taking risks and new initiatives for peace. By priding themselves on their loyalty in waiting so patiently for Hussein, Israeli leaders on both sides of the political aisle actually found a refuge from decision. Little was required in effect other than adherence to the status quo framework, professing verbally the desire for peace, and to be sure, keeping lines of communication open to Amman.

If there is thus one specific issue or area of external affairs that does seem to warrant the otherwise overly generalized critique of Israeli foreign policy as conservative, status quo oriented, unimaginative, and reactive instead of initiatory, it would be in Israeli assumptions and unquestioned answers regarding Hashemite Jordan. For how else are we to explain that not even as authoritative a denial as the July 1988 West Bank disengagement speech by King Hussein could disabuse the Israeli notion of Jordan as the key to peacemaking?

Immediate reactions to the speech in the Israeli media sought to explain away this uncoordinated move on the part of Hussein. It was viewed, for example, not in strategic terms but as merely a tactical move and therefore not to be taken too seriously. The king could still be counted upon. Similarly, concrete actions taken by Amman at the time of the speech, like canceling salary payments and funding of West Bank development projects, were interpreted by those who wanted only to work with, and through, Hussein as just the king's way of showing strength. They claimed that, far from indicating genuine disengagement, the speech and related measures were meant to chasten the PLO and to remind the West Bankers to whom they were ultimately beholden financially as well as politically, while also indicating to all and sundry, from Moscow and Washington to Tel

Aviv and Tunis, that no peace negotiations could be contemplated that did not provide for full Jordanian participation.

Months later, when events confirmed Hussein's resolve to distance himself, about the most that Israeli true believers in the Jordanian option were prepared to concede was to hyphenate the peace formula. Procedurally, they supported a joint Palestinian-Jordanian delegation to the future peace talks, while their substantive blueprint called for a Jordanian-Palestinian confederation. Twinning of Arafat and Hussein became the best way, possibly the only way, for Israelis still wedded to the option to reconcile their views. On the one hand, growing appreciation was shown toward the steadfastness of the Palestinians and their nationalist sentiments, while on the other hand, they continued to give Hussein pride of position. In spite of evidence to the contrary, as late as the summer of 1989, it remained the official stated view of the government of Israel that the legitimate interests and needs of "Jordan and the Palestinian Arabs" in Judea, Samaria, and Gaza "are not necessarily incompatible"—not necessarily incompatible with a genuine and durable peace, or seemingly with each other. Nothing would better reflect the antiquarian "most favored Arab nation" standing conferred on the Hashemites and their dynastic interests in Israel's Arab policy.

CHAPTER 10

A FOREIGN POLICY AGENDA FOR THE 1990S

Disappointment awaits us in all walks of life, but in no profession are disappointments so amply outweighed by rich opportunities as in the practice of diplomacy.

–de Callières, 1717

Israel's fifth decade already gives evidence of being the most challenging. Set squarely astride the country's path to the twenty-first century are new concerns (Islamic fundamentalism, the introduction of chemical weapons) piled atop older ones allowed to accumulate for forty years. So formidable are these impediments that they cannot be ignored or wished away; but neither can they be bulldozed over or stepped around through fancy political footwork. Least of all the middlemost peace problem.

In diagnosing the cause for Israel's torment, it is the unrelieved state of siege—the "one long war" or whatever else helps to convey the absence of peace—that has the greatest explanatory power. Conflict and insecurity serve to frame the contemporary Israeli reality, misshaping national and domestic priorities while retarding the normalization of overseas relations.

The inescapable and overwhelming conclusion is that Israeli foreign affairs are unsettled. They can be depicted as anywhere from less than satisfactory to menacing, depending on one's degree of alarmism, even though some significant diplomatic inroads have been made in salvaging Israel's international prestige and political position. Coming quickly to mind are peace with Egypt, a peaceful border policed with Jordan, and of course, close association with the United States. Also worth mentioning are repaired ties in Eastern

Europe and the Third World, active trading partnerships in Western Europe and the Far East, and a network of important yet discreet commercial and defense cooperation with a range of individual countries—all of which provide Israel with a global reach. Still, in the end, the absence of secure peace represents the single most telling indictment of efforts to date by Israel in the diplomatic arena. In operational policy terms this leads to asking what might be done to improve the situation.

At this point our discussion takes a different tack. Having surveyed Israel and the world after forty years from the comparatively safe confines of scholarly description and analysis, it is only fair by way of conclusion to join the reader in considering the future direction of Israeli foreign policy at home and Israeli foreign relations abroad.

The initial item of business on Israel's peace and normalization agenda has got to be a much clearer understanding of what diplomacy is about and a better appreciation for what foreign affairs can be expected to accomplish. Perhaps the best way to begin is with the classic "diplomat's dilemma." International threat situations in general, and the explosive Middle East conflict in particular, force the diplomat to define each situation accurately and, on this basis, to mount the most timely, appropriate, and effective response commensurate to the situation. Here the statesman has but three choices. The alternative strategies are evasion, capitulation, or initiative.

Evasive Diplomacy

When faced with an unpleasant situation the first impulse may be to adopt a policy of evasiveness. Denial of reality is one of its more dangerous expressions; belittling the severity of the situation is another. The most prevalent form of escapism, however, lies in committing the state to preserving the status quo in the belief that the situation will improve with time or at least will not get any worse. Watching, waiting, evaluating—without taking remedial decisions—becomes a policy of drift based on tactical responses without an overarching strategy. Diplomacy under such circumstances in reduced to a hopeless rear-guard action. Because of the impossibility of defending against political change, nondecision and evasiveness carry with them the risk that a much higher and perhaps fatal price eventually may be paid than had firm action been taken earlier.

Submissive Policy

The diplomat's commission lies not in freezing a situation but in redeeming it. Which leaves the two strategies for Israel of either capitulation or taking the initiative. Whatever the major differences between these strategies, at least they reflect realism. The former, however, insists on accepting the situation as it is, surrendering to the force and weight of circumstance. The aim of diplomacy is to cut one's losses. Not by resisting the inevitable but by adjusting to the new realities as soon as possible and certainly before it becomes too late. Here realism and prudence call for flexibility in redefining the national interest downward, conceding marginal or secondary goals to save the vital ones. In other words, through a pliant and submissive foreign policy you do not change the situation itself so much as concentrate on improving your own position relative to it.

The diplomacy of diktat has often been prescribed as the wisest, possibly the only, course for smaller states in particular to adopt. In Israel's case it is what in fact Ben-Gurion did at the end of 1956, bowing to international pressures in ordering withdrawal from Sinai and Gaza. Even though there is obviously an element of defeatism in such a strategy, there is something to say for it: it has the not minor virtue of allowing one to return the next day and continue participating in the game of nations, albeit from a position of weakness. Provided, that is, that the concessions called for do not touch core interests such as security and survival.

Policy Initiative

When nothing less than vital interests are at stake, the only other response is to break out of inactive or reactive diplomacy by seeking to change the situation itself. This is the policy of initiative, applying to diplomacy the belief shared by generals and sportsmen that the best defense should be a good offense. The political rationale for this third strategy goes deeper, of course. Rather than wait for outside actors or circumstance to impose its will, active diplomacy encourages attempts at arresting the negative trend and turning it to one's favor. Redressing an unfavorable balance or a disadvantageous and possibly threatening situation becomes the top priority in such a diplomatic mode. But for it to succeed, the nation's full intellectual and material resources must be mobilized and all possible openings exploited. Where diplomatic openings do not immediately present themselves, an aggressive and purposive foreign policy must create new openings and opportunities.

An initiatory policy may sound like the height of imprudence, not to mention arrogance, especially where small states on the level of Israel are concerned. In setting out to restructure the political situation more to one's liking and consistent with one's own self-interest the risks are great, but perhaps no greater than in either of the two preceding options. A policy of drift underestimates the situation; a policy of diktat underestimates the ability of state actors to affect the situation.

Evasiveness and submissiveness are unimaginative. Both are uninspiring and unworthy of the sovereign state. Both may also very well be unnecessary, at least as a first response to adversity, in light of the historical and contemporary evidence. We are reminded of how through skillful statesmanship Talleyrand brilliantly restored France to a secure position under the nineteenth-century Concert of Europe; similarly, by acting with resolve, American foreign policy fundamentally reshaped the global balance with the Soviet Union and China in the early 1970s. North Vietnam, Egypt vis-à-vis the Soviet Union, and Afghanistan further suggest how capable relatively weak states can be in revising basic power situations. These lessons about the virtue of creative, strong-willed diplomacy at moments of adversity might best apply to Israel as it goes about fashioning a foreign policy for the middle and late 1990s.

NEW OPENINGS

Moving from what Michael Brecher has called the "pole of caution" to the "pole of courage" may very well be the only way to liberate Israeli foreign relations from the straitjacket imposed by Palestinian and Arab hostility. This course of action would be worthy of political Zionism, which shed the ghetto mentality after centuries of Jewish lethargy. It also falls within the prestate tradition of denying "objective" realities and creating instead new facts on the ground, thereby transforming the situation in Palestine. Similarly, the trademark of the previous generation of Israeli statesmen as well as military commanders was in looking for strategic openings. Whenever confronted by crisis, the country always found within itself the leadership, the vision, and the strength not merely to withstand the challenge but to seize the initiative: in striking against Egypt in 1956; in breaking the ring of imposed isolation by opening bilateral ties with Ethiopia, Iran, Turkey, and most of the non-Islamic emerging nations; in launching the 1967 preemptive war; in reversing the Yom Kippur War by crossing the Suez Canal; in improving the climate of relations with Washington; in promoting the Israeli-Egyptian diplomatic initiative after 1977 to revise the entire military equation in the Middle East.

In its requirement of imagination, tactical flexibility, and initiative, this third course certainly has to be preferred over an inactive foreign policy or a reactive one. Nor is there anything to suggest it would be any less effective than in the past in helping erase the memory of war and the sense of menace that have become part of Israeli life.

Much depends, however, on first laying the groundwork for a reinvigorated diplomacy at home. Foreign policy, after all, is only as good as the society it represents. The reverse is also true. Should Israel fail on the diplomatic front, it will be as much for internal reasons under its control as for independent outside factors. Specifically, at least four improvements in the way foreign policy is made and implemented within Israel are required before a diplomatic breakthrough can be achieved and fresh openings fully exploited. National self-confidence must be restored. A greater sense of vision needs to accompany efforts by Israel among the nations. The domestic consensus, badly frayed over the last decade, has got to be repaired. Finally, the decision making apparatus could stand certain improvements.

In the current mood of discontent Israelis as a group tend to be down on themselves, questioning everything from the relevance of Judaism, Zionism, and socialism to the prospects for ever ending the conflict and experiencing genuine peace. Entirely consistent with this frame of mind are extremely low assessments of diplomacy and its utility for Israel under siege. This sentiment is doubly unfortunate, for it is not only dangerous but invalid. If world politics teach anything it is that no country lacking in self-respect can insist of others that they respect and defer to it. Moreover, dismissing foreign policy's contribution in the past and in coming years seems excessive and uncalled for. All things considered, the Jewish state has not acquitted itself that badly in the international field. Certainly, as argued here and in earlier chapters, Israeli foreign policy has been far from an unmitigated failure; on the contrary it can point with pride to many significant achievements over forty years. And in terms of the present and the immediate future, Israel is far from helpless or powerless in directing the course of events. A primary task, therefore, is to generate appreciation for how much can be gained through adept diplomacy.

Encouraging this reeducation process relates, in turn, to the larger and still unresolved debate over Israel's role in world affairs. From the triad of competing worldviews discussed in chapter 2, a diplomacy of initiative leaves no room whatsoever for the pessimistic mindset. Jewish neo-isolationism is clearly inappropriate; so, too, is a permanent chip-on-the-shoulder stance of defiance in daring to take on the entire world. While negative symptoms (fatalism, xenophobia, fundamentalism, or "we against the Gentiles") must be fought against, so is simplistic naiveté equally to be discouraged. Idealism has a place in renewed diplomatic efforts, yet it needs to be tempered by *Realpolitik*. The Arab conflict rather than global anti-Semitism is the principal barrier to international acceptability, just as an Arab peace is a long, hard, and complex political process rather than a magical formula. A realist-idealism, in short, is called for.

Retooling for the future thus puts as the highest set of priorities restoring Israel's credibility in its own eyes and, secondly, adopting an affirmative and therefore constructive worldview. Together, this would give a renewed sense of direction, of purpose to daily foreign affairs. Just as essential is operating abroad from within a fortified national consensus. This is easier said than done when both government and public are so clearly divided on the most basic issues: the nature of the Jewish state and the wages of peace. Or, what price security?

Formed in December 1988, the second national unity coalition was believed at the time to have succeeded in hammering out an agreed, bipartisan peace platform. It pledged, for instance, determined opposition by Israel to negotiations with the PLO, withdrawal to the 1967 lines, and creation of an independent state west of the Jordan. Yet it did not even take three months for this minimal working consensus to come unraveled in the face of quickly unfolding developments—the *intifada* in the territories, dissenting voices from within each of the fractious Likud and Labour Alignment camps, criticism of the Israeli position by the American Jewish community, and most notably, a budding U.S.-PLO dialogue. So long as such pressures and strains continue to bombard the Israeli policy on almost a daily basis, getting its own house in order and repairing the national consensus from the bottom up—calmly, systematically, and free of outside interferences or distractions—are certain to prove extremely difficult.

Less pardonable for going untackled are those too frequent lapses and the many inefficiencies exposed in the making, coordination, and implementation of foreign policy analyzed in chapters 5, 6, and 7. Government leaders do remarkably little during the first stages of the decision-making process to take the public into their confidence by encouraging and also framing debate over the national agenda—the goals and the options—or by preparing the public for shifts in policy. Dissent is often muted, kept harmlessly confined to sterile party or Knesset debate while decisions themselves are taken in a highly centralized setting. Modest but yet positive steps would be to encourage devil's advocacy and originality by independent think tanks, academic research, open hearings under the auspices of the

Knesset's Foreign Affairs and Security Committee, or lecture series sponsored by such groups as the Israel Council on Foreign Relations. How far even this is from reality was evidenced by the fate of a 235-page report released in March 1989 by a JCSS study group at Tel Aviv University. Based on months of staff research and team discussion, *Israel's Options for Peace* and a companion pamphlet *Israel, the West Bank and Gaza: Toward a Solution* were dismissed by Prime Minister Shamir as politicized; he refused even to accept copies. Within a week the report dropped from public attention.

Inside government, policy coordination among the concerned ministries leaves much to be desired. Individual cabinet members often seem unaware of the need to speak with one voice and for the prime minister to be the authoritative spokesman. For ministers or their aides to initiate actions on their own or to vent their dissenting views after a policy decision has been reached violates the most fundamental norms of orderly government.

Organizational disharmony can be combated to an appreciable extent through closer interministerial consultation at all levels. The Ministry for Foreign Affairs should be brought back into the center of the process, with or without a proposed national security staff to supervise longer-range policy planning and ongoing policy review. Existing laws against the irresponsible leaking to the media of confidential and highly classified materials must be strictly enforced to curb what has become commonplace. Not to put all or most of these reforms into effect adds to an embarrassing picture of improvisation and policy disarray. It consigns Israeli foreign policy to fighting with one hand figuratively tied behind its back.

Israel does better at the implementation stage, when it comes to choosing how and by what means a particular decision or policy might best be given effect. Yet even here the level of performance and effectiveness can be improved. Perhaps the most important lesson learned from the 1980s is that the use of force alone is inappropriate to most of the political situations in which Israel can expect to find itself short of border defense, counterterrorism, or a direct threat of Arab military attack. This greater political sophistication automatically places a higher premium on diplomatic prowess and skill.

Cultural diplomacy but especially economic statecraft can be impressive in breaking down barriers; they are well worth expanding in the 1990s in an era of greater international economic integration and interdependence. Meanwhile, Israel's special brand of statecraft in the dark has allowed the country quietly to lower and get around other political barriers. Here the agenda calls for promoting some of the secret, back-channel exchanges to the point of full, open relationships by a combination of tact and persistence. This cause is hardly served by Israeli indiscretions that compromise the unwritten rules for confidentiality and trust.

Arms diplomacy, on the other hand, already had begun to undergo revision, prodded by market trends in the global arms bazaar as well as the costly fallout (i.e., American pressure, world criticism, and a blow to Israel's image as a world actor) from weapons supply practices toward Khomeini's Iran, South Africa, and Central America. Any further revision, it bears noting, is unlikely to terminate the sale of defense equipment and technologies altogether. In the absence, once again, of genuine peace, the security and economic imperatives for foreign military assistance by Israel are too cogent to give up this form of trade and influence by converting to nonmilitary production exclusively. Rather, the thrust is in diversification: rechanneling military cooperation from the more dubious and less dependable arms recipients in Central America and southern Africa to the industrializing democratic powers of North America, Western Europe, and East Asia.

In a separate category is how Israel might best activate its diplomatic trump card: the invaluable Jewish bond. As in other areas, Israeli diplomacy could be less heavyhanded and more tactful. The Polland affair was an unmitigated disaster; no less so was the unfortunate "Who is a Jew?" controversy clumsily reopened in late 1988 just when Diaspora solidarity with Israel was so badly needed in contending with the PLO diplomatic-propaganda offensive aimed, in part, at driving a split between Israel and world Jewry. In specific terms of the largest, most affluent, and politically most influential American Jewish community, Jerusalem must show increasing sensitivity and greater care toward keeping the dialogue within mutually acceptable bounds. Nor will it do to remain excessively dependent on the American Jewish lobby in general, and AIPAC in particular, in promoting Israel and Israeli interests in Washington.

As far as promoting Israel goes, several neglected policy instruments should be reappraised as part of a bolder, more assertive foreign policy. High on the agenda should be a major revamping of the propaganda (*hasbara*) apparatus, leading to a revitalized overseas information campaign. Idealist-realism posits that world opinion *can* be influenced and *can* be won over, provided policies are clearly defined and reasonable, and they are disseminated by using the proper approach and effective marketing techniques on an individual country and target audience basis. It is hardly accidental that the struggle for world opinion has so little so show when, in addition to not projecting a clear and positive image, cultural activities abroad are described by government sources as "incidental and coincidental" and when the entire government budget of *hasbara* in the United States at the end of the eighties amounted to little more than $1 million a year. Throwing money around has never been a panacea; still, this gross lack of funding and professionalism has got to be remedied before Israel will enjoy its day in court before world opinion.

Nor should the United Nations be underestimated in the future or shunned. For all its structural, procedural, and partisan political defects, the United Nations and its agencies provide an exceptional forum for making Israel's presence felt and its voice heard internationally. Even given the frequently hostile atmosphere prevailing in the plenum sessions, the world body has continued to provide the opportunity for practicing quiet diplomacy in the UN corridors both in New York and Geneva, enabling the exchange of views with delegates from countries that still refrain from formal ties with Jerusalem. A return to the UN in force would symbolize better than anything else the change of direction in Israeli foreign policy from disengagement, or "holding the line," to one of active engagement.

Israel's place at the United Nations and the state of its various country relationships certainly discourage complacency. From Antigua to Zaire, each country has to be perceived as representing a past achievement, a present concern, and a potential problem. Omission of countries like Afghanistan, Albania, Algeria, and Angola (that precede Antigua alphabetically in Table 1) further indicates the hard road Israel must still travel in seeking—seeking, not awaiting—the comity and recognition due all sovereign nations.

Consider the road to Moscow that, by all accounts, is one of the main signposts on Israel's journey to normalization. It would be false idealism, even in an era of détente and *glasnost* to think Israel can easily repair its relations with the Soviets and arrive to a cordial reception in the Kremlin. Precisely because of the ideological, domestic-political, and global-strategic variances offered in chapter 8, friction will continue between Moscow and Jerusalem even after formal ties have been renewed. That much is clear also from the sheer number of contentious issues crowding the Soviet-Israeli agenda. One set of items begins with the status of Soviet church property in Israel and trade prospects, moving on by increments of political sensitivity to the exodus of Jews from the Soviet Union and their right to emigrate directly to Israel, but also the cultural and religious life of those Jews remaining in the USSR. These issues were being seriously addressed at the close of the eighties. Less discussed were objections raised by the Soviets to Israeli participation in "Star Wars" military research projects and to Israel's development of an intermediate-range ballistic missile (the Jericho) deemed capable of reaching the Soviet homeland. Soviet support for anti-Israel measures at the United Nations, Moscow's arms supplies to Syria and Iraq, and its one-sided, pro-Arab stand on Middle East conflict-related issues round out the bilateral agenda.

On the other hand, the situation is far from hopeless. In fact, there is room for guarded optimism. Working in Israel's favor are

- reaffirmed Soviet support for the existence and security of the Jewish state;
- evidence of a reorientation in Soviet foreign policy from adventurism and overextending itself to "new thinking" premised on greater caution and a framework for cooperation with the West in easing global as well as regional tensions;
- a desire to moderate and control world militarization at nuclear and conventional levels, with particular sensitivity for the adjacent Middle East zone;
- concern at the mounting Islamic threat in central Asia and on the southern flank of the USSR;
- extreme sensitivity lest the Soviet Union be excluded, as it has been by the United States on previous occasions (1974–75, 1978, 1982), from Middle East affairs and a wish to be part of the Arab-Israeli peace process, necessitating that it be on speaking terms with each side and acceptable as a broker to Israel; and
- a forced reassessment of the long-standing pro-Arab policy that the Kremlin has undergone in recent years out of an awareness that this strategy has cost the Soviet Union heavily while bringing only mixed results.

More than anything else, however, Israel's chances for mending ties probably depend on the ability of Mikhail Gorbachev and the school of Soviet economic reformists to consolidate their authority at home, to turn Soviet attention inward, and to steer Soviet Middle East and foreign policy in a direction of greater realism.

One final, procedural note of encouragement is the accessibility of a side path to Moscow. In 1967 the Kremlin led the way in breaking off relations; its East European allies dutifully followed suit. As of the late 1980s at least, the pattern reversed itself, with the assignment of changing an outdated 20-year policy falling upon countries like Hungary and Poland. Their actions have made it easier for the Soviet leadership to save face and reconcile with Israel. Clearly though, in this instance the initiative has had to come from Moscow, with

Israel's role being to encourage any Soviet indications of willingness to proceed further—and without preconditions—in regularizing and eventually resuming normal relations.

In Israel's superpower interests, the American road map is altogether different. Its emphasis is not so much on detail as on the larger contours. Also, Israel wants the Soviet Union to adopt a less mechanically hostile and a more evenhanded stance, whereas the main efforts toward the United States lie in discouraging too much evenhandedness by the American public, Congress, or administration at the direct expense and insecurity of Israel.

The question heading the Israeli-American agenda is less likely to be any particular agenda item (although the Middle East peace process claims obvious prominence) than the general atmosphere of the relationship and the ground rules for conducting it in the future. Here, there is considerable room for initiative and even imagination by Israel in (a) preventing a serious erosion; (b) asking itself the right questions; (c) heading off potential collisions with Washington; and (d) stepping forward with concrete proposals and solutions of is own. Only by doing so will Israel have done its utmost to prevent the accumulated warmth of America's friendship from slipping.

Before anything else, vigilance is called for to make sure that what had developed by the mid-1980s into a close working relationship is not eroded by disenchantment, mistrust, or still worse, nonchalance. To some extent each of these negative influences is only natural according to alliance dynamics. Israel's foreign policy agenda may run closely parallel to that of the United States, but they should never be mistaken as identical, nor should Israel's be subordinate. For example, Washington and Jerusalem may have different perceptions of the Soviets' place in peacemaking: the United States may desire burden-sharing, with Israel opposing any form of superpower condominium; or, vice versa, the United States may prefer, as Kissinger did, to exclude the USSR as a peace co-sponsor and Middle East actor, while Israeli calculations make it receptive to a role for the Soviets, either as a quid pro quo for normalizing bilateral ties or because policy strategists in Jerusalem are convinced Moscow can contribute meaningfully to a stable peace.

As a second step in minimizing potential friction, Israel should be asking itself (which it really has not) hard questions. Is dependence on one great power necessary? Is it good? Is it wise? At what point does reliance on a friendly foreign power, even one as giving as the United States, become excessive? On the other hand, is independence any longer realistic? Or, alternatively, can a framework of interdependence be pursued to the mutual advantage of both the United States and Israel? It is the responsibility of Jerusalem policy planners to be asking themselves these kinds of larger, longer-range questions that so easily get lost in the shuffle of daily cable traffic, rather than waiting for them to be raised unilaterally by their American counterparts.

Throughout such a long and fundamental policy review of where Israel wishes the relationship to go, a third priority must be the early identification of potentially divisive subjects as well as deeper economic, social, or political trends in America. This watchfulness is essential for Israel to avoid the disastrous consequences of being taken by surprise, of being out of tune, or of being dragged needlessly into a confrontation with U.S. policy over agenda-setting differences.

Reminding ourselves of the three traditional pillars of the relationship, all three—shared political ideologies, the pro-Israel domestic consensus, shared strategic concerns—are susceptible to change. For instance, Americans have always esteemed Israel for its equal commitment to democracy and to national security. But what if these two cardinal principles should conflict with each other? Israeli government policy of dealing firmly after December 1987 with the West Bank and Gaza uprising posed this very question in political rather than philosophical terms: just how far is a democracy like Israel justified in going to defend itself against the threatened breakdown of law and order? Without a universal standard or ethical ruling, many of the repressive measures taken in response to *intifada*-related provocations shocked American TV audiences and were sharply criticized in the media, blurring Israel's image as a democracy. As though this were not challenging enough, another serious dilemma arises from a different aspect of the strategic factor. Still to be addressed are the larger, long-term consequences of greater superpower understanding and détente for Israel and for the U.S.-Israeli friendship. Desirable in themselves, nevertheless, understanding and détente seem to suggest a diminution in Israel's esteem in American eyes as a military bastion in the Middle East, with all that might imply for defense aid authorizations from the American congress.

Similarly, support for Israel traditionally has derived from two profound advantages. First, Israeli leaders grasped better than almost any other country the nature of the American political system—how the process works, where power rests, what means of influence and pressure are acceptable, and those that are not. Second, they relied principally on the American Jewish community, yet wisely made it the nucleus for a much larger campaign with wider appeal. The price of success is that now the pro-Israel lobby itself becomes the target for attack; AIPAC, at its center, has been charged by outsiders and opponents with overplaying its hand on Capitol Hill, with the American media, and in administration policy toward the Middle East and Israel. As of the late 1980s there were also rumblings of internal dissent and even of individual defections as solidarity with Israel began to lose some of its popularity and support with those turned off by Israel's behavior. Also defecting were former "cold warriors" recently convinced that in an era of Soviet-American détente small and expensive security allies such as Israel are no longer needed, thereby weakening the strategic argument for the U.S.-Israeli partnership. It looks like the domestic American coalition backing Israel will be less dominant, considerably more cautious, and less united.

What Israel must do, in short, is prevent a no-win, zero-sum conflict of interests trading off democracy for security. Its U.S. friends, in turn, have got to avoid any scenario that would leave American Jews in their love of Israel and defense of the Jewish state isolated and outside the American national consensus. Meanwhile, both Israel and its friends should be accentuating the positive, which means pressing the case for complementary strategic interests in eastern Mediterranean stability, in the intelligence field, and in defensive weapons development.

To head off unnecessary strains in the relationship, Israel is the one that should be proposing initiatives and concrete suggestions on at least two major topics on the U.S.-Israeli agenda: the American assistance program and the peace process. Concerning the former, reductions in economic and military aid from the United States have been forecast since the mid-1980s, with American economics experts or congressmen suggesting it was merely a matter of time. Rather than waiting until funding is cut, Israel ought to be taking measures now to make sure it can manage without that income. Restructuring its economy, stimulating private investment, insisting on defense budget efficiencies, and possibly even revising its national security doctrine are but a few alternatives. In addition, it should be proposing that representatives of both countries negotiate a phased reduction in grants. And it should be showing originality in suggesting indirect compensation by expanded bilateral trade plus joint defense industrialization ventures as part of an Israeli strategy for economic recovery through industrial and export growth.

In the final analysis, however, Israel's superpower relations are unavoidably linked to its regional ones. Or to put if differently: either Israel will be forced to become entirely dependent on the United States economically, militarily, and politically, or it will have to resolve the Middle East dispute. And while there is some truth to the argument that this dispute is really two-tiered—the Israeli-Arab conflict involving the Arab states, and the Israeli-Palestinian intercommunal conflict—nevertheless, the conflict must end where it began: in an accommodation between Jewish and Palestinian nationalism.

If any sense of urgency was needed for Israel to initiate a settlement, it came not only in the *intifada* but from a remark in December 1988 by retiring U.S. ambassador to the United Nations, Vernon Walters. Speaking with undiplomatic bluntness on America's behalf, he said: "We must tell the parties . . . that we are tired of the conflict." Translated into political terms, this tiredness can only mean one of two things: a waning of U.S. interest in and support for Israel or the implied threat of an imposed settlement.

True, Israel has known moments of diplomatic isolation in its history: 1956, May–June 1967, October 1973, 1975, 1982. Yet never in its first forty years did it stand internationally so alone as at the start of 1989, running after events in the West Bank and Gaza and practicing damage control to the PLO's own brand of initiatory diplomacy launched at Algiers, Stockholm, and Geneva, which won new allies for the Palestinian cause while increasing pressure on Israel. It is too much to ask of any small state's foreign policy to challenge simultaneously the world organization, world opinion, the Arab and Islamic worlds, the Palestinians, the United States, and even segments of the Jewish world. Hence, the imperative for an Israeli peace blueprint appropriate to the 1990s.

ISRAEL AT PEACE

For the past decade at least Israel has been pursuing two foreign policies: a concerted and energetic effort toward further cementing ties with the United States; a defensive one toward the Arabs that is especially condescending toward Palestinian nationalism. Both policies assume cooperation from the other side: America's cooperation, in the form of moral and material support; Jordanian cooperation by adhering to tacit functional understandings reached over the years; Palestinian cooperation in the sense of disqualifying themselves politically through their traditional course of extremism, intransigence, and indiscriminate terrorism.

The time for indecision and relying on others has passed. Israeli diplomacy must now prove no less attentive and forthcoming to the Palestinian dimension of foreign affairs than to the U.S. connection. In this regard King Hussein's July 1988 declaration of nonintent toward the contested West Bank becomes profoundly important. The shift from Jordan to the PLO as the sole legitimate interlocutor for the Palestinians marks a fundamental change in the Arab balance of power. It is a new reality that Israel can either refuse to accept or accept and convert into a positive peace gain. It is the opportunity for redesigning the national agenda, and with it foreign relations. "Israel ought not to cleave to all its former positions on the Middle East," confided Foreign Minister Moshe Arens to a Knesset committee in January 1989. "We must not erect a stone wall and refuse to make any changes." His words indicate the kind of hard, pragmatic idealist-realism needed by Israel to see it safely through the nineties.

A willingness to contemplate change leads one back to fundamentals: who are the parties to peace and, secondly, what might be the framework for peace between them? With regard to the first, it was clear that Israel had lost the struggle against legitimization of the PLO. Moreover, in the absence of a Jordanian partner, Israel will be negotiating directly with the Palestinians and their representatives. That much seemed certain by the start of the fifth Israeli decade, in spite of Prime Minister Yitzchak Shamir's December 1988 oath: "We are not ready and will never be ready to talk to the PLO."

Such finality is inappropriate to the art of diplomacy, as is Shamir's corollary avowal: "There will never be a Palestinian state." The real question, rather, is the earthly, geopolitical one of appropriately siting such a state. One peace model might imagine Jordan's transformation into a Palestine state, with most of the West Bank becoming a condominium shared in by the Palestinian state and Israel. As imperfect as any other solution, nevertheless, a grand design of this sort at least bears within it the seeds for future cooperation between Palestinians and Israelis. Not unimportant is the logic behind the design: a two-party negotiation and a two-state solution within the historical, geographic, and demographic boundaries of East Bank–West Bank *eretz Yisrael* / Filastin. Here, in seeking to advance this strategy as cautiously as possible, secret diplomatic channels might provide an invaluable service both for Israel and the cause of peace. Used successfully in the past as a tool of Israeli national interests and foreign relations, backdoor statecraft would permit the two frustrated and suspicious antagonists at least to face each other directly, to probe intentions, and to seek areas of accord, small or large, without being forced either to lose face or to concede major bargaining cards in advance.

Over time Israel has been more successful in maneuvering internationally than in disciplining itself into choosing between Hashemites and Palestinians. With the necessity for choice at hand, there is wisdom for Israel in holding Yasir Arafat to his statement of 14 December 1988: "Self-determination means survival for the Palestinians. And our survival does not destroy the survival of the Israelis."

❑

If all goes well, on 14 May 1998 the state and people of Israel will pause to duly and appropriately mark the first half-century of reborn Jewish sovereign independence. Among its other achievements will be fifty years of foreign affairs. Israeli foreign policy since 1948 has embodied a complex mixture of change and continuity. Its alignments, power position, degree of involvement in world affairs and satisfaction with the international system have all changed, sometimes dramatically, over the years. But there remain notable continuities in Israel's view of the world, centering on Jerusalem's ceaseless striving for the three "elusives" of peace, security, and normalcy.

By that historic occasion Israel, we hope, will have broken with the past in realizing these goals by solidifying friendship and cooperation with the United States, restoring ties with the Soviet bloc, enjoying respectability in international forums, strengthening the peace with Egypt, living in coexistence with its Arab and Palestinian neighbors, and last but by no means least, fulfilling the ideal of making Israel the safe home of the Jewish people. Although there is little profit in prophesying what the exact political situation will be in May 1998, one observation seems beyond doubt. Whether upon looking back or in looking ahead, it is Israeli diplomacy, rooted in vigilant self-defense and idealist-realism, that will have the last word.

SUGGESTED READINGS

The bibliographical references listed here are not meant to provide an exhaustive inventory of the literature on Israeli international relations. Although much of the author's research involved extensive Hebrew readings, the items given here are confined to sources available to a wider audience in English. Also, rather than arranged by chapter, the material is organized by specific aspects of Israel's foreign policy to assist the student or general reader who may be interested in pursuing any of the subjects discussed in this book.

Documentary and Periodical References

The Israeli Ministry for Foreign Affairs has published a series of selected documents entitled *Israel's Foreign Relations.* Edited by Meron Medzini, these five volumes of official policy speeches and government statements extensively cover the period 1947 to 1979. The Israel State Archives, although falling behind the 30-year schedule for declassifying state papers, thus far has released five volumes of the series *Documents on the Foreign Policy of Israel* (Yehoshua Freundlich, editor) that provide detailed information for the years 1947 to 1951, particularly internal government papers, memorandums, and diplomatic cables. Itamar Rabinovich and Jehuda Reinharz have co-edited a useful book of documents and readings, *Israel and the Middle East* (Oxford University Press, 1984), dealing with society, politics, and foreign relations from 1948 to the early 1980s. The two best documentary compilations on the specific Arab-Israeli dispute are John Norton Moore (ed.), *The Arab-Israeli Conflict* (Princeton University Press, 1977), and Yehuda Lukacs (ed.), *Documents on the*

Israeli-Palestinian Conflict, 1967–1983 (Cambridge University Press, 1984).

Articles on Israeli diplomatic history and contemporary problems by Israeli scholars frequently appear in such English-language journals as the *Jerusalem Quarterly* and the *Jerusalem Journal of International Relations*. More widely circulated scholarly or policy-oriented periodicals that tend to feature topics relating to Israel's security and foreign affairs include *Foreign Affairs, Foreign Policy, Orbis, Commentary,* the *Middle East Review,* the *Middle East Journal,* and *World Politics.* Both the Hebrew University's Leonard Davis Institute for International Relations and Tel Aviv University's Jaffee Center for Strategic Studies publish a series of monographs: the Jerusalem Papers on Peace Problems and the JCSS Studies.

The History of Zionism and Israel

Paul Johnson, in his *A History of the Jews* (Harper & Row, 1987), offers a sympathetic review not only of Jewish history into the twentieth century but of the contribution and role of the Jewish people in world history. The political development of Zionism from Herzl until the First World War is ably traced by David Vital in a three-part comprehensive study published by Oxford University Press: *The Origins of Zionism* (1975), *Zionism: The Formative Years* (1982), and *Zionism: The Crucial Phase* (1987). The best single-volume general study is Walter Laqueur's *A History of Zionism* (Holt, Rinehart and Winston, 1972). Major treatments of Zionism's intellectual sources include Ben Halpern, *The Idea of the Jewish State* (Harvard University Press, 1961); Arthur Hertzberg's anthology and insightful introductory essay, *The Zionist Idea* (Meridian Books, 1969); and Shlomo Avineri, *The Making of Modern Zionism* (Basic Books, 1981). A wealth of original supplementary material is now available thanks to *The Rise of Israel: A Documentary Record From the Nineteenth Century to 1948,* Howard M. Sachar, series editor (Garland Publishing, 1987).

Samuel J. Roberts traces the historical and intellectual roots of Israeli foreign policy back to the Jewish kingdoms of Judah and Israel. Posing the question, *Survival or Hegemony?* (The Johns Hopkins University Press, 1973), he opts for the latter. Prestate Zionist diplomacy is at the center of Dr. Chaim Weizmann's autobiography, *Trial and Error* (Harper & Brothers, 1949). *The Balfour Declaration* (Simon & Schuster, 1961) by Leonard Stein remains a classic, while Christopher Sykes traces the political efforts by Zionist representatives during the British mandate period in *Crossroads to Israel* (World

Publishing Company, 1965). Arab contacts during this period by *yishuv* representatives are discussed in Aharon Cohen, *Israel and the Arab World* (W.H. Allen, 1970); Yosef Gorny, *Zionism and the Arabs, 1882–1948* (Oxford University Press, 1987); and Neil Caplan's two-volume analysis, *Futile Diplomacy:* Vol. 1, *Early Arab-Zionist Negotiation Attempts, 1913–1931* (Frank Cass, 1983) and Vol. 2, *Arab-Zionist Negotiations and the End of the Mandate* (Frank Cass, 1986).

The final showdown and combined diplomatic-military struggle for independence in 1947–48 have received considerable scholarly attention. Among those most recommended are J.C. Hurewitz, *The Struggle for Palestine* (W.W. Norton, 1950); Martin Gilbert, *Exile and Return* (Steimatsky's, 1978); and David Horowitz, *State in the Making* (Alfred A. Knopf, 1953), an observer's first-person account of the dramatic events. The history of Israel since statehood can be studied from any of the following: Conor Cruise O'Brien's popularized rendition, *The Siege: The Saga of Israel and Zionism* (Simon & Schuster, 1986); Howard M. Sachar, *A History of Israel:* Vol. I, *From the Rise of Zionism to Our Time* (Alfred A. Knopf, 1976) and Vol. II, *From the Aftermath of the Yom Kippur War* (Oxford University Press, 1987); and Nadav Safran, *Israel: The Embattled Ally* (Harvard University Press, 1978), which looks at the transformation of Israel through three decades of Middle East crises and wars while analyzing the shaping of American-Israeli relations. Colorful descriptive accounts by two men present at the creation are Abba Eban's *My Country—The Story of Modern Israel* (Weidenfeld & Nicolson, 1972) and two works penned by David Ben-Gurion: *Israel: Years of Challenge* (Holt, Rinehart & Winston, 1963) and *Israel: A Personal History* (Funk & Wagnalls, 1971).

Chronicles of Israel's many wars take up more than one library shelf, attesting to the greater emphasis on military events at the expense of its diplomatic undertakings. Among the better military studies are Chaim Herzog, *The Arab-Israeli Wars* (Random House, 1982); Netanel Lorch, *One Long War* (Keter Books, 1976) ever since 1920; and Colonel Trevor N. Dupuy, *Elusive Victory: The Arab-Israeli Wars, 1947–1974 (Harper & Row, 1978).* Useful as a supplement is Martin Gilbert's *The Arab-Israeli Conflict: Its History in Maps* (Weidenfeld & Nicolson, 1974). On the diplomatic side, among the few offerings are Walter Eytan, *The First Ten Years* (Simon & Schuster, 1958), written by the first director-general of the Foreign Ministry; and a personal memoir by a retired career diplomat, Gideon Rafael, *Destination Peace: Three Decades of Israeli Foreign Policy* (Weidenfeld & Nicolson, 1981). In a class by themselves are the two books published by Michael Brecher: *The Foreign Policy System of*

Israel (Yale University Press, 1972) and *Decisions in Israel's Foreign Policy* (Oxford University Press, 1974). The latter contains separate chapters on specific issues: Jerusalem, German reparations, the Korean War and China, Jordan waters diversion, the Sinai campaign, the Six-Day War, and the Rogers proposals.

Critics and Defenders

A recent phenomenon is the growth in Israeli revisionist historiography, reopening as well as reinterpreting earlier events. Representative of this genre of history is Simcha Flapan, *The Birth of Israel* (Pantheon Books, 1987), which in an effort to shatter old myths has created new and unfounded ones. Benjamin Beit-Hallahmi, in his book, *The Israeli Connection: Who Israel Arms and Why* (Pantheon Books, 1987), reveals more about the excesses of the revisionist approach than about the origins and motivation behind Israel's defense exports. Far more judicious and scholarly are Benny Morris, *The Birth of the Palestinian Refugee Problem 1947–1949* (Cambridge University Press, 1988), and Avi Shlaim, *Collusion Across the Jordan* (Columbia University Press, 1988), which reappraises secret negotiations with Abdullah for partitioning Palestine. Both should be read in conjunction with *Britain and the Arab-Israeli Conflict, 1948–1951* (St. Martin's Press, 1988) by Ilan Pappé.

Israel's diplomatic record does not lack for non-Israeli critics either. One type of criticism is suggested in the writings, for example, of George W. Ball, "How to Save Israel in Spite of Herself," *Foreign Affairs* 55, no. 3 (April 1977): 453–71, and George W. Ball, "The Coming Crisis in Israel-American Relations," *Foreign Affairs*, 58, no. 2 (Winter 1979–80): 231–56; Seth Tillman, *The United States in the Middle East: Interests and Obstacles* (Indiana University Press, 1982); James Lee Ray, *The Future of American-Israeli Relations: A Parting of the Ways?* (University Press of Kentucky, 1985); Cheryl A. Rubenberg, *Israel and the American National Interest* (University of Illinois Press, 1986). The tone of such works is often strident and uniformly uncharitable in interpreting the motives behind Israeli behavior. More moderate and constructive forms of criticism are mirrored by Nahum Goldmann, "Zionist Ideology and the Reality of Israel," *Foreign Affairs* 57, no. 1 (Fall 1978): 70–82; Stanley Hoffmann, "A New Policy for Israel," *Foreign Affairs* 53, no. 3 (April 1975): 405–31.

Israel's ambassadors to the United Nations have always been a first line of defense. Some of them subsequently compiled and published their speeches and writings. See Abba Eban, *Voice of Israel*

(Horizon Press, 1957); Yosef Tekoah, *In the Face of the Nations: Israel's Struggle for Peace* (Simon & Schuster, 1976); and Chaim Herzog, *Who Stands Accused?* (Random House, 1978). Another such collection is by former Israeli ambassador to Britain Shlomo Argov, *An Ambassador Speaks Out* (Weidenfeld & Nicolson, 1983). The author's personal favorite is the late Dr. Yaacov Herzog's *A People That Dwells Alone* (Weidenfeld & Nicolson, 1975), published posthumously and including his famous debate with historian Arnold Toynbee when Herzog served as Israel's envoy to Canada.

Memoirs and Biographies

The researcher can benefit from autobiographies written by makers of Israeli policy, although these tend to detail their early careers more than periods in power. Memoirs of Israeli prime ministers include Golda Meir, *My Life* (G.P. Putnam's Sons, 1975) and Golda Meir, *A Land of Our Own* (G.P. Putnam's Sons, 1973), an oral autobiography; Yitzhak Rabin, *The Rabin Memoirs* (Little, Brown & Co., 1979); Menachem Begin, *The Revolt* (Henry Schuman, 1951); and Shimon Peres, *David's Sling* (Randon House, 1970), which is particularly good on Israel's early arms acquisitions and how the French connection was forged in the early 1950s. Of some value is Henry M. Christman (ed.), *The State Papers of Levi Eshkol* (Funk & Wagnalls, 1969). Other top leaders who have published autobiographical material are former Foreign Minister Abba Eban, *An Autobiography* (Steimatsky's, 1977); the late Defense Minister and Foreign Minister Moshe Dayan, *Story of My Life* (William Morrow, 1976); and former Defense Minister Ezer Weizman, *On Eagles' Wings* (Weidenfeld & Nicolson, 1976).

Supplementing these memoirs are a number of biographies, some of which, however, tend to be laudatory of their subjects. Two of the best are on David Ben-Gurion, the first by Michael Bar-Zohar, *Ben-Gurion: A Biography* (Delacorte Press, 1977), and the second by Shabtai Teveth, *Ben-Gurion: The Burning Ground, 1886–1948* (Houghton Mifflin, 1987), with a companion volume scheduled for publication covering Ben-Gurion's premiership. Both biographers had access to Ben-Gurion's personal diaries and correspondence reposited in Sde Boker. Works on those who succeeded the Old Man are in print for Eshkol, Meir, Rabin, Begin, and Peres. Curiously missing as yet are studies of second Prime Minister Moshe Sharett and of Yitzhak Shamir. See, however, Terence Prittie, *Eshkol—The Man and the Nation* (Pitman, 1969); Marie Syrkin, *Golda Meir: Woman with a Cause* (G.P. Putnam's Sons, 1963); Robert Slater, *Rabin of*

Israel (Robson Books, 1977); Eric Silver, *Begin: The Haunted Prophet* (Random House, 1984) and another biography by Amos Perlmutter, *The Life and Times of Menachem Begin* (Doubleday, 1987); and Matti Golan, *Shimon Peres* (Weidenfeld & Nicolson, 1982). Two other biographies that are noteworthy are Shabtai Teveth, *Moshe Dayan: A Biography* (Houghton & Mifflin, 1973), and Uzi Benziman, *Sharon: An Israeli Caesar* (Adam Books, 1985).

Menachem Begin in particular has always been a figure of controversy, which explains the number of books in print assessing his impact on Israeli politics. The reader interested in the subject may find the following insightful: Robert O. Freedman (ed.), *Israel in the Begin Era* (Praeger Publishers, 1982); Steven Heydemann (ed.), *The Begin Era* (Westview Press, 1984); Melvin R. Friedlander, *Sadat and Begin: The Domestic Politics of Peacemaking* (Westview Press, 1983); and Dan Caspi, Abraham Diskin, Emanuel Gutmann, *The Roots of Begin's Success* (Croom Helm, 1984). Two books have concentrated on foreign policy under Begin. One is Ofira Seliktar, *New Zionism and the Foreign Policy System of Israel* (Southern Illinois University Press, 1986). The other is Ilan Peleg, *Begin's Foreign Policy: 1977–1983* (Greenwood Press, 1987). Both are by former Israelis critical of Begin's nationalism and intransigence to the point of insisting that 1977 marks a break in the country's diplomatic continuity. Indicative of Begin's knack for arousing extreme sentiment, he is faulted for being too compromising by a disillusioned former comrade-in-arms, Shmuel Katz, *The Hollow Peace* (The Jerusalem Post, 1981).

Politics and Society

General background information is available for understanding the foreign policy-making process as part of the wider political system and how Israeli democracy works. A good starting point is Alan Arian, *Politics in Israel: The Second Generation* (Chatham House, 1985). Insight is provided into the role of political and ideological parties, public opinion, the influence of ethnic and economic interest groups, elections, the Knesset, and government coalitions. An earlier book edited by Arian includes five essays on foreign policy and strategic questions: *Israel: A Developing Society* (Van Gorcum, 1980). Three additional surveys are Bernard Reich, *Israel: Land of Tradition and Conflict* (Westview Press, 1985); Michael Wolffsohn, *Israel: Polity, Society and Economy, 1882–1986* (Humanities Press, 1987); and Daniel J. Elazar *Israel: Building a New Society* (Indiana University Press, 1986).

Israel is a society deep in transition. The nature of this transformation since independence and how it may have affected Israeli views of the world are themes developed in several useful works. These include Peter Grose, *A Changing Israel* (Vintage Books, 1985), which presents some of the new political, economic, and social realities; Rafael Patai, *Israel Between East and West* (Greenwood Press, 1953), with its emphasis on human relations and the impact of early large-scale immigration; Amos Perlmutter, *Israel: The Partitioned State* (Charles Scribner's Sons, 1985), providing a political history since 1900; and the best-selling *The Israelis: Founders & Sons* (Weidenfeld & Nicolson, 1971) by Amos Elon. An interesting look at Israel in the first full year of independence is Tom Segev's *1949: The First Israelis* (The Free Press, 1986).

The national mood reflects this intensity of change, compounded by crisis, war, and stress. These shifting attitudes on the part of the country's leaders and public toward the world at large and toward the Arabs and the Arab-Israeli conflict in particular have been well researched. One of the earliest and most introspective surveys were a number of interviews conducted among second-generation Israelis following the 1967 crisis, edited by Avraham Shapira and published in English as *The Seventh Day: Soldiers Talk about the Six-Day War* (Charles Scribner's Sons, 1970). Two sets of impressions gathered from travel and interviews around the country toward the end of the 1980s by Israeli authors, and which generated a good deal of controversy upon publication both in Israel and abroad, are Amos Oz, *In the Land of Israel* (Harcourt, Brace, Jovanovich, 1983), and David Grossman, *The Yellow Wind* (Farrar, Straus & Giroux, 1988). A more recent study employing scientific survey techniques was done by Asher Arian, Ilan Talmud, and Tamar Hermann, *National Security and Public Opinion in Israel,* JCSS Study No. 9 (Westview Press, 1988).

On Israeli views toward the Arabs, see David K. Shipler, *Arabs and Jews: Wounded Spirits in a Promised Land* (Random House, 1986). A study of Arab animosity toward Israel that probably influenced more than any other the perceptions of Israelis in earlier years was Yehoshafat Harkabi's *Arab Attitudes to Israel* (Vallentine, Mitchell, 1972), followed by *Arab Strategies and Israel's Response* (The Free Press, 1977). Harkabi, whose main conclusion then was that the Arab-Muslim world took seriously its verbal pledges to eliminate the Jewish state, has since radically changed his thinking. Turning completely around, he has written a book criticizing Israelis for not being more flexible and conciliatory in reply to expressions of peace by various Arabs and Palestinians, *Israel's Fateful Hour* (Harper & Row, 1988).

The psychological obstacles to peace are indentified and analyzed in David Heradstreit, *The Arab-Israeli Conflict* (Universitiets for Laget, 1979). Also, John Edwin Mroz, *Beyond Security* (Pergamon Press, 1981). On the divisive issue of the administered territories, see Shmuel Sandler and Hillel Frisch, *Israel, the Palestinians and the West Bank* (D.C. Heath, 1984). The ideology and political activities of *Gush Emunim* have generated a good deal of critical analysis, as represented in Ehud Sprinzak, *Gush Emunim: The Politics of Zionist Fundamentalism in Israel* (The American Jewish Committee, 1986), and Ian Lustick, *For the Land and the Lord: Jewish Fundamentalism in Israel* (The Council on Foreign Relations, 1988). Surprising, considering the number of Israeli social scientists who identify with it, is the absence of any comparable inquiry into the motivation and activism of "Peace Now" and smaller protest movements on the political left urging withdrawal from the territories back to the 1967 line.

National Security

The foremost consideration in the Israeli national interest is security. The country's approach to security and its evolving military doctrine in the absence of peace have been analyzed in several studies. Recommended are Michael Handel, *Israel's Political-Military Doctrine* (Harvard University Press, 1973), published as Occasional Papers in International Affairs No. 30 by Harvard's Center for International Affairs; Ya'ar Ben-Horin and Barry Posen, *Israel's Strategic Doctrine* (The Rand Corporation, 1981); Efraim Inbar, *Israeli Strategic Thought in the Post 1973 Period* (Israel Research Institute of Contemporary Society, 1982); Israel Tal, "Israel's Security in the Eighties," the *Jerusalem Quarterly*, no. 17 (Fall 1980): 13–19.

The question of Israel's final borders still remains unresolved. Different conceptions have been offered of what might constitute secure lines and of the distinction between political and security borders. The reader's attention is drawn to the following: Nissim Bar-Yaakov, *The Israel-Syrian Armistice* (Magnes Press, 1967) on the problem of implementing the post-1949 armistice regime; Moshe Dayan, "Israel's Border and Security Problems," *Foreign Affairs* 33, no. 2 (January 1955): 250–267. After 1967 *Foreign Affairs* printed an interesting exchange of views sparked by Colonel Merrill A. McPeak's "Israel: The Case for Defensible Borders," *Foreign Affairs*

55, no. 1 (October 1976): 38–53. Two worthwhile essays on the border question to appear in recent years are Saul Cohen, *The Geopolitics of Israel's Border Question*, JCSS Study No. 7 (Westview Press, 1986), and a book-length treatment by Aryeh Shalev, *The West Bank: Line of Defense* (Praeger Publishers, 1985).

Israel's strategy is premised on conventional deterrence, although presumed nuclear development on the part of Israel has led to an academic debate over the merits of conventional vs. nuclear capabilities in the context of the Middle East. Indicative of the argumentation on each side are Avner Yaniv, *Deterrence Without the Bomb* (Lexington Books, 1987); Yair Evron, *War and Intervention in Lebanon: The Israeli-Syrian Deterrence Dialogue* (Johns Hopkins, 1987); Louis René Beres (ed.), *Security or Armageddon: Israel's Nuclear Strategy* (Lexington Books, 1986); and Jonathan Shimshoni, *Israel and Conventional Deterrence* (Cornell University Press, 1988). The logic of going for a nuclear option was first raised by Shai Feldman in 1982 in his book entitled *Israeli Nuclear Deterrence* (Columbia University Press).

The Decision-making Process

Foreign policy studies of Israel are still few in number. Aside from Brecher's *The Foreign Policy System of Israel*, there is a general outline of the policy-making process in chapter 5, "Israeli Foreign Policy," in *Foreign Policy Making in the Middle East* edited by R.D. McLaurin, Mohammed Mughisuddin, and Abraham R. Wagner (Praeger Publishers, 1977). Its emphasis is on domestic influences on policy. A shorter essay but more incisive is Avi Shlaim and Avner Yaniv, "Domestic Politics and Foreign Policy in Israel," *International Affairs* (Spring 1980): 242–62. The Knesset's role in the realm of foreign policy is discussed in Netanel Lorch, "The Knesset and Israel's Foreign Relations," the *Jerusalem Journal of International Relations* 9, no. 2 (June 1987): 117–31; also, Samuel Sager, *The Parliamentary System of Israel* (Syracuse University Press, 1985).

There are, by contrast, a growing number of case studies of Israeli crisis decision making and crisis behavior. In addition to those dealt with by Brecher in his other book, *Decisions in Israel's Foreign Policy*, the reader is encouraged to look at the following: Abraham R. Wagner, *Crisis Decision-Making: Israel's Experience in 1967 and 1973* (Praeger Publishers, 1974); Janice Gross Stein and Raymond Tanter, *Rational Decision-Making: Israel's Security Choices, 1967* (Ohio University Press, 1980); Theodore Draper, *Israel and World*

Politics (The Viking Press, 1968), treating the roots of Israel's third war, the 1967 crisis. Insights into one of the lesser-known episodes, the war of attrition, is provided by Avi Shlaim and Raymond Tanter, "Decision Process, Choice and Consequences: Israel's Deep-Penetration Bombing in Egypt, 1970," *World Politics* 30, no. 4 (July 1978): 483–516. The story of how Israel foiled Iraq's attempt to "go nuclear" in 1981 is told in Shlomo Nakdimon, *First Strike* (Summit Books, 1987), written with the assistance of people obviously involved in the government's decision to destroy the reactor. A similar behind-the-scenes treatment of the 1982 Lebanon intervention is Ze'ev Schiff and Ehud Ya'ari, *Israel's Lebanon War* (Simon & Schuster, 1984). As detailed, but also broader in scope, is the later study by Avner Yaniv, *Dilemmas of Security* (Oxford University Press, 1987), subtitled "Politics, strategy and the Israeli experience in Lebanon."

Israel's handling of foreign policy in noncrisis as in crisis tends to highlight the clash of personalities and the clash of bureaucratic organizations. A useful starting essay in Uri Bialer's *"Our Place in the World"—Mapai and Israel's Foreign Policy Orientation, 1947–1952* (Jerusalem, 1981), published as Jerusalem Papers on Peace Problems No. 33 by the Leonard Davis Institute for International Relations. The early clash between Ben-Gurion and Sharett has fascinated Israeli academics drawing from Ben-Gurion's papers and Sharett's equally voluminous and deeply introspective diaries. Unfortunately, little of this scholarly debate has appeared in English. One of the few pieces to do so is Gabriel Sheffer, *Resolution vs. Management of the Middle East Conflict* (Jerusalem, 1980), Paper No. 32, also done for the Davis Institute. The reader interested in Ben-Gurion will also find interesting his exchange of letters with President Charles de Gaulle of France at the end of 1967 printed in *Midstream* (February, 1968): 11–26. Ben-Gurion felt compelled to respond to a remark by the French leader on 27 November 1967 describing the Jews as "an elite people, self-assured and dominating." A characterization of Ben-Gurion as "Israel's democratic Bismark" is offered by Shlomo Aronson, *Conflict & Bargaining* (The Johns Hopkins University Press, 1978).

The theme of strong individuals interacting to determine policy is resumed by Amos Perlmutter in his two articles in *Foreign Affairs:* "Begin's Strategy and Dayan's Tactics: The Conduct of Israeli Foreign Policy," 56, no. 2 (January 1978): 357–72, and "Begin's Rhetoric and Sharon's Tactics," 61, no. 1 (Fall 1982): 67–83. Both can be read in tandem with Samuel W. Lewis, "Israel: The Peres Era and Its Legacy," *Foreign Affairs* 65, no. 3 (1987): 582–610.

The interdepartmental clash, a subject unto itself, features competition between two leading bureaucratic actors, the Foreign Ministry and the Defense Ministry. On the former's strengths and weaknesses, see Nissan Oren, "The Origins of the Israeli Foreign Ministry," *Public Administration in Israel and Abroad, 1968* (Jerusalem, 1969); Mordechai Gazit, "The Role of the Israeli Foreign Ministry," *The Jerusalem Quarterly,* no. 18 (Winter 1981): 3–14, written with the insights of a former director-general of the ministry; and Martin Mayer, *The Diplomats* (Doubleday & Co., 1983), in which chapter 11 is called "Special Case II: The Israeli Foreign Ministry." The dominance of the Defense Ministry at the head of a vast defense establishment is well covered in the following works: Amos Perlmutter, *Military and Politics in Israel* (Frank Cass, 1969); Yoram Peri, *Between Battles and Ballots* (Cambridge, University Press, 1983); Moshe Lissak (ed.), *Israeli Society and Its Defense Establishment* (Frank Cass, 1984).

Two particular bones of contention at the organizational level are policy planning and intelligence activity. On the lack of systematic planning see Lewis Brownstein, "Decision-Making in Israeli Foreign Policy: An Unplanned Process," *Political Science Quarterly* 93, no. 2 (Summer 1977): 259–79. Although the article is outdated, the central thesis still holds true and is borne out in other studies, such as Major General (res.) Avraham Tamir, *A Soldier in Search of Peace* (Harper & Row, 1988), giving an inside look at Israel's strategy and the peace problem that stimulated an effort at introducing more structured policy planning. Also important in this regard is Zvi Lanir (ed.), *Israeli Security Planning in the 1980s* (Praeger Publishers, 1984). For obvious reasons the 1973 war has encouraged a closer look at the connection between intelligence assessment and policy. The fruits of this analysis are apparent in each of the following scholarly efforts: Abraham Ben-Zvi, "Hindsight and Foresight: A Conceptual Framework for the Analysis of Surprise Attack," *World Politics* 27 (1976): 381–95, followed by Avi Shlaim, "Failure in National Intelligence Estimates: The Case of the Yom Kippur War," *World Politics* 28 (1976): 348–80; Ephraim Kam, *Strategic Surprise* (Harvard University Press, 1988). Recommendations for making policy making more efficient are offered in Yehuda Ben-Meir, *National Security Decision-making: the Israeli Case,* JCSS Study No. 8 (Westview Press, 1986).

Israel and the Superpowers

From birth Israel has been forced to pursue its own national interest against the backdrop of the larger superpower contest that eventually extended into the Middle East region itself. These cold war constraints are one major determinant of Israel's foreign policy that has been exhaustively documented and analyzed in a number of books. Merely representative are any of the following: Yair Evron, *The Middle East: Nations, Superpowers and War* (Elek Publications, 1973); Peter Mangold, *Superpower Intervention in the Middle East* (St. Martin's Press, 1978); J.C. Hurewitz (ed.), *Soviet-American Rivalry in the Middle East* (Columbia University Press, 1969); Robert O. Freedman, *World Politics and the Arab-Israeli Conflict* (Pergamon Press, 1979); and Yaacov Bar-Siman-Tov, *Israel, the Superpowers, and the War in the Middle East* (Praeger Publishers, 1987).

At the bilateral level, the Israeli-Soviet relationship has been considered from a number of different angles. The early "honeymoon" is dealt with by Uri Bialer in his article, "The Czech-Israeli Arms Deal Revisited," *The Journal of Strategic Studies* 8, no. 3 (September 1985): 307–15. The 1947–54 period is treated extensively in the work of Yaacov Roi, *Soviet Decision-Making: The USSR and Israel* (Transaction Books, 1980), and in an earlier study by Arnold Paul Krammer, *The Forgotten Friendship: Israel and the Soviet Bloc, 1947–1953* (University of Illinois Press, 1974). Avigdor Dagan, a former Israeli ambassador to Poland and Yugoslavia and head of the Foreign Ministry's Eastern European department, looks back over the first twenty years of relations with the Soviet Union and the Warsaw Pact countries in *Moscow and Jerusalem* (Abelard-Schuman, 1970). Later strained ties are competently analyzed by Galia Golan in her book, *Yom Kippur and After: The Soviet Union and the Middle East Crisis* (Cambridge University Press, 1977), and the picture is updated and rounded out in Arthur Jay Klinghoffer, *Israel and the Soviet Union: Alienation or Reconciliation?* (Westview Press, 1985).

The study of Israeli-American relations has assumed the dimensions of an academic industry in Israel as well as in the United States, indicative of the special interest in the subject while keeping pace with the expanded bilateral ties. Presenting a forceful defense of shared U.S.-Israeli values and interests are three articles worth reading: Eugene V. Rostow, "The American Stake in Israel," *Commentary* 63, no. 4 (April 1977): 32–46; Aaron Wildavsky, "What's In It For Us? America's National Interest in Israel," *The Middle East Review* 10, no. 1 (Fall 1977): 5–13; and Steven L. Spiegel, "Israel as a Strategic Asset," *Commentary* 75, no. 6 (June 1983): 51–55. An iconoclastic view of the early period, and of the Truman administration, is presented by historian Shlomo Slonim in a piece done for the *Political Science Quarterly*, "The 1948 American Embargo on Arms to Palestine" 94, no. 3 (Fall 1979): 495–514. According to another historian this earlier legacy of cold shouldering Israel was abandoned in the Kennedy-Johnson era: Mitchell G. Bard, "The Turning Point in United States Relations with Israel: The 1968 Sale of Phantom Jets,"*Middle East Review* (Summer 1988): 50–58. Tensions remained thereafter, however, as pointed out in Avi Ben-Zvi, *Alliance Politics and the Limits of Influence: The Case of the US and Israel, 1975–1983*, JCSS. Study No. 25 (Westview Press, 1984), and carried over into the late 1980s by Ze'ev Schiff, "U.S. and Israel: Friendship Under Strain," *The National Interest* (Winter 1987/8): 3–12.

Beyond these shorter monographs and articles, the interested reader is fortunate in being able to benefit from other more comprehensive and detailed reviews of the complex partnership. Worthy of mention are two contributions by Bernard Reich: *Quest for Peace* (Transaction Books, 1977) and *The United States and Israel* (Praeger Publishers, 1984). The making of America's Middle East policy from Truman to Reagan is meticulously developed in Steven L. Spiegel, *The Other Arab-Israeli Conflict* (University of Chicago Press, 1985). Attitudes toward Israel are the subject of Eytan Gilboa's book on *American Public Opinion Toward Israel and the Arab-Israeli Conflict* (D.C. Heath, 1987), while Nimrod Novik considers the domestic determinants of a changing American commitment toward Israel in his *The United States and Israel* (Westview Press, 1986). Israeli dependency in underscored in a collection of essays edited by Gabriel Sheffer, *Dynamics of Dependence* (Westview Press, 1987).

Israel and the Middle East

Over the years Israeli interaction with its Arab neighbors has extended to three modes: conflict, conflict management, and exploring peace prospects. The conflict side of this interaction has been exhaustively covered; less so the other two dimensions. Techniques for moderating the dispute are examined in Gabriel Ben-Dor and David B. Dewitt (eds.), *Conflict and Management in the Middle East* (Lexington Books, 1987). A comprehensive yearly data base and in-depth analysis of regional strategic issures centering on Israel is published by the Jaffee Center for Strategic Studies and Westview Press under the title *The Middle East Military Balance*. The impact of the "no war, no peace" situation on Israeli policy behavior after 1967 is the focus of *Israel the Peaceful Belligerent, 1967–1979* (St. Martin's Press, 1986), coauthored by Amnon Sella and Yael Yishai. The role of third-party intermediaries in advancing interim agreements, and Israel's reactions to such initiatives, is traced in Saadia Touval, *The Peace Brokers* (Princeton University Press, 1982).

The shift in emphasis from ameliorating the conflict to terminating it peacefully gained momentum with the 1977 initiative. What brought Egypt's President Sadat to Israel is explained in Michael I. Handel, *The Diplomacy of Surprise* (Harvard University Press, 1981), and in a monograph by Martin Indyk, *"To the Ends of the Earth": Sadat's Jerusalem Initiative,* Harvard Middle East Papers, Modern Series No. 1 (Center for Middle Eastern Studies, 1984). Indispensable is Moshe Dayan's own account of the secret prelude and subsequent open diplomacy, *Breakthrough* (Alfred A. Knopf, 1981). The Camp David phase of the negotiations is dealt with in William B. Quandt, *Camp David: Peacemaking and Politics* (The Brookings Institution, 1986) and a retrospective, William B. Quandt (ed.), *Ten Years after Camp David* (The Brookings Institution, 1988); also Harold H. Saunders, *The Other Walls: The Politics of the Arab-Israeli Peace Process* (American Enterprise Institute for Public Policy Research, 1985). A journalistic treatment of divided counsel within the Israeli delegation is given in Eitan Haber, Zeev Schiff, and Ehud Yaari, *The Year of the Dove* (Bantam, 1979).

At the core of Israel's Middle East policy is its triangular relationship with Jordan and the Palestinians. This model was adopted in the author's earlier work: Aaron S. Klieman, *Israel, Jordan, Palestine: The Search for a Durable Peace,* Washington Papers No. 83 (Georgetown University's Center for Strategic and International Studies, 1981). A neglected issue is earlier Israeli positions toward the Palestinians as a national movement and rival territorial claimant. Recent attempts at filling this gap include Ilan Pappé, "Moshe Sharett, David Ben-Gurion and the 'Palestinian Option,' 1948–1956," *Studies in Zionism* 7, no. 1 (Spring 1986): 64–77; and Shabtai Teveth, *Ben-Gurion and the Palestinian Arabs* (Oxford University Press, 1985). The shift of Zionist thinking away from the Palestinians to the Hashemites is fully documented in Avi Shlaim's *Collusion Across the Jordan,* mentioned previously. Thereafter, efforts concentrated on building the functional network of ties with King Hussein that are the subject of two noteworthy efforts: one, by Ian Lustick, *Israel and Jordan: The Implications of an Adversarial Partnership,* Policy Papers in International Affairs No. 6 (University of California Institute of International Studies, 1978); the other by the most knowledgeable student of the discreet dialogue spanning the Jordan, journalist Moshe Zak, "Israeli-Jordanian Negotiations," *The Washington Quarterly* 8, no. 1 (Winter 1985): 167–76. Renewed questioning of the Palestinians' status by Israeli scholars begins with Shlomo Avineri (ed.), *Israel and the Palestinians* (St. Martin's Press, 1971), and continues in such works as Joel S. Migdal and others, *Palestinian Society and Politics* (Princeton University Press, 1980); Shaul Mishal, *West Bank/East Bank: The Palestinians in Jordan, 1949–1967* (Yale University Press, 1978); and Mark Heller, *A Palestinian State* (Harvard University Press, 1983).

Israel's Other Foreign Relations

Preoccupation with the superpowers and the Arabs should not denigrate the wide range of ties pursued by Israel. One expression of this global approach to foreign affairs is Israel at the UN and in related international organizations. On this multilateral dimension, and Israel's mixed results, see Avi Beker, *The U.N. and Israel* (Lexington Books, 1988), the long-overdue first study of the subject. Israeli hopes for the world organization, before both fell prey to coalition politics at the UN, today seem quaint. Nevertheless, they are worth recalling for the sake of perspective. Jacob Robinson, *Palestine and the United Nations,* (Public Affairs Press, 1947) and *Israel and the United Nations,* a report of a study group set up by the Hebrew University of Jerusalem (Carnegie Endowment for International Peace, 1956). The disillusionment with the UN is understandable in light of the 1975 anti-Israel action; see Bernard Lewis, "The Anti-Zionist Resolution," *Foreign Affairs* 55, no. 1 (October 1976), 54–64.

Few studies exist on Israel's relations with Western European countries as a distinctive group. Perhaps the only one is a brief sketch by Yaacov Shimoni, "Israel and Europe," *The Jerusalem Quarterly,* no. 18 (Spring 1981): 92–107, although another uneven effort is David Allen and Alfred Pijpers (eds.), *European Foreign Policy-Making and the Arab-Israeli Conflict* (Martinus Nijhoff, 1984). The scholarly record on Israel and the EEC is not much better, an exception being Avner Yaniv, "The European Community and Israel Since October 1973," in Avigdor Levy (ed.), *The Arab-Israeli Conflict: Risks and Opportunities* (Statis, 1975). Two books deal with Israel's associate status in the Common Market: Pierre Uri (ed.), *Israel and the Common Market* (Weindenfeld and Nicolson, 1971), and Herbert Giersch (ed.), *The Economic Integration of Israel in the E.E.C.* (J.C.B. Mohr, 1980). Both, however, are outdated by now and are economics oriented, giving little attention to the political dynamics of the relationship.

Most disappointing is the state of research on the history of Israeli relations with individual European countries. No book has ever been done, for example, on Great Britain and Israel. Of the several works on West Germany, all are limited to the reparations agreement reached in 1952. Inge Deutschkorn, *Bonn and Jerusalem: The Strange Coalition* (Chilton Books, 1970), and Nicholas Balabkins, *West German Reparations to Israel* (Rutgers University Press, 1971). An important exception is Lily Gardner Feldman, *The Special Relationship between West Germany and Israel* (George Allen & Unwin, 1984). There is one book on France, by Sylvia Kowitt-Crosbie, *A Tacit Alliance* (Princeton University Press, 1974), that as its subtitle indicates, is restricted to *France and Israel from the Suez to the Six-Day War*. The influence of the religious factor on European policy toward Israel likewise is unresearched. See Livia Rokach, *The Catholic Church and the Question of Palestine* (Sagi Books, 1987).

Moving beyond Europe to the developing Third World countries the scholarly record is slightly better. General treatments of Israel's 1960s initiative toward the Afro–Asian bloc of nonaligned nations, and of the techniques used rather effectively, are Leopold Laufer, *Israel and the Developing Countries* (Twentieth Century Fund, 1967); Shimeon Amir, *Israel's Developing Cooperation with Africa, Asia and Latin America* (Praeger Publishers, 1974); Edy Kaufman, Yoram Shapira, and Joel Barromi, *Israel-Latin American Relations* (Transaction Books, 1979); and Michael Curtis and Susan Aurelia Gitelson (eds.), *Israel in the Third World* (Transaction Books, 1976). An early doctoral dissertation by Samuel Decalo, "Israel and Africa" (1971), looked at the initial politics of cooperation in terms of the link made by Israel between foreign policy and technical assistance. A comparable regional perspective was adopted in an article by Moshe Yegar, "Israel in Asia," *The Jerusalem Quarterly*, no. 18 (Winter 1981); 15–29.

Most studies tend to gloss over the use of weapons sales and back channels for gaining access to many of the Third World nations and for extending Israeli influence worldwide. Two research projects by the author on these less publicized initiatives are Aaron S. Klieman, *Israel's Global Reach: Arms Sales as Diplomacy* (Pergamon-Brassey's, 1985) and Aharon Klieman, *Statecraft in the Dark: Israel's Practice of Quiet Diplomacy* JCSS Study No. 10 (Westview Press, 1988). One disclosed episode was secret efforts in bringing 16,000 Ethiopian Jews to Israel. For an account of the operation, see Claire Safran, *Secret Exodus* (Prentice-Hall Press, 1987).

Of the few country-by-country studies, the reader might consider George E. Gruen, "Turkey, Israel and the Palestine Question, 1948–1960: A Study in the Diplomacy of Ambivalence" (unpublished Ph.D. dissertation, 1970), superseded now by Amikam Lachmani's more recent and comparative study entitled *Israel, Turkey and*

Greece: Uneasy Relations in the East Mediterranean (Frank Cass, 1987); on Iran: Robert B. Reppa, Sr., *Israel and Iran* (Praeger Publishers, 1974); Uri Bialer, "The Iranian Connection in Israel's Foreign Policy—1948–1951," *Middle East Journal* 39, no. 2 (Spring 1985): 292–315; Samuel Segev, *The Iranian Triangle* (The Free Press, 1988). Morocco may also warrant membership in Israel's "periphery policy" of tacit relationships—an impression conveyed by Mark Tessler, "Moroccan-Israel Relations and the Reasons for Moroccan Receptivity to Contact with Israel," *The Jerusalem Journal of International Relations* 10, no. 2 (June 1988): 76–108. In the category of mischievous attempts at exposing Israeli nefarious undercover activity abroad are James Adams, *The Unnatural Alliance: Israel and South Africa* (Quartet Books, 1984), and Bishara Bahbah, *Israel and Latin America: The Military Connection* (St. Martin's Press, 1986). For the sake of contrast see the firsthand account of discreet contacts in 1954–55, prior to the Bandung Conference of nonaligned countries, with Chinese officials of the Beijing government in David Hacohen, "Behind the Scenes of Negotiations Between Israel and China," *New Outlook* 6, no.7 (58) (November–December 1963): 29–44. At the time Hacohen, Israel's ambassador to Burma, was entrusted with pursuing these contacts. Fresh prospects are analyzed in Yitzchak Shichor, *The Middle East in China's Foreign Policy* (Cambridge University Press, 1980).

Left appropriately for last is the special relationship of Israel with world Jewry. Israeli statecraft, and the Zionist forerunner, in the service of the Diaspora is the theme of David Vital, *Diplomacy in the Jewish Interest* (Tel Aviv University, 1983), in a paper prepared by the first incumbent of the Nahum Goldmann Chair in Diplomacy. The unique partnership is further developed in a number of learned essays by distinguished contributors on Jewish identification with Israel, the centrality of Israel, and interactions among world Jewish communities in Moshe Davis (ed.), *World Jewry and the State of Israel* (Arno Press, 1977). Several years before, Professor Davis had edited a volume of papers investigating the impact of the 1973 war, *The Yom Kippur War: Israel and Jewish People* (Arno Press, 1974). Solidarity is the message behind Melvin I. Urofsky's *We Are One! American Jewry and Israel* (Doubleday, 1978). A less sanguine view is taken toward the premise of an identity of interests in a debate between two Hebrew University academics in the pages of the *Jerusalem Quarterly*. Shlomo Avineri, "Ideology and Israel's Foreign Policy," no. 37 (1986); 3–13, argues that sensitivity for the delicate situation of many Jewish communities acts as a restraint on Jerusalem's freedom of action; whereas Gabriel Sheffer takes the opposite position, criticizing Israeli policy makers for insensitivity, "The Elusive Question: Jews and Jewry in Israeli Foreign Policy," no. 46 (Spring 1988); 104–14. The influence of world Jewry on Israeli policy rather than vice versa is considered by Charles S. Liebman in his book, *Pressure Without Sanctions* (Fairleigh Dickinson University Press, 1977). Illustrating the Jewish stake in an Israel at peace with itself and its external environment is a report of the International Economic and Racial Commission of the World Jewish Congress, *The Implications of Israeli-Arab Peace for World Jewry* (Waldon Press, 1981).

INDEX

THE AUTHOR

Aaron S. Klieman is professor of international relations in the Department of Political Science at Tel Aviv University.

His publications include *Foundations of British Policy in the Arab World, Soviet Russia and the Middle East,* and *Israel's Global Reach: Arms Sales as Diplomacy,* as well as a number of monographs and two books in Hebrew. He has twice been visiting professor at Georgetown University in Washington, D.C.